The Wisdom of Thomas Troward Vol I

The Wisdom of Thomas Troward Vol I

By Thomas Troward

The Edinburgh Lectures on Mental Science
Dore Lectures on Mental Science
The Law and the Word
The Creative Process in the Individual

Start Publishing PD is a registered trademark of Start Publishing PD LLC
Manufactured in the United States of America

Cover art: Shutterstock/Taisiya Kozorez

Cover design: Jennifer Do

10 9 8 7 6 5 4 3 2 1

ISBN 979-8-8809-2295-6

The Edinburgh Lectures on Mental Science

The Writer Affectionately Dedicates this Little Volume to His Wife

Foreword

This book contains the substance of a course of lectures recently given by the writer in the Queen Street Hall, Edinburgh. Its purpose is to indicate the *Natural Principles* governing the relation between Mental Action and Material Conditions, and thus to afford the student an intelligible starting-point for the practical study of the subject.

T.T.
March, 1904.

Table of Contents

SPIRIT AND MATTER

In commencing a course of lectures on Mental Science, it is somewhat difficult for the lecturer to fix upon the best method of opening the subject. It can be approached from many sides, each with some peculiar advantage of its own; but, after careful deliberation, it appears to me that, for the purpose of the present course, no better starting-point could be selected than the relation between Spirit and Matter. I select this starting-point because the distinction—or what we believe to be such— between them is one with which we are so familiar that I can safely assume its recognition by everybody; and I may, therefore, at once state this distinction by using the adjectives which we habitually apply as expressing the natural opposition between the two—*living* spirit and *dead* matter. These terms express our current impression of the opposition between spirit and matter with sufficient accuracy, and considered only from the point of view of outward appearances this impression is no doubt correct. The general consensus of mankind is right in trusting the evidence of our senses, and any system which tells us that we are not to do so will never obtain a permanent footing in a sane and healthy community. There is nothing wrong in the evidence conveyed to a healthy mind by the senses of a healthy body, but the point where error creeps in is when we come to judge of the meaning of this testimony. We are accustomed to judge only by external appearances and by certain limited significances which we attach to words; but when we begin to enquire into the real meaning of our words and to analyse the causes which give rise to the appearances, we find our old notions gradually falling off from us, until at last we wake up to the fact that we are living in an entirely different world to that we formerly recognized. The old limited mode of thought has imperceptibly slipped away, and we discover that we have stepped out into a new order of things where all is liberty and life. This is the work of an enlightened intelligence resulting from persistent determination to discover what truth really is irrespective of any preconceived notions from whatever source derived, the determination to think honestly for ourselves instead of endeavouring to get our thinking done for us. Let us then commence by enquiring what we really mean by the livingness which we attribute to spirit and the deadness which we attribute to matter.

At first we may be disposed to say that livingness consists in the power of motion and deadness in its absence; but a little enquiry into the most recent researches of science will soon show us that this distinction does not go deep enough. It is now one of the fully-established facts of physical science that no atom of what we call "dead matter" is without motion. On the table before me lies a solid lump of steel, but in the light of up-to-date science I know that the atoms of that seemingly inert mass are vibrating with the most intense energy, continually dashing hither and thither, impinging upon and rebounding from one another, or circling round like miniature solar systems, with a ceaseless rapidity whose complex activity is enough to bewilder the imagination. The mass, as a mass, may lie inert upon the table; but so far from being destitute of the element of motion it is the abode of the never-tiring energy moving the particles with a swiftness to which the speed of an express train is as nothing. It is, therefore, not the mere fact of motion that is at the root of the distinction which we draw instinctively between spirit and matter; we must go deeper than that. The solution of the problem will never be found by comparing Life with what we call deadness, and the reason for this will become apparent later on; but the true key is to be found by comparing one degree of livingness with another. There is, of course, one sense in which the quality of livingness does not admit of degrees; but there is another sense in which it is entirely a question of degree. We have no doubt as to the livingness of a plant, but we realize that it is something very different from the livingness of an animal. Again, what average boy would not prefer a fox-terrier to a goldfish for a pet? Or, again, why is it that the boy himself is an advance upon the dog? The plant, the fish, the dog, and the boy are all equally *alive*; but there is a difference in the quality of their livingness about which no one can have any doubt, and no one would hesitate to say that this difference is in the degree of intelligence. In whatever way we turn the subject we shall always find that what we call the "livingness" of any individual life is ultimately measured by its intelligence. It is the possession of greater intelligence that places the animal higher in the scale of being than the plant, the man higher than the animal, the intellectual man higher than the savage. The increased intelligence calls into activity modes of motion of a higher order corresponding to itself. The higher the intelligence, the more completely the mode of motion is under its control: and as we descend in the scale of intelligence, the descent is marked by a corresponding increase in *automatic* motion not subject to the control of a self-conscious intelligence. This descent is gradual from the expanded self-recognition of the highest human personality to that lowest order of visible forms which we speak of as "things," and from which self-recognition is entirely absent.

We see, then, that the livingness of Life consists in intelligence—in other words, in the power of Thought; and we may therefore say that the distinctive quality of spirit is Thought, and, as the opposite to this, we may say that the distinctive quality of matter is Form. We cannot conceive of matter without form. Some form there must be, even though invisible to the physical eye; for matter, to be matter at all, must occupy space, and to occupy any particular space necessarily implies a corresponding form. For these reasons we may lay it down as a fundamental proposition that the distinctive quality of spirit is Thought and the distinctive quality of matter is Form. This is a radical distinction from which important consequences follow, and should, therefore, be carefully noted by the student.

Form implies extension in space and also limitation within certain boundaries. Thought implies neither. When, therefore, we think of Life as existing in any particular *form* we associate it with the idea of extension in space, so that an elephant may be said to consist of a vastly larger amount of living substance than a mouse. But if we think of Life as the fact of livingness we do not associate it with any idea of extension, and we at once realize that the mouse is quite as much alive as the elephant, notwithstanding the difference in size. The important point of this distinction is that if we can conceive of anything as entirely devoid of the element of extension in space, it must be present in its entire totality anywhere and everywhere—that is to say, at every point of space simultaneously. The scientific definition of time is that it is the period occupied by a body in passing from one given point in space to another, and, therefore, according to this definition, when there is no space there can be no time; and hence that conception of spirit which realizes it as devoid of the element of space must realize it as being devoid of the element of time also; and we therefore find that the conception of spirit as pure Thought, and not as concrete Form, is the conception of it as subsisting perfectly independently of the elements of time and space. From this it follows that if the idea of anything is conceived as existing on this level it can only represent that thing as being actually present here and now. In this view of things nothing can be remote from us either in time or space: either the idea is entirely dissipated or it exists as an actual present entity, and not as something that *shall* be in the future, for where there is no sequence in time there can be no future. Similarly where there is no space there can be no conception of anything as being at a distance from us. When the elements of time and space are eliminated all our ideas of things must necessarily be as subsisting in a universal here and an everlasting now. This is, no doubt, a highly abstract conception, but I would ask the student to endeavour to grasp it thoroughly, since it is of vital importance in the practical application of Mental Science, as will appear further on.

The opposite conception is that of things expressing themselves through conditions of time and space and thus establishing a variety of *relations* to other things, as of bulk, distance, and direction, or of sequence in time. These two conceptions are respectively the conception of the abstract and the concrete, of the unconditioned and the conditioned, of the absolute and the relative. They are not opposed to each other in the sense of incompatibility, but are each the complement of the other, and the only reality is in the combination of the two. The error of the extreme idealist is in endeavouring to realize the absolute without the relative, and the error of the extreme materialist is in endeavouring to realize the relative without the absolute. On the one side the mistake is in trying to realize an inside without an outside, and on the other in trying to realize an outside without an inside; both are necessary to the formation of a substantial entity.

THE HIGHER MODE OF INTELLIGENCE CONTROLS THE LOWER

We have seen that the descent from personality, as we know it in ourselves, to matter, as we know it under what we call inanimate forms, is a gradual descent in the scale of intelligence from that mode of being which is able to realize its own will-power as a capacity for originating new trains of causation to that mode of being which is incapable of recognizing itself at all. The higher the grade of life, the higher the intelligence; from which it follows that the supreme principle of Life must also be the ultimate principle of intelligence. This is clearly demonstrated by the grand natural order of the universe. In the light of modern science the principle of evolution is familiar to us all, and the accurate adjustment existing between all parts of the cosmic scheme is too self-evident to need insisting upon. Every advance in science consists in discovering new subtleties of connection in this magnificent universal order, which already exists and only needs our recognition to bring it into practical use. If, then, the highest work of the greatest minds consists in nothing else than the recognition of an already existing order, there is no getting away from the conclusion that a paramount intelligence must be inherent in the Life-Principle, which manifests itself *as* this order; and thus we see that there must be a great cosmic intelligence underlying the totality of things.

The physical history of our planet shows us first an incandescent nebula dispersed over vast infinitudes of space; later this condenses into a central sun surrounded by a family of glowing planets hardly yet consolidated from the plastic primordial matter; then succeed untold millenniums of slow geological formation; an earth peopled by the lowest forms of life, whether vegetable or animal; from which crude beginnings a majestic, unceasing, unhurried, forward movement brings things stage by stage to the condition in which we know them now. Looking at this steady progression it is clear that, however we may conceive the nature of the evolutionary principle, it unerringly provides for the continual advance of the race. But it does this by creating such numbers of each kind that, after allowing a wide margin for all possible accidents to individuals, the race shall still continue:—

So careful of the type it seems
So careless of the single life."

In short, we may say that the cosmic intelligence works by a Law of Averages which allows a wide margin of accident and failure to the individual.

But the progress towards higher intelligence is always in the direction of narrowing down this margin of accident and taking the individual more and more out of the law of averages, and substituting the law of individual selection. In ordinary scientific language this is the survival of the fittest. The reproduction of fish is on a scale that would choke the sea with them if every individual survived; but the margin of destruction is correspondingly enormous, and thus the law of averages simply keeps up the normal proportion of the race. But at the other end of the scale, reproduction is by no means thus enormously in excess of survival. True, there is ample margin of accident and disease cutting off numbers of human beings before they have gone through the average duration of life, but still it is on a very different scale from the premature destruction of hundreds of thousands as against the survival of one. It may, therefore, be taken as an established fact that in proportion as intelligence advances the individual ceases to be subject to a mere law of averages and has a continually increasing power of controlling the conditions of his own survival.

We see, therefore, that there is a marked distinction between the cosmic intelligence and the individual intelligence, and that the factor which differentiates the latter from the former is the presence of *individual* volition. Now the business of Mental Science is to ascertain the relation of this individual power of volition to the great cosmic law which provides for the maintenance and advancement of the race; and the point to be carefully noted is that the power of individual volition is itself the outcome of the cosmic evolutionary principle at the point where it reaches its highest level. The effort of Nature has always been upwards from the time when only the lowest forms of life peopled the globe, and it has now culminated in the production of a being with a mind capable of abstract reasoning and a brain fitted to be the physical instrument of such a mind. At this stage the all-creating Life-principle reproduces itself in a form capable of recognizing the working of the evolutionary law, and the unity and continuity of purpose running through the whole progression until now indicates, beyond a doubt, that the place of such a being in the universal scheme must be to introduce the operation of that factor which, up to this point, has been, conspicuous by its absence—the factor, namely, of intelligent individual volition. The evolution which has brought us up to this standpoint has worked by a cosmic law of averages; it has been a process in which the individual himself has not taken a conscious part. But because he is what he is, and leads the van of the evolutionary procession, if man is to evolve further, it can now only be by his own conscious co-operation with the law which has brought him up to the standpoint where he is able to realize that such a law exists. His evolution in the future must be by conscious participation in the great work, and this can only be effected by his own individual intelligence and effort. It is a process of intelligent growth. No one else can grow for us: we must each grow for ourselves; and this intelligent growth consists in our increasing recognition of the universal law, which has brought us as far as we have yet got, and of our own individual relation to that law, based upon the fact that we ourselves are the most advanced product of it. It is a great maxim that Nature obeys us precisely in proportion as we first obey Nature. Let the electrician try to go counter to the principle that electricity must always pass from a higher to a lower potential and he will effect nothing; but let him submit in all things to this one fundamental law, and he can make whatever particular applications of electrical power he will.

These considerations show us that what differentiates the higher from the lower degree of intelligence is the recognition of its own self-hood, and the more intelligent that recognition is, the greater will be the power. The lower degree of self-recognition is that which only realizes itself as an entity separate from all other entities, as the *ego* distinguished from the *non-ego*. But the higher degree of self-recognition is that which, realizing its own spiritual nature, sees in all other forms, not so much the *non-ego*, or that which is not itself, as the *alter-ego*, or that which is itself in a different mode of expression. Now, it is this higher degree of self-recognition that is the power by which the Mental Scientist produces his results. For this reason it is imperative that he should clearly understand the difference between Form and Being; that the one is the mode of the relative and, the mark of subjection to conditions, and that the other is the truth of the absolute and is that which controls conditions.

Now this higher recognition of self as an individualization of pure spirit must of necessity control all modes of spirit which have not yet reached the same level of self-recognition. These lower modes of spirit are in bondage to the law of their own being because they do not know the law; and, therefore, the individual who has attained to this knowledge can control them through that law. But to understand this we must inquire a little further into the nature of spirit. I have already shown that the grand scale of adaptation and adjustment of all parts of the cosmic scheme to one another exhibits the presence *somewhere* of a marvellous intelligence, underlying the whole, and the question is, where is this intelligence to be found? Ultimately we can only conceive of it as inherent in some primordial substance which is the root of all those grosser modes of matter which are known to us, whether visible to the physical eye, or necessarily inferred by science from their perceptible effects. It is that power which, in every species and in every individual, becomes that which that species or individual is; and thus we can only conceive of it as a self-forming intelligence inherent in the ultimate substance of which each thing is a particular manifestation. That this primordial substance must be considered as self-forming by an inherent intelligence abiding in itself becomes evident from the fact that intelligence is the essential quality of spirit; and if we were to conceive of the primordial substance as something apart from spirit, then we should have to postulate some other power which is neither spirit nor matter, and originates both; but this is only putting the idea of a self-evolving power a step further back and asserting the production of a lower grade of undifferentiated spirit by a higher, which is both a purely gratuitous assumption and a contradiction of any idea we can form of undifferentiated spirit at all. However far back, therefore, we may relegate the original starting-point, we cannot avoid the conclusion that, at that point, spirit contains the primary substance in itself, which brings us back to the common statement that it made everything out of nothing. We thus find two factors to the making of all things, Spirit and—Nothing; and the addition of Nothing to Spirit leaves *only* spirit: $x + 0 = x$.

From these considerations we see that the ultimate foundation of every form of matter is spirit, and hence that a universal intelligence subsists throughout Nature inherent in every one of its manifestations. But this cryptic intelligence does not belong to the particular *form* excepting in the measure in which it is physically fitted for its concentration into self-recognizing individuality: it lies hidden in that primordial substance of which the visible form is a grosser manifestation. This primordial substance is a philosophical necessity, and we can only picture it to ourselves as something infinitely finer than the atoms which are themselves a philosophical inference of physical science: still, for want of a better word, we may conveniently speak of this primary intelligence inherent in the very substance of things as the Atomic Intelligence. The term may, perhaps, be open to some objections, but it will serve our present purpose as distinguishing *this* mode of spirit's intelligence from that of the opposite pole, or Individual Intelligence. This distinction should be carefully noted because it is by the response of the atomic intelligence to the individual intelligence that thought-power is able to produce results on the material plane, as in the cure of disease by mental treatment, and the like. Intelligence manifests itself by responsiveness, and the whole action of the cosmic mind in bringing the evolutionary process from its first beginnings up to its present human stage is nothing else but a continual intelligent response to the demand which each stage in the progress has made for an adjustment between itself and its environment. Since, then, we have recognized the presence of a universal intelligence permeating all things, we must also recognize a corresponding responsiveness hidden deep down in their nature and ready to be called into action when appealed to. All mental treatment depends on this responsiveness of spirit in its lower degrees to higher degrees of itself. It is here that the difference between the mental scientist and the uninstructed person comes in; the former knows of this responsiveness and makes use of it, and the latter cannot use it because he does not know it.

THE UNITY OF THE SPIRIT

We have now paved the way for understanding what is meant by "the unity of the spirit." In the first conception of spirit as the underlying origin of all things we see a universal substance which, at this stage, is not differentiated into any specific forms. This is not a question of some bygone time, but subsists at every moment of all time in the *innermost* nature of all being; and when we see this, we see that the division between one specific form and another has below it a deep essential unity, which acts as the supporter of all the several forms of individuality arising out of it. And as our thought penetrates deeper into the nature of this all-producing spiritual substance we see that it cannot be limited to any one portion of space, but must be limitless as space itself, and that the idea of any portion of space where it is not is inconceivable. It is one of those intuitive perceptions from which the human mind can never get away that this primordial, all-generating living spirit must be commensurate with infinitude, and we can therefore never think of it otherwise than as universal or infinite. Now it is a mathematical truth that the infinite must be a unity. You cannot have two infinites, for then neither would be infinite, each would be limited by the other, nor can you split the infinite up into fractions. The infinite is mathematically essential unity. This is a point on which too much stress cannot be laid, for there follow from it the most important consequences. Unity, as such, can be neither multiplied nor divided, for either operation destroys the unity. By multiplying, we produce a plurality of units of the same scale as the original; and by dividing, we produce a plurality of units of a smaller scale; and a plurality of units is not unity but multiplicity. Therefore if we would penetrate below the outward nature of the individual to that innermost principle of his being from which his individuality takes its rise, we can do so only by passing beyond the conception of individual existence into that of the unity of universal being. This may appear to be a merely philosophical abstraction, but the student who would produce practical results must realize that these abstract generalizations are the foundation of the practical work he is going to do.

Now the great fact to be recognized about a unity is that, *because* it is a single unit, wherever it is at all the *whole* of it must be. The moment we allow our mind to wander off to the idea of extension in space and say that one part of the unit is here and another there, we have descended from the idea of unity into that of parts or fractions of a single unit, which is to pass into the idea of a multiplicity of smaller units, and in that case we are dealing with the relative, or the relation subsisting between two or more entities which are therefore *limited by each other*, and so have passed out of the region of simple unity which is the absolute. It is, therefore, a mathematical necessity that, because the originating Life- principle is infinite, it is a single unit, and consequently, wherever it is at all, the *whole* of it must be present. But because it is *infinite*, or limitless, it is everywhere, and therefore it follows that the *whole* of spirit must be present at every point in space at the same moment. Spirit is thus omnipresent *in its entirety*, and it is accordingly logically correct that at every moment of time *all* spirit is concentrated at any point in space that we may choose to fix our thought upon. This is the fundamental fact of all being, and it is for this reason that I have prepared the way for it by laying down the relation between spirit and matter as that between idea and form, on the one hand the absolute from which the elements of time and space are entirely absent, and on the other the relative which is entirely dependent on those elements. This great fact is that pure spirit continually subsists in the absolute, whether in a corporeal body or not; and from it all the phenomena of being flow, whether on the mental plane or the physical. The knowledge of this fact regarding spirit is the basis of all conscious spiritual operation, and therefore in proportion to our increasing recognition of it our power of producing outward visible results by the action of our thought will grow. The whole is greater than its part, and therefore, if, by our recognition of this unity, we can concentrate *all* spirit into any given point at any moment, we thereby include any individualization of it that we may wish to deal with. The practical importance of this conclusion is too obvious to need enlarging upon.

Pure spirit is the Life-principle considered apart from the matrix in which it takes relation to time and space in a particular form. In this aspect it is pure intelligence undifferentiated into individuality. As pure intelligence it is infinite responsiveness and susceptibility. As devoid of relation to time and space it is devoid of individual personality. It is, therefore, in this aspect a purely impersonal element upon which, by reason of its inherent intelligence and susceptibility, we can impress any recognition of personality that we will. These are the great facts that the mental scientist works with, and the student will do well to ponder deeply on their significance and on the responsibilities which their realization must necessarily carry with it.

SUBJECTIVE AND OBJECTIVE MIND

Up to this point it has been necessary to lay the foundations of the science by the statement of highly abstract general principles which we have reached by purely metaphysical reasoning. We now pass on to the consideration of certain natural laws which have been established by a long series of experiments and observations, the full meaning and importance of which will become clear when we see their application to the general principles which have hitherto occupied our attention. The phenomena of hypnosis are now so fully recognized as established scientific facts that it is quite superfluous to discuss the question of their credibility. Two great medical schools have been founded upon them, and in some countries they have become the subject of special legislation. The question before us at the present day is, not as to the credibility of the facts, but as to the proper inferences to be drawn from them, and a correct apprehension of these inferences is one of the most valuable aids to the mental scientist, for it confirms the conclusions of purely *a priori* reasoning by an array of experimental instances which places the correctness of those conclusions beyond doubt.

The great truth which the science of hypnotism has brought to light is the dual nature of the human mind. Much conflict exists between different writers as to whether this duality results from the presence of two actually separate minds in the one man, or in the action of the same mind in the employment of different functions. This is one of those distinctions without a difference which are so prolific a source of hindrance to the opening out of truth. A man must be a single individuality to be a man at all, and, so, the net result is the same whether we conceive of his varied modes of mental action as proceeding from a set of separate minds strung, so to speak, on the thread of his one individuality and each adapted to a particular use, or as varied functions of a single mind: in either case we are dealing with a single individuality, and how we may picture the wheel-work of the mental mechanism is merely a question of what picture will bring the nature of its action home to us most clearly. Therefore, as a matter of convenience, I shall in these lectures speak of this dual action as though it proceeded from two minds, an outer and an inner, and the inner mind we will call the subjective mind and the outer the objective, by which names the distinction is most frequently indicated in the literature of the subject.

A long series of careful experiments by highly-trained observers, some of them men of world-wide reputation, has fully established certain remarkable differences between the action of the subjective and that of the objective mind which may be briefly stated as follows. The subjective mind is only able to reason *deductively* and not inductively, while the objective mind can do both. Deductive reasoning is the pure syllogism which shows why a third proposition must necessarily result if two others are assumed, but which does not help us to determine whether the two initial statements are true or not.

To determine this is the province of inductive reasoning which draws its conclusions from the observation of a series of facts. The relation of the two modes of reasoning is that, first by observing a sufficient number of instances, we inductively reach the conclusion that a certain principle is of general application, and then we enter upon the deductive process by assuming the truth of this principle and determining what result must follow in a particular case on the hypothesis of its truth. Thus deductive reasoning proceeds on the assumption of the correctness of certain hypotheses or suppositions with which it sets out: it is not concerned with the truth or falsity of those suppositions, but only with the question as to what results must necessarily follow supposing them to be true. Inductive reasoning; on the other hand, is the process by which we compare a number of separate instances with one another until we see the common factor that gives rise to them all. Induction proceeds by the comparison of facts, and deduction by the application of universal principles. Now it is the deductive method only which is followed by the subjective mind. Innumerable experiments on persons in the hypnotic state have shown that the subjective mind is utterly incapable of making the selection and comparison which are necessary to the inductive process, but will accept any suggestion, however false, but having once accepted any suggestion, it is strictly logical in deducing the proper conclusions from it, and works out every suggestion to the minutest fraction of the results which flow from it.

As a consequence of this it follows that the subjective mind is entirely under the control of the objective mind. With the utmost fidelity it reproduces and works out to its final consequences whatever the objective mind impresses upon it; and the facts of hypnotism show that ideas can be impressed on the subjective mind by the objective mind of another as well as by that of its own individuality. This is a most important point, for it is on this amenability to suggestion by the thought of another that all the phenomena of healing, whether present or absent, of telepathy and the like, depend. Under the control of the practised hypnotist the very personality of the subject becomes changed for the time being; he believes himself to be whatever the operator tells him he is: he is a swimmer breasting the waves, a bird flying in the air, a soldier in the tumult of battle, an Indian stealthily tracking his victim: in short, for the time being, he identifies himself with any personality that is impressed upon him by the will of the operator, and acts the part with inimitable accuracy. But the experiments of hypnotism go further than this, and show the existence in the subjective mind of powers far transcending any exercised by the objective mind through the medium of the physical senses; powers of thought-reading, of thought-transference, of clairvoyance, and the like, all of which are frequently manifested when the patient is brought into the higher mesmeric state; and we have thus experimental proof of the existence in ourselves of transcendental faculties the full development and conscious control of which would place us in a perfectly new sphere of life.

But it should be noted that the control must be *our own* and not that of any external intelligence whether in the flesh or out of it.

But perhaps the most important fact which hypnotic experiments have demonstrated is that the subjective mind is the builder of the body. The subjective entity in the patient is able to diagnose the character of the disease from which he is suffering and to point out suitable remedies, indicating a physiological knowledge exceeding that of the most highly trained physicians, and also a knowledge of the correspondences between diseased conditions of the bodily organs and the material remedies which can afford relief. And from this it is but a step further to those numerous instances in which it entirely dispenses with the use of material remedies and itself works directly on the organism, so that complete restoration to health follows as the result of the suggestions of perfect soundness made by the operator to the patient while in the hypnotic state.

Now these are facts fully established by hundreds of experiments conducted by a variety of investigators in different parts of the world, and from them we may draw two inferences of the highest importance: one, that the subjective mind is in itself absolutely impersonal, and the other that it is the builder of the body, or in other words it is the creative power in the individual. That it is impersonal in itself is shown by its readiness to assume any personality the hypnotist chooses to impress upon it; and the unavoidable inference is that its realization of personality proceeds from its association with the particular objective mind of its own individuality. Whatever personality the objective mind impresses upon it, that personality it assumes and acts up to; and since it is the builder of the body it will build up a body in correspondence with the personality thus impressed upon it. These two laws of the subjective mind form the foundation of the axiom that our body represents the aggregate of our beliefs. If our fixed belief is that the body is subject to all sorts of influences beyond our control, and that this, that, or the other symptom shows that such an uncontrollable influence is at work upon us, then this belief is impressed upon the subjective mind, which by the law of its nature accepts it without question and proceeds to fashion bodily conditions in accordance with this belief. Again, if our fixed belief is that certain material remedies are the only means of cure, then we find in this belief the foundation of all medicine. There is nothing unsound in the theory of medicine; it is the strictly logical correspondence with the measure of knowledge which those who rely on it are as yet able to assimilate, and it acts accurately in accordance with their belief that in a large number of cases medicine will do good, but also in many instances it fails. Therefore, for those who have not yet reached a more interior perception of the law of Nature, the healing agency of medicine is a most valuable aid to the alleviation of physical maladies. The error to be combated is not the belief that, in its own way, medicine is capable of doing good, but the belief that there is no higher or better way.

Then, on the same principle, if we realize that the subjective mind is the builder of the body, and that the body is subject to no influences except those which reach it through the subjective mind, then what we have to do is to impress *this* upon the subjective mind and habitually think of it as a fountain of perpetual Life, which is continually renovating the body by building in strong and healthy material, in the most complete independence of any influences of any sort, save those of our own desire impressed upon our own subjective mind by our own thought. When once we fully grasp these considerations we shall see that it is just as easy to externalize healthy conditions of body as the contrary. Practically the process amounts to a belief in our own power of life; and since this belief, if it be thoroughly domiciled within us, will necessarily produce a correspondingly healthy body, we should spare no pains to convince ourselves that there are sound and reasonable grounds for holding it. To afford a solid basis for this conviction is the purpose of Mental Science.

FURTHER CONSIDERATIONS REGARDING SUBJECTIVE AND OBJECTIVE MIND

An intelligent consideration of the phenomena of hypnotism will show us that what we call the hypnotic state is the *normal* state of the subjective mind. It *always* conceives of itself in accordance with some suggestion conveyed to it, either consciously or unconsciously to the mode of objective mind which governs it, and it gives rise to corresponding external results. The abnormal nature of the conditions induced by experimental hypnotism is in the removal of the normal control held by the individual's own objective mind over his subjective mind and the substitution of some other control for it, and thus we may say that the normal characteristic of the subjective mind is its perpetual action in accordance with some sort of suggestion. It becomes therefore a question of the highest importance to determine in every case what the nature of the suggestion shall be and from what source it shall proceed; but before considering the sources of suggestion we must realize more fully the place taken by subjective mind in the order of Nature.

If the student has followed what has been said regarding the presence of intelligent spirit pervading all space and permeating all matter, he will now have little difficulty in recognizing this all-pervading spirit as universal subjective mind. That it cannot *as universal mind* have the qualities of objective mind is very obvious. The universal mind is the creative power throughout Nature; and as the originating power it must first give rise to the various *forms* in which objective mind recognizes its own individuality, before these individual minds can re-act upon it; and hence, as pure spirit or *first cause*, it cannot possibly be anything else than subjective mind; and the fact which has been abundantly proved by experiment that the subjective mind is the builder of the body shows us that the power of creating by growth from within is the essential characteristic of the subjective mind. Hence, both from experiment and from *a priori* reasoning, we may say that where-ever we find creative power at work there we are in the presence of subjective mind, whether it be working on the grand scale of the cosmos, or on the miniature scale of the individual. We may therefore lay it down as a principle that the universal all-permeating intelligence, which has been considered in the second and third sections, is purely subjective mind, and therefore follows the law of subjective mind, namely that it is amenable to any suggestion, and will carry out any suggestion that is impressed upon it to its most rigorously logical consequences. The incalculable importance of this truth may not perhaps strike the student at first sight, but a little consideration will show him the enormous possibilities that are stored up in it, and in the concluding section I shall briefly touch upon the very serious conclusions resulting from it. For the present it will be sufficient to realize that the subjective mind in ourselves is *the same* subjective mind which is at work throughout the universe giving rise to the infinitude of natural forms with which we are surrounded, and in like manner giving rise *to ourselves also*. It may be called the supporter of our individuality; and we may loosely speak of our individual subjective mind as our personal share in the universal mind. This, of course, does not imply the splitting up of the universal mind into fractions, and it is to avoid this error that I have discussed the essential unity of spirit in the third section, but in order to avoid too highly abstract conceptions in the present stage of the student's progress we may conveniently employ the idea of a personal share in the universal subjective mind.

To realize our individual subjective mind in this manner will help us to get over the great metaphysical difficulty which meets us in our endeavour to make conscious use of first cause, in other words to create external results by the power of our own thought. Ultimately there can be only one first cause which is the universal mind, but because it is universal it cannot, *as universal*, act on the plane of the individual and particular. For it to do so would be for it to cease to be universal and therefore cease to be the creative power which we wish to employ. On the other hand, the fact that we are working for a specific definite object implies our intention to use this universal power in application to a particular purpose, and thus we find ourselves involved in the paradox of seeking to make the universal act on the plane of the particular. We want to effect a junction between the two extremes of the scale of Nature, the innermost creative spirit and a particular external form. Between these two is a great gulf, and the question is how is it to be bridged over. It is here, then, that the conception of our individual subjective mind as our personal share in the universal subjective mind affords the means of meeting the difficulty, for on the one hand it is in immediate connection with the universal mind, and on the other it is immediate connection with the individual objective, or intellectual mind; and this in its turn is in immediate connection with the world of externalization, which is conditioned in time and space; and thus the relation between the subjective and objective minds in the individual forms the bridge which is needed to connect the two extremities of the scale.

The individual subjective mind may therefore be regarded as the organ of the Absolute in precisely the same way that the objective mind is the organ of the Relative, and it is in order to regulate our use of these two organs that it is necessary to understand what the terms "absolute" and "relative" actually mean. The absolute is that idea of a thing which contemplates it as existing *in itself* and not in relation to something else, that is to say, which contemplates the essence of it; and the relative is that idea of a thing which contemplates it as related to other things, that is to say as circumscribed by a certain environment. The absolute is the region of causes, and the relative is the region of conditions; and hence, if we wish to control conditions, this can only be done by our thought-power operating on the plane of the absolute, which it can do only through the medium of the subjective mind. The conscious use of the creative power of thought consists in the attainment of the power of Thinking in the Absolute, and this can only be attained by a clear conception of the interaction between our different mental functions. For this purpose the student cannot too strongly impress upon himself that subjective mind, on whatever scale, is intensely sensitive to suggestion, and as creative power works accurately to the externalization of that suggestion which is most deeply impressed upon it. If then, we would take any idea out of the realm of the relative, where it is limited and restricted by conditions imposed upon it through surrounding circumstances, and transfer it to the realm of the absolute where it is not thus limited, a right recognition of our mental constitution will enable us to do this by a clearly defined method.

The object of our desire is necessarily first conceived by us as bearing some relation to existing circumstances, which may, or may not, appear favourable to it; and what we want to do is to eliminate the element of contingency and attain something which is certain in itself. To do this is to work upon the plane of the absolute, and for this purpose we must endeavour to impress upon our subjective mind the idea of that which we desire quite apart from any conditions. This separation from the elements of condition implies the elimination of the idea of *time*, and consequently we must think of the thing as already in actual existence. Unless we do this we are not consciously operating upon the plane of the absolute, and are therefore not employing the creative power of our thought. The simplest practical method of gaining the habit of thinking in this manner is to conceive the existence in the spiritual world of a spiritual prototype of every existing thing, which becomes the root of the corresponding external existence. If we thus habituate ourselves to look on the spiritual prototype as the essential being of the thing, and the material form as the growth of this prototype into outward expression, then we shall see that the initial step to the production of any external fact must be the creation of its spiritual prototype. This prototype, being purely spiritual, can only be formed by the operation of *thought*, and in order to have substance on the spiritual plane it *must* be thought of as actually existing there. This conception has been elaborated by Plato in his doctrine of archetypal ideas, and by Swedenborg in his doctrine of correspondences; and a still greater teacher has said "All things whatsoever ye pray and ask for, believe that ye *have* received them, and ye *shall* receive them." (Mark xi. 24, R.V.) The difference of the tenses in this passage is remarkable. The speaker bids us first to believe that our desire *has* already been fulfilled, that it is a thing already accomplished, and then its accomplishment *will* follow as a thing in the future. This is nothing else than a concise direction for making use of the creative power of thought by impressing upon the universal subjective mind the particular thing which we desire as an already existing fact. In following this direction we are thinking on the plane of the absolute and eliminating from our minds all consideration of conditions, which imply limitation and the possibility of adverse contingencies; and we are thus planting a seed which, if left undisturbed, will infallibly germinate into external fruition.

By thus making intelligent use of our subjective mind, we, so to speak, create a *nucleus*, which is no sooner created than it begins to exercise an attractive force, drawing to itself material of a like character with its own, and if this process is allowed to go on undisturbed, it will continue until an external form corresponding to the nature of the nucleus comes out into manifestation on the plane of the objective and relative. This is the universal method of Nature on every plane. Some of the most advanced thinkers in modern physical science, in the endeavour to probe the great mystery of the first origin of the world, have postulated the formation of what they call "vortex rings" formed from an infinitely fine primordial substance. They tell us that if such a ring be once formed on the minutest scale and set rotating, then, since it would be moving in pure ether and subject to no friction, it must according to all known laws of physics be indestructible and its motion perpetual. Let two such rings approach each other, and by the law of attraction, they would coalesce into a whole, and so on until manifested matter as we apprehend it with our external senses, is at last formed. Of course no one has ever seen these rings with the physical eye. They are one of those abstractions which result if we follow out the observed law of physics and the unavoidable sequences of mathematics to their necessary consequences. We cannot account for the things that we *can* see unless we assume the existence of other things which we *cannot*; and the "vortex theory" is one of these assumptions. This theory has not been put forward by mental scientists but by purely physical scientists as the ultimate conclusion to which their researches have led them, and this conclusion is that all the innumerable forms of Nature have their origin in the infinitely minute nucleus of the vortex ring, by whatever means the vortex ring may have received its initial impulse, a question with which physical science, as such, is not concerned.

As the vortex theory accounts for the formation of the inorganic world, so does biology account for the formation of the living organism. That also has its origin in a primary nucleus which, as soon as it is established, operates as a centre of attraction for the formation of all those physical organs of which the perfect individual is composed. The science of embryology shows that this rule holds good without exception throughout the whole range of the animal world, including man; and botany shows the same principle at work throughout the vegetable world. All branches of physical science demonstrate the fact that every completed manifestation, of whatever kind and on whatever scale, is started by the establishment of a nucleus, infinitely small but endowed with an unquenchable energy of attraction, causing it to steadily increase in power and definiteness of purpose, until the process of growth is completed and the matured form stands out as an accomplished fact. Now if this be the universal method of Nature, there is nothing unnatural in supposing that it must begin its operation at a stage further back than the formation of the material nucleus. As soon as that is called into being it begins to operate by the law of attraction on the material plane; but what is the force which originates the material nucleus? Let a recent work on physical science give us the answer; "In its ultimate essence, energy may be incomprehensible by us except as an exhibition of the direct operation of that which we call Mind or Will." The quotation is from a course of lectures on "Waves in Water, Air and Æther," delivered in 1902, at the Royal Institution, by J. A. Fleming. Here, then, is the testimony of physical science that the originating energy is Mind or Will; and we are, therefore, not only making a logical deduction from certain unavoidable intuitions of the human mind, but are also following on the lines of the most advanced physical science, when we say that the action of Mind plants that nucleus which, if allowed to grow undisturbed, will eventually attract to itself all the conditions necessary for its manifestation in outward visible form. Now the only action of Mind is Thought; and it is for this reason that by our thoughts we create corresponding external conditions, because we thereby create the nucleus which attracts to itself its own correspondences in due order until the finished work is manifested on the external plane. This is according to the strictly scientific conception of the universal law of growth; and we may therefore briefly sum up the whole argument by saying that our thought of anything forms a spiritual prototype of it, thus constituting a nucleus or centre of attraction for all conditions necessary to its eventual externalization by a law of growth inherent in the prototype itself.

THE LAW OF GROWTH

A correct understanding of the law of growth is of the highest importance to the student of Mental Science. The great fact to be realized regarding Nature is that it is natural. We may pervert the order of Nature, but it will prevail in the long run, returning, as Horace says, by the back door even though we drive it out with a pitchfork; and the beginning, the middle, and the end of the law of Nature is the principle of growth from a vitality inherent in the entity itself. If we realize this from the outset we shall not undo our own work by endeavouring to *force* things to become that which by their own nature they are not. For this reason when the Bible says that "he who believeth shall not make haste," it is enunciating a great natural principle that success, depends on our using, and not opposing, the universal law of growth. No doubt the greater the vitality we put into the germ, which we have agreed to call the spiritual prototype, the quicker it will germinate; but this is simply because by a more realizing conception we put more growing-power into the seed than we do by a feebler conception. Our mistakes always eventually resolve themselves into distrusting the law of growth. Either we fancy we can hasten it by some exertion of our own from *without*, and are thus led into hurry and anxiety, not to say sometimes into the employment, of grievously wrong methods; or else we give up all hope and so deny the germinating power of the seed we have planted. The result in either case is the same, for in either case we are in effect forming a fresh spiritual prototype of an opposite character to our desire, which therefore neutralizes the one first formed, and disintegrates it and usurps its place. The law is always the same, that our Thought forms a spiritual prototype which, if left undisturbed, will reproduce itself in external circumstances; the only difference is in the sort of prototype we form, and thus evil is brought to us by precisely the same law as good.

These considerations will greatly simplify our ideas of life. We have no longer to consider two forces, but only one, as being the cause of all things; the difference between good and evil resulting simply from the direction in which this force is made to flow. It is a universal law that if we reverse the action of a cause we at the same time reverse the effect. With the same apparatus we can commence by mechanical motion which will generate electricity, or we can commence with electricity which will generate mechanical motion; or to take a simple arithmetical instance: if $10/2 = 5$, then $10/5 = 2$; and therefore if we once recognize the power of thought to produce any results at all, we shall see that the law by which negative thought produces negative results is the same by which positive thought produces positive results. Therefore all our distrust of the law of growth, whether shown in the anxious endeavour to bring pressure to bear from without, or in allowing despair to take the place of cheerful expectation, is reversing the action of the original cause and consequently reversing the nature of the results. It is for this reason that the

Bible, which is the most deeply occult of all books, continually lays so much stress upon the efficiency of faith and the destructive influence of unbelief; and in like manner, all books on every branch of spiritual science emphatically warn us against the admission of doubt or fear. They are the inversion of the principle which builds up, and they are therefore the principle which pulls down; but the Law itself never changes, and it is on the unchangeableness of the law that all Mental Science is founded. We are accustomed to realize the unchangeableness of natural law in our every day life, and it should therefore not be difficult to realize that the same unchangeableness of law which obtains on the visible side of nature obtains on the invisible side as well. The variable factor is, not the law, but our own volition; and it is by combining this variable factor with the invariable one that we can produce the various results we desire. The principle of growth is that of inherent vitality in the seed itself, and the operations of the gardener have their exact analogue in Mental Science. We do not *put* the self-expansive vitality into the seed, but we must sow it, and we may also, so to speak, water it by quiet concentrated contemplation of our desire as an actually accomplished fact. But we must carefully remove from such contemplation any idea of a strenuous effort on our part to *make* the seed grow. Its efficacy is in helping to keep out those negative thoughts of doubt which would plant tares among our wheat, and therefore, instead of anything of effort, such contemplation should be accompanied by a feeling of pleasure and restfulness in foreseeing the certain accomplishment of our desires. This is that making our requests known to God *with thanksgiving* which St. Paul recommends, and it has its reason in that perfect wholeness of the Law of Being which only needs our recognition of it to be used by us to any extent we wish.

Some people possess the power of visualization, or making mental pictures of things, in a greater degree than others, and by such this faculty may advantageously be employed to facilitate their realization of the working of the Law. But those who do not possess this faculty in any marked degree, need not be discouraged by their want of it, for visualization is not the only way of realizing that the law is at work on the invisible plane. Those whose mental bias is towards physical science should realize this Law of Growth as the creative force throughout all nature; and those who have a mathematical turn of mind may reflect that all solids are generated from the movement of a point, which, as our old friend Euclid tells us, is that which has no parts nor magnitude, and is therefore as complete an abstraction as any spiritual nucleus could be. To use the apostolic words, we are dealing with the substance of things not seen, and we have to attain that habit of mind by which we shall see its reality and feel that we are mentally manipulating the only substance there ultimately is, and of which all visible things are only different modes. We must therefore regard our mental creations as spiritual realities and then implicitly trust the Law of Growth to do the rest.

RECEPTIVITY

In order to lay the foundations for practical work, the student must endeavour to get a clear conception of what is meant by the intelligence of undifferentiated spirit. We want to grasp the idea of intelligence apart from individuality, an idea which is rather apt to elude us until we grow accustomed to it. It is the failure to realize this quality of spirit that has given rise to all the theological errors that have brought bitterness into the world and has been prominent amongst the causes which have retarded the true development of mankind. To accurately convey this conception in words, is perhaps, impossible, and to attempt definition is to introduce that very idea of limitation which is our object to avoid. It is a matter of feeling rather than of definition; yet some endeavour must be made to indicate the direction in which we must feel for this great truth if we are to find it. The idea is that of realizing personality without that selfhood which differentiates one individual from another. "I am not that other because I am myself"—this is the definition of individual selfhood; but it necessarily imparts the idea of limitation, because the recognition of any other individuality at once affirms a point at which our own individuality ceases and the other begins. Now this mode of recognition cannot be attributed to the Universal Mind. For it to recognize a point where itself ceased and something else began would be to recognize itself as *not* universal; for the meaning of universality is the including of *all* things, and therefore for this intelligence to recognize anything as being *outside itself* would be a denial of its own being. We may therefore say without hesitation that, whatever may be the nature of its intelligence, it must be entirely devoid of the element of self-recognition *as an individual personality* on any scale whatever. Seen in this light it is at once clear that the originating all-pervading Spirit is the grand impersonal principle of Life which gives rise to all the particular manifestations of Nature. Its absolute impersonalness, in the sense of the entire absence of any consciousness of *individual* selfhood, is a point on which it is impossible to insist too strongly. The attributing of an impossible individuality to the Universal Mind is one of the two grand errors which we find sapping the foundations of religion and philosophy in all ages. The other consists in rushing to the opposite extreme and denying the quality of personal intelligence to the Universal Mind. The answer to this error remains, as of old, in the simple question, "He that made the eye shall He not see? He that planted the ear shall He not hear?"—or to use a popular proverb, "You cannot get out of a bag more than there is in it;" and consequently the fact that we ourselves are centres of personal intelligence is proof that the infinite, from which these centres are concentrated, must be infinite intelligence, and thus we cannot avoid attributing to it the two factors which constitute personality, namely, intelligence and volition. We are therefore brought to the conclusion that this universally diffused essence, which we might think of as a sort of spiritual protoplasm, must possess all the qualities of personality without that conscious recognition of self which constitutes separate individuality: and since the word "personality" has became so associated in our ordinary talk with the idea of "individuality" it will perhaps be better to coin a new word, and speak of the personalness of the Universal Mind as indicating its personal *quality*, apart from individuality. We must realize that this universal spirit permeates all space and all manifested substance, just as physical scientists tell us that the ether does, and that wherever it is, there it must carry with it all that it is in its own being; and we shall then see that we are in the midst of an ocean of undifferentiated yet intelligent Life, above, below, and all around, and permeating ourselves both mentally and corporeally, and all other beings as well.

Gradually as we come to realize the truth of this statement, our eyes will begin to open to its immense significance. It means that all Nature is pervaded by an interior personalness, infinite in its potentialities of intelligence, responsiveness, and power of expression, and only waiting to be called into activity by our recognition of it. By the terms of its nature it can respond to us only as we recognize it. If we are at that intellectual level where we can see nothing but chance governing the world, then this underlying universal mind will present to us nothing but a fortuitous confluence of forces without any intelligible order. If we are sufficiently advanced to see that such a confluence could only produce a chaos, and not a cosmos, then our conceptions expand to the idea of universal Law, and we find *this* to be the nature of the all-underlying principle. We have made an immense advance from the realm of mere accident into a world where there are definite principles on which we can calculate with certainty *when we know them*. But here is the crucial point. The laws of the universe are there, but we are ignorant of them, and only through experience gained by repeated failures can we get any insight into the laws with which we have to deal. How painful each step and how slow the progress! Æons upon æons would not suffice to grasp all the laws of the universe in their totality, not in the visible world only, but also in the world of the unseen; each failure to know the true law implies suffering arising from our ignorant breach of it; and thus, since Nature is infinite, we are met by the paradox that we must in some way contrive to compass the knowledge of the infinite with our individual intelligence, and we must perform a pilgrimage along an unceasing Via Dolorosa beneath the lash of the inexorable Law until we find the solution to the problem. But it will be asked, May we not go on until at last we attain the possession of all knowledge? People do not realize what is meant by "the infinite," or they would not ask such questions. The infinite is that which is limitless and exhaustless. Imagine the vastest capacity you will, and having filled it with the infinite, what remains of the infinite is just as infinite as before. To the mathematician this may be put very clearly. Raise x to any power you will, and however vast may be the disparity between it and the lower powers of x, both are equally incommensurable with x^n. The universal reign of Law is a magnificent truth; it is one of the two great pillars of the universe symbolized by the two pillars that stood at the entrance to Solomon's temple: it is Jachin, but Jachin must be equilibriated by Boaz.

It is an enduring truth, which can never be altered, that every infraction of the Law of Nature must carry its punitive consequences with it. We can never get beyond the range of cause and effect. There is no escaping from the law of punishment, except by knowledge. If we know a law of Nature and work with it, we shall find it our unfailing friend, ever ready to serve us, and never rebuking us for past failures; but if we ignorantly or wilfully transgress it, it is our implacable enemy, until we again become obedient to it; and therefore the only redemption from perpetual pain and servitude is by a self-expansion which can grasp infinitude itself. How is this to be accomplished? By our progress to that kind and degree of intelligence by which we realize the inherent *personalness* of the divine all-pervading Life, which is at once the Law and the Substance of all that is. Well said the Jewish rabbis of old, "The Law is a Person." When we once realize that the universal Life and the universal Law are one with the universal Personalness, then we have established the pillar Boaz as the needed complement to Jachin; and when we find the common point in which these two unite, we have raised the Royal Arch through which we may triumphantly enter the Temple. We must dissociate the Universal Personalness from every conception of individuality. The universal can never be the individual: that would be a contradiction in terms. But because the universal personalness is the root of all individual personalities, it finds its highest expression in response to those who realize its personal nature. And it is this recognition that solves the seemingly insoluble paradox. The only way to attain that knowledge of the Infinite Law which will change the Via Dolorosa into the Path of Joy is to embody in ourselves a *principle* of knowledge commensurate with the infinitude of that which is to be known; and this is accomplished by realizing that, infinite as the law itself, is a universal Intelligence in the midst of which we float as in a living ocean. Intelligence without individual personality, but which, in producing us, concentrates itself into the personal individualities which we are. What should be the relation of such an intelligence towards us? Not one of favouritism: not any more than the Law can it respect one person above another, for itself is the root and support for each alike. Not one of refusal to our advances; for without individuality it can have no personal object of its own to conflict with ours; and since it is itself the origin of all individual intelligence, it cannot be shut off by inability to understand. By the very terms of its being, therefore, this infinite, underlying, all-producing Mind must be ready immediately to respond to all who realize their true relation to it. As the very principle of Life itself it must be infinitely susceptible to feeling, and consequently it will reproduce with absolute accuracy whatever conception of itself we impress upon it; and hence if we realize the human mind as that stage in the evolution of the cosmic order at which an individuality has arisen capable of expressing, not merely the livingness, but also the personalness of the universal underlying spirit, then we see that its most perfect mode of self-expression must be by identifying itself with these individual personalities.

The identification is, of course, limited by the measure of the individual intelligence, meaning, not merely the intellectual perception of the sequence of cause and effect, but also that indescribable reciprocity of *feeling* by which we instinctively recognize something in another making them akin to ourselves; and so it is that when we intelligently realize that the innermost principle of being, must by reason of its universality, have a common nature with our own, then we have solved the paradox of universal knowledge, for we have realized our identity of being with the Universal Mind, which is commensurate with the Universal Law. Thus we arrive at the truth of St. John's statement, "Ye know all things," only this knowledge is primarily on the spiritual plane. It is not brought out into intellectual statement whether needed or not; for it is not in itself the specific knowledge of particular facts, but it is the undifferentiated principle of knowledge which we may differentiate in any direction that we choose. This is a philosophical necessity of the case, for though the action of the individual mind consists in differentiating the universal into particular applications, to differentiate the *whole* universal would be a contradiction in terms; and so, because we cannot exhaust the infinite, our possession of it must consist in our power to differentiate it as the occasion may require, the only limit being that which we ourselves assign to the manifestation.

In this way, then, the recognition of the community of *personality* between ourselves and the universal undifferentiated Spirit, which is the root and substance of all things, solves the question of our release from the iron grasp of an inflexible Law, not by abrogating the Law, which would mean the annihilation of all things, but by producing in us an intelligence equal in affinity with the universal Law itself, and thus enabling us to apprehend and meet the requirements of the Law in each particular as it arises. In this way the Cosmic Intelligence becomes individualized, and the individual intelligence becomes universalized; the two became one, and in proportion as this unity is realized and acted on, it will be found that the Law, which gives rise to all outward conditions, whether of body or of circumstances, becomes more and more clearly understood, and can therefore be more freely made use of, so that by steady, intelligent endeavour to unfold upon these lines we may reach degrees of power to which it is impossible to assign any limits. The student who would understand the rationale of the unfoldment of his own possibilities must make no mistake here. He must realize that the whole process is that of bringing the universal within the grasp of the individual by raising the individual to the level of the universal and not vice-versa. It is a mathematical truism that you cannot contract the infinite, and that you *can* expand the individual; and it is precisely on these lines that evolution works. The laws of nature cannot be altered in the least degree; but we can come into such a realization of our own relation to the universal principle of Law that underlies them as to be able to press all particular laws, whether of the visible or invisible side of Nature, into our service and so find ourselves masters of the situation. This is to be accomplished by knowledge; and the only knowledge which will effect this purpose in all its measureless immensity is the knowledge of the personal element in Universal Spirit in its reciprocity to our own personality. Our recognition of this Spirit must therefore be twofold, as the principle of necessary sequence, order or Law, and also as the principle of Intelligence, responsive to our own recognition of it.

RECIPROCAL ACTION OF THE UNIVERSAL AND INDIVIDUAL MINDS.

It must be admitted that the foregoing considerations bring us to the borders of theological speculation, but the student must bear in mind that as a Mental Scientist it is his business to regard even the most exalted spiritual phenomena from a purely scientific standpoint, which is that of the working of a universal natural Law. If he thus simply deals with the facts as he finds them, there is little doubt that the true meaning of many theological statements will become clear to him: but he will do well to lay it down as a general rule that it is not necessary either to the use or understanding of any law, whether on the personal or the impersonal side of Nature, that we should give a theological explanation of it: although, therefore, the personal quality inherent in the universal underlying spirit, which is present in all things, cannot be too strongly insisted upon, we must remember that in dealing with it we are still dealing with a purely natural power which reappears at every point with protean variety of form, whether as person, animal, or thing. In each case what it becomes to any individual is exactly measured by that individual's recognition of it. To each and all it bears the relation of supporter of the race, and where the individual development is incapable of realizing anything more, this is the limit of the relation; but as the individual's power of recognition expands, he finds a reciprocal expansion on the part of this intelligent power which gradually develops into the consciousness of intimate companionship between the individualized mind and the unindividualized source of it.

Now this is exactly the relation which, on ordinary scientific principles, we should expect to find between the individual and the cosmic mind, on the supposition that the cosmic mind is subjective mind, and for reasons already given we can regard it in no other light. As subjective mind it must reproduce exactly the conception of itself which the objective mind of the individual, acting through his own subjective mind, impresses upon it; and at the same time as creative mind, it builds up external facts in correspondence with this conception. "Quot homines tot sententiæ": each one externalizes in his outward circumstances precisely his idea of the Universal Mind; and the man who realizes that by the natural law of mind he can bring the Universal Mind into perfectly reciprocal action with its own, will on the one hand make it a source of infinite instruction, and on the other a source of infinite power. He will thus wisely alternate the personal and impersonal aspects respectively between his individual mind and the Universal Mind; when he is seeking for guidance or strength he will regard his own mind as the impersonal element which is to *receive personality* from the superior wisdom and force of the Greater Mind; and when, on the other hand, he is to give out the stores thus accumulated, he must reverse the position and consider his own mind as the personal element, and the Universal Mind as the impersonal, which he can therefore *direct* with certainty by impressing his own personal desire upon it. We need not be staggered at the greatness of this conclusion, for it follows necessarily from the natural relation between the subjective and the objective minds; and the only question is whether we will limit our view to the lower level of the latter, or expand it so as to take in the limitless possibilities which the subjective mind presents to us.

I have dealt with this question at some length because it affords the key to two very important subjects, the Law of Supply and the nature of Intuition. Students often find it easier to understand how the mind can influence the body with which it is so intimately associated, than how it can influence circumstances. If the operation of thought-power were confined exclusively to the individual mind this difficulty might arise; but if there is one lesson the student of Mental Science should take to heart more than another, it is that the action of thought-power is not limited to a circumscribed individuality. What the individual does is to *give direction* to something which is unlimited, to call into action a force infinitely greater than his own, which because it is in itself impersonal though intelligent, will receive the impress of his personality, and can therefore make its influence felt far beyond the limits which bound the individual's objective perception of the circumstances with which he has to deal. It is for this reason that I lay so much stress on the combination of two apparent opposites in the Universal Mind, the union of intelligence with impersonality. The intelligence not only enables it to receive the impress of our thought, but also causes it to devise exactly the right *means* for bringing it into accomplishment. This is only the logical result of the hypothesis that we are dealing with infinite Intelligence which is also infinite Life. Life means Power, and infinite life therefore means limitless power; and limitless power moved by limitless intelligence cannot be conceived of as ever stopping short of the accomplishment of its object; therefore, given the *intention* on the part of the Universal Mind, there can be no doubt as to its ultimate accomplishment. Then comes the question of intention. How do we know what the intention of the Universal Mind may be? Here comes in the element of impersonality. It has *no intention*, because it is *impersonal*. As I have already said, the Universal mind works by a law of averages for the advancement of the race, and is in no way concerned with the particular wishes of the individual. If his wishes are in line with the forward movement of the everlasting principle, there is nowhere in Nature any power to restrict him in their fulfilment. If they are opposed to the general forward movement, then they will bring him into collision with it, and it will crush him. From the relation between them it results that the same principle which shows itself in the individual mind as Will, becomes in the universal mind a Law of Tendency; and the direction of this tendency must always be to life-givingness, because the universal mind is the undifferentiated Life-spirit of the universe. Therefore in every case the test is whether our particular intention is in this same lifeward direction: and if it is, then we may be absolutely certain that there is no intention on the part of the Universal Mind to thwart the intention of our own individual mind; we are dealing with a purely impersonal force, and it will no more oppose us by specific plans of its own than will steam or electricity. Combining then, these two aspects of the Universal Mind, its utter impersonality and its perfect intelligence, we find precisely the sort of natural force we are in want of, something which will undertake whatever we put into its hands without asking questions or bargaining for terms, and which, having undertaken our business, will bring to bear on it an intelligence to which the united knowledge of the whole human race is as nothing, and a power equal to this intelligence. I may be using a rough and ready mode of expression, but my object is to bring home to the student the nature of the power he can employ and the method of employing it, and I may therefore state the whole position thus:—Your object is not to run the whole cosmos, but to draw particular benefits, physical, mental, moral, or financial into your own or someone else's life. From this individual point of view the universal creative power has no mind of its own, and therefore you can make up its mind for it. When its mind is thus made up for it, it never abrogates its place as the creative power, but at once sets to work co carry out the purpose for which it has thus been concentrated; and unless this concentration is dissipated by the same agency (yourself) which first produced it, it will work on by the law of growth to complete manifestation on the outward plane.

In dealing with this great impersonal intelligence, we are dealing with the infinite, and we must fully realize infinitude as that which touches all points, and if it does, there should be no difficulty in understanding that this intelligence can draw together the means requisite for its purpose even from the ends of the world; and therefore, realizing the Law according to which the result can be produced, we must resolutely put aside all questioning as to the specific means which will be employed in any case. To question this is to sow that very seed of doubt which it is our first object to eradicate, and our intellectual endeavour should therefore be directed, not to the attempt to foretell the various secondary causes which will eventually combine to produce the desired result, laying down beforehand what particular causes should be necessary, and from what quarter they should come; but we should direct our intellectual endeavour to seeing more clearly the rationale of the general law by which trains of secondary causes are set in motion. Employed in the former way our intellect becomes the greatest hindrance to our success, for it only helps to increase our doubts, since it is trying to grasp particulars which, at the time are entirely outside its circle of vision; but employed in the latter it affords the most material aid in maintaining that nucleus without which there is no centre from which the principle of growth can assert itself. The intellect can only deduce consequences from facts which it is able to state, and consequently cannot deduce any assurance from facts of whose existence it cannot yet have any knowledge through the medium of the outward senses; but for the same reason it can realize the existence of a *Law* by which the as yet unmanifested circumstances may be brought into manifestation. Thus used in its right order, the intellect becomes the handmaid of that more interior power within us which manipulates the unseen substance of all things, and which we may call relative first cause.

CAUSES AND CONDITIONS

The expression *"relative* first cause" has been used in the last section to distinguish the action of the creative principle in the *individual* mind from Universal First Cause on the one hand and from secondary causes on the other. As it exists in *us*, primary causation is the power to initiate a train of causation directed to an individual purpose. As the power of initiating a fresh sequence of cause and effect it is first cause, and as referring to an individual purpose it is relative, and it may therefore be spoken of as relative first cause, or the power of primary causation manifested by the individual. The understanding and use of this power is the whole object of Mental Science, and it is therefore necessary that the student should clearly see the relation between causes and conditions. A simple illustration will go further for this purpose than any elaborate explanation. If a lighted candle is brought into a room the room becomes illuminated, and if the candle is taken away it becomes dark again. Now the illumination and the darkness are both conditions, the one positive resulting from the presence of the light, and the other negative resulting from its absence: from this simple example we therefore see that every positive condition has an exactly opposite negative condition corresponding to it, and that this correspondence results from their being related to the *same cause*, the one positively and the other negatively; and hence we may lay down the rule that all positive conditions result from the active presence of a certain cause, and all negative conditions from the absence of such a cause. A condition, whether positive or negative, is never *primary* cause, and the *primary* cause of any series can never be negative, for negation is the condition which arises from the absence of active causation. This should be thoroughly understood as it is the philosophic basis of all those "denials" which play so important a, part in Mental Science, and which may be summed up in the statement that evil being negative, or privation of good, has no substantive existence in itself. Conditions, however, whether positive or negative, are no sooner called into existence than they become causes in their turn and produce further conditions, and so on *ad infinitum*, thus giving rise to the whole train of secondary causes. So long as we judge only from the information conveyed to us by the outward senses, we are working on the plane of secondary causation and see nothing but a succession of conditions, forming part of an endless train of antecedent conditions coming out of the past and stretching away into the future, and from this point of view we are under the rule of an iron destiny from which there seems no possibility of escape. This is because the outward senses are only capable of dealing with the relations which one mode of limitation bears to another, for they are the instruments by which we take cognizance of the relative and the conditioned. Now the only way of escape is by rising out of the region of secondary causes into that of primary causation, where the originating energy is to be found before it has yet passed into manifestation as a condition. This region is to be found *within ourselves*; it is the region of pure ideas; and it is for this reason that I have laid stress on the two aspects of spirit as pure thought and manifested form. The thought-image or ideal pattern of a thing is the *first cause* relatively to that thing; it is the substance of that thing untrammelled, by any antecedent conditions.

If we realize that all visible things *must* have their origin in spirit, then the whole creation around us is the standing evidence that the starting-point of all things is in thought-images or ideas, for no other action than the formation of such images can be conceived of spirit prior to its manifestation in matter. If, then, this is spirit's modus operandi for self-expression, we have only to transfer this conception from the scale of cosmic spirit working on the plane of the universal to that of individualized spirit working on the plane of the particular, to see that the formation of an ideal image by means of our thought is setting first cause in motion with regard to this specific object. There is no difference in kind between the operation of first cause in the universal and in the particular, the difference is only a difference of scale, but the power itself is identical. We must therefore always be very clear as to whether we are *consciously* using first cause or not. Note the word "consciously" because, whether consciously or unconsciously, we are always using first cause; and it was for this reason I emphasized the fact that the Universal Mind is purely subjective and therefore bound by the laws which apply to subjective mind on whatever scale. Hence we are *always* impressing some sort of ideas upon it, whether we are aware of the fact or not, and all our existing limitations result from our having habitually impressed upon it that idea of limitation which we have imbibed by restricting all possibility to the region of secondary causes. But now when investigation has shown us that conditions are never causes in *themselves*, but only the subsequent links of a chain started on the plane of the pure ideal, what we have to do is to reverse our method of thinking and regard the ideal as the real, and the outward manifestation as a mere reflection which must change with every change of the object which casts it. For these reasons it is essential to know whether we are consciously making use of first cause with a definite purpose or not, and the criterion is this. If we regard the fulfilment of our purpose as contingent upon any *circumstances*, past, present, or future, we are not making use of first cause; we have descended to the level of secondary causation, which is the region of doubts, fears, and limitations, all of which we are impressing upon the universal subjective mind with the inevitable result that it will build up corresponding external conditions. But if we realize that the region of secondary causes is the region of mere reflections we shall not think of our purpose as contingent on any conditions whatever, but shall know that by forming the idea of it in the absolute, and maintaining that idea, we have shaped the first cause into the desired form and can await the result with cheerful expectancy.

It is here that we find the importance of realizing spirit's independence of time and space. An ideal, as such, cannot be formed in the future. It must either be formed here and now or not be formed at all; and it is for this reason that every teacher, who has ever spoken with due knowledge of the subject, has impressed upon his followers the necessity of picturing to themselves the fulfilment of their desires as *already accomplished* on the spiritual plane, as the indispensable condition of fulfilment in the visible and concrete.

When this is properly understood, any anxious thought as to the *means* to be employed in the accomplishment of our purposes is seen to be quite unnecessary. If the end is already secured, then it follows that all the steps leading to it are secured also. The means will pass into the smaller circle of our conscious activities day by day in due order, and then we have to work upon them, not with fear, doubt, or feverish excitement, but calmly and joyously, because we *know* that the end is already secured, and that our reasonable use of such means as present themselves in the desired direction is, only one portion of a much larger co-ordinated movement, the final result of which admits of no doubt. Mental Science does not offer a premium to idleness, but it takes, all work out of the region of anxiety and toil by assuring the worker of the success of his labour, if not in the precise form he anticipated, then in some other still better suited to his requirements. But suppose, when we reach a point where some momentous decision has to be made, we happen to decide wrongly? On the hypothesis that the end is already secured you cannot decide wrongly. Your right decision is as much one of the necessary steps in the accomplishment of the end as any of the other conditions leading up to it, and therefore, while being careful to avoid rash action, we may make sure that the same Law which is controlling the rest of the circumstances in the right direction will influence our judgment in that direction also. To get good results we must properly understand our relation to the great impersonal power we are using. It is intelligent and we are intelligent, and the two intelligences must co-operate. We must not fly in the face of the Law by expecting it to do *for* us what it can only do *through* us; and we must therefore use our intelligence with the knowledge that it is acting *as the instrument of a greater intelligence*; and because we have this knowledge we may, and should, cease from all anxiety as to the final result. In actual practice we must first form the ideal conception of our object with the definite intention of impressing it upon the universal mind—it is this intention which takes such thought out of the region of mere casual fancies—and then affirm that our knowledge of the Law is sufficient reason for a calm expectation of a corresponding result, and that therefore all necessary conditions will come to us in due order. We can then turn to the affairs of our daily life with the calm assurance that the initial conditions are either there already or will soon come into view. If we do not at once see them, let us rest content with the knowledge that the spiritual prototype is already in existence and wait till some circumstance pointing in the desired direction begins to show itself. It may be a very small circumstance, but it is the direction and not the magnitude which is to be taken into consideration. As soon as we see it we should regard it as the first sprouting of the seed we have sown in the Absolute, and do calmly, and without excitement, whatever the circumstances may seem to require, and then later on we shall see that this doing will in turn lead to further circumstances in the same direction until we find ourselves conducted step by step to the accomplishment of our object. In this way the understanding of the great principle of the Law of Supply will, by repeated experiences, deliver us more and more completely out of the region of anxious thought and toilsome labour and bring us into a new world where the useful employment of all our powers, whether mental or physical, will only be an unfolding of our individuality upon the lines of its own nature, and therefore a perpetual source of health and happiness; a sufficient inducement, surely, to the careful study of the laws governing the relation between the individual and the Universal Mind.

INTUITION

We have seen that the subjective mind is amenable to suggestion by the objective mind; but there is also an action of the subjective mind upon the objective. The individual's subjective mind is his own innermost self, and its first care is the maintenance of the individuality of which it is the foundation; and since it is pure spirit it has its continual existence in that plane of being where all things subsist in the universal here and the everlasting now, and consequently can, inform the lower mind of things removed from its ken either by distance or futurity. As the absence of the conditions of time and space must logically concentrate all things into a present focus, we can assign no limit to the subjective mind's power of perception, and therefore the question arises, why does it not keep the objective mind continually informed on all points? And the answer is that it would do so if the objective mind were sufficiently trained to recognize the indications given, and to effect this training is one of the purposes of Mental Science. When once we recognize the position of the subjective mind as the supporter of the whole individuality we cannot doubt that much of what we take to be the spontaneous movement of the objective mind has its origin in the subjective mind prompting the objective mind in the right direction without our being consciously aware of it. But at times when the urgency of the case seems to demand it, or when, for some reason yet unknown, the objective mind is for a while more closely *en rapport* with the subjective mind, the interior voice is heard strongly and persistently; and when this is the case we do well to pay heed to it. Want of space forbids me to give examples, but doubtless such will not be wanting in the reader's experience.

The importance of understanding and following the intuition cannot be exaggerated, but I candidly admit the great practical difficulty of keeping the happy mean between the disregard of the interior voice and allowing ourselves to be run away with by groundless fancies. The best guide is the knowledge that comes of personal experience which gradually leads to the acquisition of a sort of inward sense of touch that enables us to distinguish the true from the false, and which appears to grow with the sincere desire for truth and with the recognition of the spirit as its source. The only general principles the writer can deduce from his own experience are that when, in spite of all appearances pointing in the direction of a certain line of conduct, there is still a persistent *feeling* that it should not be followed, in the majority of instances it will be found that the argument of the objective mind, however correct on the facts objectively known, was deficient from ignorance of facts which could not be objectively known at the time, but which were known to the intuitive faculty. Another principle is that our *very first* impression of feeling on any subject is generally correct. Before the objective mind has begun to argue on the subject it is like the surface of a smooth lake which clearly reflects the light from above; but as soon as it begins to argue from outside appearances these also throw their reflections upon its surface, so that the original image becomes blurred and is no longer recognizable. This first conception is very speedily lost, and it should therefore be carefully observed and registered in the memory with a view to testing the various arguments which will subsequently arise on the objective plane. It is however impossible to reduce so interior an action as that of the intuition to the form of hard and fast rules, and beyond carefully noting particular cases as they occur, probably the best plan for the student will be to include the whole subject of intuition in the general principle of the Law of Attraction, especially if he sees how this law interacts with that personal quality of universal spirit of which we have already spoken.

HEALING

The subject of healing has been elaborately treated by many writers and fully deserves all the attention that has been given to it, but the object of these lectures is rather to ground the student in those general principles on which *all* conscious use of the creative power of thought is based, than to lay down formal rules for specific applications of it. I will therefore examine the broad principles which appear to be common to the various methods of mental healing which are in use, each of which derives its efficacy, not from the peculiarity of the method, but from it being such a method as allows the higher laws of Nature to come into play. Now the principle universally laid down by all mental healers, in whatever various terms they may explain it, is that the basis of all healing is a change in belief. The sequence from which this results is as follows:—the subjective mind is the creative faculty within us, and creates whatever the objective mind impresses upon it; the objective mind, or intellect, impresses its thought upon it; the thought is the expression of the belief; hence whatever the subjective mind creates is the reproduction externally of our beliefs. Accordingly our whole object is to change our beliefs, and we cannot do this without some solid ground of conviction of the falsity of our old beliefs and of the truth of our new ones, and this ground we find in that law of causation which I have endeavoured to explain. The wrong belief which externalizes as sickness is the belief that some secondary cause, which is really only a condition, is a primary cause. The knowledge of the law shows that there is only *one* primary cause, and this is the factor which in our own individuality we call subjective or sub-conscious mind. For this reason I have insisted on the difference between placing an idea in the sub-conscious mind, that is, on the plane of the absolute and without reference to time and space, and placing the same idea in the conscious intellectual mind which only perceives things as related to time and space. Now the only conception you can have of *yourself* in the absolute, or unconditioned, is as *purely living Spirit*, not hampered by conditions of any sort, and therefore not subject to illness; and when this idea is firmly impressed on the sub-conscious mind, it will externalize it. The reason why this process is not always successful at the first attempt is that all our life we have been holding the false belief in sickness as a substantial entity in itself and thus being a primary cause, instead of being merely a negative *condition* resulting from the *obsence* of a primary cause; and a belief which has become ingrained from childhood cannot be eradicated at a moment's notice. We often find, therefore, that for some time after a treatment there is an improvement in the patient's health, and then the old symptoms return. This is because the new belief in his own creative faculty has not yet had time to penetrate down to the innermost depths of the subconscious mind, but has only partially entered it. Each succeeding treatment strengthens the sub-conscious mind in its hold of the new belief until at last a permanent cure is effected. This is the method of self-treatment based on the patient's own knowledge of the law of his being.

But "there is not in all men this knowledge," or at any rate not such a full recognition of it as will enable them to give successful treatment to themselves, and in these cases the intervention of the healer becomes necessary. The only difference between the healer and the patient is that the healer has learnt how to control the less self-conscious modes of the spirit by the more self-conscious mode, while the patient has not yet attained to this knowledge; and what the healer does is to substitute his own objective or conscious mentality, which is will joined to intellect, for that of the patient, and in this way to find entrance to his sub-conscious mind and impress upon it the suggestion of perfect health.

The question then arises, how can the healer substitute his own conscious mind for that of the patient? and the answer shows the practical application of those very abstract principles which I have laid down in the earlier sections. Our ordinary conception of ourselves is that of an individual personality which ends where another personality begins, in other words that the two personalities are entirely separate. This is an error. There is no such hard and fast line of demarcation between personalities, and the boundaries between one and another can be increased or reduced in rigidity according to will, in fact they may be temporarily removed so completely that, for the time being, the two personalities become merged into one. Now the action which takes place between healer and patient depends on this principle. The patient is asked by the healer to put himself in a receptive mental attitude, which means that he is to exercise his volition for the purpose of removing the barrier of his own objective personality and thus affording entrance to the mental power of the healer. On his side also the healer does the same thing, only with this difference, that while the patient withdraws the barrier on his side with the intention of admitting a flowing-in, the healer does so with the intention of allowing a flowing-out: and thus by the joint action of the two minds the barriers of both personalities are removed and the direction of the flow of volition is determined, that is to say, it flows from the healer as actively willing to give, towards the patient as passively willing to receive, according to the universal law of Nature that the flow must always be from the *plenum* to the *vacuum*. This mutual removal of the external mental barrier between healer and patient is what is termed establishing a *rapport* between them, and here we find one most valuable practical application of the principle laid down earlier in this book, that pure spirit is present in its entirety at every point simultaneously. It is for this reason that as soon as the healer realizes that the barriers of external personality between himself and his patient have been removed, he can then speak to the sub-conscious mind of the patient as though it were his own, for both being pure spirit the *thought* of their identity *makes* them identical, and both are concentrated into a single entity at a single point upon which the conscious mind of the healer can be brought to bear, according to the universal principle of the control of the subjective mind by the objective mind through suggestion. It is for this reason I have insisted on the distinction between *pure* spirit, or spirit conceived of apart from extension in any matrix and the conception of it as so extended. If we concentrate our mind upon the diseased condition of the patient we are thinking of him as a separate personality, and are not fixing our mind upon that conception of him as pure spirit which will afford us effectual entry to his springs of being. We must therefore withdraw our thought from the contemplation of symptoms, and indeed from his corporeal personality altogether, and must think of him as a purely spiritual individuality, and as such entirely free from subjection to any conditions, and consequently as voluntarily externalizing the conditions most expressive of the vitality and intelligence which pure spirit is. Thinking of him thus, we then make mental affirmation that he shall build up outwardly the correspondence of that perfect vitality which he knows himself to be inwardly; and this suggestion being impressed by the healer's conscious thought, while the patient's conscious thought is at the same time impressing the fact that he is receiving the active thought of the healer, the result is that the patient's sub-conscious mind becomes thoroughly imbued with the recognition of its own life-giving power, and according to the recognized law of subjective mentality proceeds to work out this suggestion into external manifestation, and thus health is substituted for sickness.

It must be understood that the purpose of the process here described is to strengthen the subject's individuality, not to dominate it. To use it for domination is *inversion*, bringing its appropriate penalty to the operator.

In this description I have contemplated the case where the patient is consciously co-operating with the healer, and it is in order to obtain this co-operation that the mental healer usually makes a point of instructing the patient in the broad principles of Mental Science, if he is not already acquainted with them. But this is not always advisable or possible. Sometimes the statement of principles opposed to existing prejudices arouses opposition, and any active antagonism on the patient's part must tend to intensify the barrier of conscious personality which it is the healer's first object to remove. In these cases nothing is so effective as *absent treatment*. If the student has grasped all that has been said on the subject of spirit and matter, he will see that in mental treatment time and space count for nothing, because the whole action takes place on a plane where these conditions do not obtain; and it is therefore quite immaterial whether the patient be in the immediate presence of the healer or in a distant country. Under these circumstances it is found by experience that one of the most effectual modes of mental healing is by treatment during sleep, because then the patient's whole system is naturally in a state of relaxation which prevents him offering any conscious opposition to the treatment. And by the same rule the healer also is able to treat even more effectively during his own sleep than while waking. Before going to sleep he firmly impresses on his subjective mind that it is to convey curative suggestion to the subjective mind of the patient, and then, by the general principles of the relation between subjective and objective mind this suggestion is carried out during all the hours that the conscious individuality is wrapped in repose. This method is applicable to young children to whom the principles of the science cannot be explained; and also to persons at a distance: and indeed the only advantage gained by the personal meeting of the patient and healer is in the instruction that can be orally given, or when the patient is at that early stage of knowledge where the healer's visible presence conveys the suggestion that something is then being done which could not be done in his absence; otherwise the presence or absence of the patient are matters perfectly indifferent. The student must always recollect that the sub- conscious mind does not have to work *through* the intellect or conscious mind to produce its curative effects. It is part of the all-pervading creative force of Nature, while the intellect is not creative but distributive.

From mental healing it is but a step to telepathy, clairvoyance and other, kindred manifestations of transcendental power which, are from time to time exhibited by the subjective entity and which follow laws as accurate as those which govern what we are accustomed to consider our more normal faculties; but these subjects do not properly fall within the scope of a book whose purpose is to lay down the broad principles which underlie *all* spiritual phenomena. Until these are clearly understood the student cannot profitably attempt the detailed study of the more interior powers; for to do so without a firm foundation of knowledge and some experience in its practical application would only be to expose himself to unknown dangers, and would be contrary to the scientific principle that the advance into the unknown can only be made from the standpoint of the known, otherwise we only come into a confused region of guess-work without any clearly defined principles for our guidance.

THE WILL

The Will is of such primary importance that the student should be on his guard against any mistake as to the position which it holds in the mental economy. Many writers and teachers insist on will-power as though that were the creative faculty. No doubt intense will-power can evolve certain external results, but like all other methods of compulsion it lacks the permanency of natural growth. The appearances, forms, and conditions produced by mere intensity of will-power will only hang together so long as the compelling force continues; but let it be exhausted or withdrawn, and the elements thus forced into unnatural combination will at once fly back to their proper affinities; the form created by compulsion never had the germ of vitality *in itself* and is therefore dissipated as soon as the external energy which supported it is withdrawn. The mistake is in attributing the creative power to the will, or perhaps I should say in attributing the creative power to ourselves at all. The truth is that man never creates anything. His function is, not to create, but to combine and distribute that which is already in being, and what we call our creations are new combinations of already existing material, whether mental or corporeal. This is amply demonstrated in the physical sciences. No one speaks of creating energy, but only of transforming one form of energy into another; and if we realize this as a universal principle, we shall see that on the mental plane as well as on the physical we never create energy but only provide the conditions by which the energy already existing in one mode can exhibit itself in another: therefore what, relatively to man, we call his creative power, is that receptive attitude of expectancy which, so to say, makes a mould into which the plastic and as yet undifferentiated substance can flow and take the desired form. The will has much the same place in our mental machinery that the tool-holder has in a power-lathe: it is not the power, but it keeps the mental faculties in that position relatively to the power which enables it to do the desired work. If, using the word in its widest sense, we may say that the imagination is the creative function, we may call the will the centralizing principle. Its function is to keep the imagination centred in the right direction. We are aiming at consciously controlling our mental powers instead of letting them hurry us hither and thither in a purposeless manner, and we must therefore understand the relation of these powers to each other for the production of external results. First the whole train of causation is started by some emotion which gives rise to a desire; next the judgment determines whether we shall externalize this desire or not; then the desire having been approved by the judgment, the will comes forward and directs the imagination to form the necessary spiritual prototype; and the imagination thus centred on a particular object creates the spiritual nucleus, which in its turn acts as a centre round which the forces of attraction begin to work, and continue to operate until, by the law of growth, the concrete result becomes perceptible to our external senses.

The business of the will, then, is to retain the various faculties of our mind in that position where they are really doing the work we wish, and this position may be generalized into the three following attitudes; either we wish to act upon something, or be acted on by it, or to maintain a neutral position; in other words we either intend to project a force, or receive a force or keep a position of inactivity relatively to some particular object. Now the judgment determines which of these three positions we shall take up, the consciously active, the consciously receptive, or the consciously neutral; and then the function of the will is simply to maintain the position we have determined upon; and if we maintain any given mental attitude we may reckon with all certainty on the law of attraction drawing us to those correspondences which exteriorly symbolize the attitude in question. This is very different from the semi-animal screwing-up of the nervous forces which, with some people, stands for will-power. It implies no strain on the nervous system and is consequently not followed by any sense of exhaustion. The will-power, when transferred from the region of the lower mentality to the spiritual plane, becomes simply a calm and peaceful determination to retain a certain mental attitude in spite of all temptations to the contrary, knowing that by doing so the desired result will certainly appear.

The training of the will and its transference from the lower to the higher plane of our nature are among the first objects of Mental Science. The man is summed up in his will. Whatever he does by his own will is his own act; whatever he does without the consent of his will is not his own act but that of the power by which his will was coerced; but we must recognize that, on the mental plane, no other individuality can obtain control over our will unless we first allow it to do so; and it is for this reason that all legitimate use of Mental Science is towards the strengthening of the will, whether in ourselves or others, and bringing it under the control of an enlightened reason. When the will realizes its power to deal with first cause it is no longer necessary for the operator to state to himself *in extenso* all the philosophy of its action every time he wishes to use it, but, knowing that the trained will is a tremendous spiritual force acting on the plane of first cause, he simply expresses his desire with the intention of operating on that plane, and knows that the desire thus expressed will in due time externalize itself as concrete fact. He now sees that the point which really demands his earnest attention is not whether he possesses the power of externalizing any results he chooses, but of learning to choose wisely what results to produce. For let us not suppose that even the highest powers will take us out of the law of cause and effect. We can never set any cause in motion without calling forth those effects which it already contains in embryo and which will again become causes in their turn, thus producing a series which must continue to flow on until it is cut short by bringing into operation a cause of an opposite character to the one which originated it. Thus we shall find the field for the exercise of our intelligence continually expanding with the expansion of our powers; for, granted a good intention, we shall always wish to contemplate the results of our action as far as our intelligence will permit. We may not be able to see very far, but there is one safe general principle to be gained from what has already been said about causes and conditions, which is that the whole sequence always partakes of the same character as the initial cause: if that character is negative, that is, destitute of any desire to externalize kindness, cheerfulness, strength, beauty or some other sort of good, this negative quality will make itself felt all down the line; but if the opposite affirmative character is in the original motive, then it will reproduce its kind in forms of love, joy, strength and beauty with unerring precision. Before setting out, therefore, to produce new conditions by the exercise of our thought-power we should weigh carefully what further results they are likely to lead to; and here, again, we shall find an ample field for the training of our will, in learning to acquire that self-control which will enable us to postpone an inferior present satisfaction to a greater prospective good.

These considerations naturally lead us to the subject of concentration. I have just now pointed out that all duly controlled mental action consists in holding the mind in one of three attitudes; but there is a fourth mental condition, which is that of letting our mental functions run on without our will directing them to any definite purpose. It is on this word *purpose* that we must fix our whole attention; and instead of dissipating our energies, we must follow an intelligent method of concentration. The, word means being gathered up at a centre, and the centre of anything is that point in which all its forces are equally balanced. To concentrate therefore means first to bring our minds into a condition of equilibrium which will enable us to consciously direct the flow of spirit to a definitely recognized purpose, and then carefully to guard our thoughts from inducing a flow in the opposite direction. We must always bear in mind that we are dealing with a wonderful *potential* energy which is not yet differentiated into any particular mode, and that by the action of our mind we can differentiate it into any specific mode of activity that we will; and by keeping our thought fixed on the fact that the inflow of this energy *is* taking place and that by our mental attitude we *are* determining its direction, we shall gradually realize a corresponding externalization. Proper concentration, therefore, does not consist of strenuous effort which exhausts the nervous system and defeats its own object by suggesting the consciousness of an adverse force to be fought against, and thus creating the adverse circumstances we dread; but in shutting out all thoughts of a kind that would disperse the spiritual nucleus we are forming and dwelling cheerfully on the knowledge that, because the law is certain in its action, our desire is certain of accomplishment. The other great principle to be remembered is that concentration is for the purpose of determining the *quality* we are going to give to the previously undifferentiated energy rather than to arrange the *specific circumstances* of its manifestation. *That* is the work of the creative energy itself, which will build up its own forms of expression quite naturally if we allow it, thus saving us a great deal of needless anxiety. What we really want is expansion in a certain direction, whether of health, wealth, or what not: and so long as we get this, what does it matter whether it reaches us through some channel which we thought we could reckon upon or through some other whose existence we had not suspected. It is the fact that we are concentrating energy of a particular kind for a particular purpose that we should fix our minds upon, and not look upon any specific details as essential to the accomplishment of our object.

These are the two golden rules regarding concentration; but we must not suppose that because we have to be on our guard against idle drifting there is to be no such thing as repose; on the contrary it is during periods of repose that we accumulate strength for action; but repose does not mean a state of purposelessness. As pure spirit the subjective mind never rests: it is only the objective mind in its connection with the physical body that needs rest; and though there are no doubt times when the greatest possible rest is to be obtained by stopping the action, of our conscious thought altogether, the more generally advisable method is by changing the direction of the thought and, instead of centering it upon something we intend to *do*, letting it dwell quietly upon what we *are*. This direction of thought might, of course, develop into the deepest philosophical speculation, but it is not necessary that we should be always either consciously projecting our forces to produce some external effect or working out the details of some metaphysical problem; but we may simply realize ourselves as part of the universal livingness and thus gain a quiet centralization, which, though maintained by a conscious act of the volition, is the very essence of rest. From this standpoint we see that all is Life and all is Good, and that Nature, from her clearly visible surface to her most arcane depths, is one vast storehouse of life and good entirely devoted to our individual use. We have the key to all her treasures, and we can now apply our knowledge of the law of being without entering into all those details which are only needed for purposes of study, and doing so we find it results in our having acquired the consciousness of our *oneness with the whole*. This is the great secret: and when we have once fathomed it we can enjoy our possession of the whole, or of any part of it, because by our recognition we have made it, and can increasingly make it, our own. Whatever most appeals to us at any particular time or place is that mode of the universal living spirit with which at that moment we are most in touch, and realizing this, we shall draw from it streams of vital energy which will make the very sensation of livingness a joy and will radiate from us as a sphere of vibration that can deflect all injurious suggestion on whatever plane. We may not have literary, artistic, or scientific skill to present to others the results of our communings with Nature, but the joy of this sympathetic indrawing will nevertheless produce a corresponding outflow manifesting itself in the happier look and kindlier mien of him who thus realizes his oneness with every aspect of the whole. He realizes—and this is the great point in that attitude of mind which is not directed to any specific external object—that, for himself, he is, and always must be the centre of all this galaxy of Life, and thus he contemplates himself as seated at the centre of infinitude, not an infinitude of blank space, but pulsating with living being, in all of which he knows that the true essence is nothing but good. This is the very opposite to a selfish self-centredness; it, is the centre where we find that we both receive from all and flow out to all. Apart from this principle of circulation there is no true life, and if we contemplate our central position only as affording us greater advantages for in-taking, we have missed the whole point of our studies by missing the real nature of the Life-principle, which is action and re-action. If we would have life enter into us, we ourselves must enter into life—enter into the spirit of it, just as we must enter into the spirit of a book or a game to enjoy it. There can be no action at a centre only. There must be a perpetual flowing out towards the circumference, and thence back again to the centre to maintain a vital activity; otherwise collapse must ensue either from anaemia or congestion. But if we realize the reciprocal nature of the vital pulsation, and that the outflowing consists in the habit of mind which gives itself to the good it sees in others, rather than in any specific actions, then we shall find that the cultivation of this disposition will provide innumerable avenues for the universal livingness to flow through us, whether as giving or receiving, which we had never before suspected: and this action and re-action will so build up our own vitality that each day will find us more thoroughly alive than any that had preceded it. This, then, is the attitude of repose in which we may enjoy all the beauties of science, literature and art or may peacefully commune with the spirit of nature without the aid of any third mind to act as its interpreter, which is still a purposeful attitude although not directed to a specific object: we have not allowed the will to relax its control, but have merely altered its direction; so that for action and repose alike we find that our strength lies in our recognition of the unity of the spirit and of ourselves as individual concentrations of it.

IN TOUCH WITH THE SUBCONSCIOUS MIND

The preceding pages have made the student in some measure aware of the immense importance of our dealings with the sub-conscious mind. Our relation to it, whether on the scale of the individual or the universal, is the key to all that we are or ever can be. In its unrecognized working it is the spring of all that we can call the automatic action of mind and body, and on the universal scale it is the silent power of evolution gradually working onwards to that "divine event, to which the whole creation moves"; and by our conscious recognition of it we make it, relatively to ourselves, all that we believe it to be. The closer our *rapport* with it becomes, the more what we have hitherto considered automatic action, whether in our bodies or our circumstances, will pass under our control, until at last we shall control our whole individual world. Since, then, this is the stupendous issue involved, the question how we are to put ourselves practically in touch with the sub-conscious mind is a very important one. Now the clue which gives us the right direction is to be found in the *impersonal* quality of sub-conscious mind of which I have spoken. Not impersonal as lacking the *elements* of personality; nor even, in the case of individual subjective mind, as lacking the sense of individuality; but impersonal in the sense of not recognizing the particular external relations which appear to the objective mind to constitute its personality, and having a realization of itself quite independent of them. If, then, we would come in touch with it we must meet it on its own ground. It can see things only from the deductive standpoint, and therefore cannot take note of the inductive standpoint from which we construct the idea of our external personality; and accordingly if we would put ourselves in touch with it, we cannot do so by bringing it down to the level of the external and non-essential but only by rising to its own level on the plane of the interior and essential. How can this be done? Let two well-known writers answer. Rudyard Kipling tells us in his story of "Kim" how the boy used at times to lose his sense of personality by repeating to himself the question, *Who* is Kim? Gradually his personality would seem to fade and he would experience a feeling of passing into a grander and a wider life, in which the boy Kim was unknown, while his own conscious individuality remained, only exalted and expanded to an inconceivable extent; and in Tennyson's life by his son we are told that at times the poet had a similar experience. We come into touch with the absolute exactly in proportion as we withdraw ourselves from the relative: they vary inversely to each other.

For the purpose, then, of getting into touch with our sub-conscious mind we must endeavour to think of ourselves as pure being, as that entity which interiorly supports the outward manifestation, and doing so we shall realize that the essential quality of pure being must be good. It is in itself *pure Life*, and as such cannot desire anything detrimental to pure Life under whatever form manifested. Consequently the purer our intentions the more readily we

shall place ourself *en rapport* with our subjective entity; and *a fortiori* the
same applies to that Greater Sub-conscious Mind of which our individual
subjective mind is a particular manifestation. In actual practice the process
consists in first forming a clear conception in the objective mind of the idea we
wish to convey to the subjective mind: then, when this has been firmly
grasped, endeavour to lose sight of all other facts connected with the external
personality except the one in question, and then mentally address the
subjective mind as though it were an independent entity and impress upon it
what you want it to do or to believe. Everyone must formulate his own way of
working, but one method, which is both simple and effective is to say to the
subjective mind, "This is what I want you to do; you will now step into my
place and do it, bringing all your powers and intelligence to bear, and
considering yourself to be none other than myself." Having done this return
to the realization of your own objective personality and leave the subjective
mind to perform its task in full confidence that, by the law of its nature, it will
do so if not hindered by a repetition of contrary messages from the objective
mind. This is not a mere fancy but a truth daily proved by the experience of
increasing numbers. The facts have not been fabricated to fit the theory, but
the theory has been built up by careful observation of the facts; and since it
has been shown both by theory and practice that such is the law of the
relation between subjective and objective mind, we find ourselves face to face
with a very momentous question. Is there any reason why the laws which hold
good of the individual subjective mind should not hold good of the Universal
Mind also? and the answer is that there is not. As has been already shown the
Universal Mind must, by its very universality, be purely subjective, and what
is the law of a part must also be the law of the whole: the qualities of fire are
the same whether the centres of combustion be great or small, and therefore
we may well conclude these lectures by considering what will be the result if
we apply what we have learnt regarding the individual subjective mind to the
Universal Mind.

We have learnt that the three great facts regarding subjective mind are
its creative power, its amenableness to suggestion, and its inability to work by
any other than the deductive method. This last is an exceedingly important
point, for it implies that the action of the subjective mind is in no way limited
by precedent. The inductive method works on principles inferred from an
already existing pattern, and therefore at the best only produces the old thing
in a new shape. But the deductive method works according to the essence or
spirit of the principle, and does not depend on any previous concrete
manifestation for its apprehension of it; and this latter method of working
must necessarily be that of the all-originating Mind, for since there could be
no prior existing pattern from which it could learn the principles of
construction, the want of a pattern would have prevented its creating
anything had its method been inductive instead of deductive. Thus by the
necessity of the case the Universal Mind must act deductively, that is,
according to the law which has been found true of individual subjective mind.
It is thus not bound by any precedent, which means that its creative power is
absolutely unlimited; and since it is essentially subjective mind, and not
objective mind, it is entirely amenable to suggestion. Now it is an unavoidable

inference from the identity of the law governing subjective mind, whether in the individual or the universal, that just as we can by suggestion impress a certain character of personality upon the individual subjective mind, so we can, and do, upon the Universal Mind; and it is for this reason that I have drawn attention to the inherent personal *quality* of pure spirit when contemplated in its most interior plane. It becomes, therefore, the most important of all considerations with what character we invest the Universal Mind; for since our relation to it is *purely subjective* it will infallibly bear *to us* exactly that character which we impress upon it; in other words it will be to us exactly what we believe it to be. This is simply a logical inference from the fact that, as subjective mind, our primary relation to it can only be on the subjective plane, and indirectly our objective relations must also spring from the same source. This is the meaning of that remarkable passage twice repeated in the Bible, "With, the pure thou wilt show thyself pure, and with the froward thou wilt show thyself froward." (Ps. xviii., 26, and II. Sam. xxii., 27), for the context makes it clear that these words are addressed to the Divine Being. The spiritual kingdom is *within* us, and as we realize it *there* so it becomes to us a reality. It is the unvarying law of the subjective life that "as a man thinketh in his heart so is he," that is to say, his inward subjective states are the only true reality, and what we call external realities are only their objective correspondences. If we thoroughly realize the truth that the Universal Mind must be to us exactly according to our conception of it, and that this relation is not merely imaginary but by the law of subjective mind must be to us an actual fact and the foundation of all other facts, then it is impossible to over-estimate the importance of the conception of the Universal Mind which we adopt. To the uninstructed there is little or no choice: they form a conception in accordance with the tradition they have received from others, and until they have learnt to think for themselves, they have to abide by the results of that tradition: for natural laws admit of no exceptions, and however faulty the traditional idea may be, its acceptance will involve a corresponding reaction upon the Universal Mind, which will in turn be reflected into the conscious mind and external life of the individual. But those who understand the law of the subject will have no one but themselves to blame if they do not derive all possible benefits from it. The greatest Teacher of Mental Science the world has ever seen has laid down sufficiently plain rules for our guidance. With a knowledge of the subject whose depth can be appreciated only by those who have themselves some practical acquaintance with it, He bids His unlearned audiences, those common people who heard Him gladly, picture to themselves the Universal Mind as a benign Father, tenderly compassionate of all and sending the common bounties of Nature alike on the evil and the good; but He also pictured It as exercising a special and peculiar care over those who recognize Its willingness to do so:—"the very hairs of your head are all numbered," and "ye are of more value than many sparrows." Prayer was to be made to the unseen Being, not with doubt or fear, but with the absolute assurance of a certain answer, and no limit was to be set to its power or willingness to work for us. But to those who did not thus realize it, the Great Mind is necessarily the adversary who casts them into prison until they have paid the uttermost farthing; and thus in all cases the Master impressed upon his hearers the exact correspondence of the attitude of this unseen Power towards *them* with their own attitude towards *it*. Such teaching was not a narrow anthropomorphism but the adaptation to the intellectual capacity of the unlettered multitude of the very deepest truths of what we now call Mental Science. And the basis of it all is the cryptic personality of spirit hidden throughout the infinite of Nature under every form of manifestation. As unalloyed Life and Intelligence it *can* be no other than good, it can entertain no intention of evil, and thus all intentional evil must put us in opposition to it, and so deprive us of the consciousness of its guidance and strengthening and thus leave us to grope our own way and fight our own battle single-handed against the universe, odds which at last will surely prove too great for us. But remember that the opposition can never be on the part of the Universal Mind, for in itself it is sub-conscious mind; and to suppose any active opposition taken on its own initiative would be contrary to all we have learnt as to the nature of sub-conscious mind whether in the individual or the universal; the position of the Universal Mind towards us is always the reflection of our own attitude. Therefore although the Bible is full of threatening against those who persist in conscious opposition to the Divine Law of Good, it is on the other hand full of promises of immediate and full forgiveness to all who change, their attitude and desire to co-operate with the Law of Good so far as they know it. The laws of Nature do not act vindictively; and through all theological formularies and traditional interpretations let us realize that what we are dealing with is the supreme law of our own being; and it is on the basis of this natural law that we find such declarations as that in Ezek. xviii., 22, which tells that if we forsake our evil ways our past transgressions shall never again be mentioned to us. We are dealing with the great principles of our subjective being, and our misuse of them in the past can never make them change their inherent law of action. If our method of using them in the past has brought us sorrow, fear and trouble, we have only to fall back on the law that if we reverse the cause the effects will be reversed also; and so what we have to do is simply to reverse our mental attitude and then endeavour to act up to the new one. The sincere endeavour to act up to our new mental attitude is essential, for we cannot really think in one way and act in another; but our repeated failures to fully act as we would wish must not discourage us. It is the sincere intention that is the essential thing, and this will in time release us from the bondage of habits which at present seem almost insuperable.

The initial step, then, consists in determining to picture the Universal Mind as the ideal of all we could wish it to be both to ourselves and to others, together with the endeavour to reproduce this ideal, however imperfectly, in our own life; and this step having been taken, we can then cheerfully look upon it as our ever-present Friend, providing all good, guarding from all danger, and guiding us with all counsel. Gradually as the habit of thus regarding the Universal Mind grows upon us, we shall find that in accordance with the laws we have been considering, it will become more and more *personal* to us, and in response to our desire its inherent intelligence will make itself more and more clearly perceptible within as a power of perceiving truth far beyond any statement of it that we could formulate by merely intellectual investigation. Similarly if we think of it as a great power devoted to supplying all our needs, we shall impress this character also upon it, and by the law of subjective mind it will proceed to enact the part of that special providence which we have credited it with being; and if, beyond the general care of our concerns, we would draw to ourselves some particular benefit, the same rule holds good of impressing our desire upon the Universal Subjective Mind. And if we realize that above and beyond all this we want something still greater and more enduring, the building-up of character and unfolding of our powers so that we may expand into fuller and yet fuller measures of joyous and joy-giving Life, still the same rule holds good: convey to the Universal Mind the suggestion of the desire, and by the law of relation between subjective and objective mind this too will be fulfilled. And thus the deepest problems of philosophy bring us back to the old statement of the Law:—Ask and ye shall receive, seek and ye shall find, knock and it shall be opened unto you. This is the summing-up of the natural law of the relation between us and the Divine Mind. It is thus no vain boast that Mental Science can enable us to make our lives what we will. We must start from where we are now, and by rightly estimating our relation to the Divine Universal Mind we can gradually grow into any conditions we desire, provided we first make ourselves in habitual mental attitude the person who corresponds to those conditions: for we can never get over the law of correspondence, and the externalization will always be in accord with the internal principle that gives rise to it. And to this law there is no limit. What it can do for us to-day it can do to-morrow, and through all that procession of to-morrows that loses itself in the dim vistas of eternity. Belief in limitation is the one and only thing that causes limitation, because we thus impress limitation upon the creative principle; and in proportion as we lay that belief aside our boundaries will expand, and increasing life and more abundant blessing will be ours.

But we must not ignore our responsibilities. Trained thought is far more powerful than untrained, and therefore the more deeply we penetrate into Mental Science the more carefully we must guard against all thoughts and words expressive of even the most modified form of ill-will. Gossip, tale-bearing, sneering laughter, are not in accord with the principles of Mental Science; and similarly even our smallest thoughts of good carry with them a seed of good which will assuredly bear fruit in due time. This is not mere "goodie, goodie," but an important lesson in Mental Science, for our subjective mind takes its colour from our settled mental habits, and an occasional affirmation or denial will not be sufficient to change it; and we must therefore cultivate that tone which we wish to see reproduced in our conditions whether of body, mind, or circumstance.

In these lectures my purpose has been, not so much to give specific rules of practice as to lay down the broad general principles of Mental Science which will enable the student to form rules for himself. In every walk in life, book knowledge is only a means to an end. Books can only direct us where to look and what to look for, but we must do the finding *for ourselves*; therefore, if you have really grasped the principles of the science, you will frame rules of your own which will give you better results than any attempt to follow somebody else's method, which was successful in their hands precisely because it was theirs. Never fear to be yourself. If Mental Science does not teach you to be yourself it teaches you nothing. Yourself, more yourself, and yet more yourself is what you want; only with the knowledge that the true self includes the inner and higher self which is always in immediate touch with the Great Divine Mind.

As Walt Whitman says:—"You are not all included between your hat and your boots."

The growing popularity of the Edinburgh Lectures on Mental Science has led me to add to the present edition three more sections on Body, Soul, and Spirit, which it is hoped will prove useful by rendering the principles of the interaction of these three factors somewhat clearer.

THE BODY

Some students find it difficult to realize that mental action can produce any real effect upon material substance; but if this is not possible there is no such thing as Mental Science, the purpose of which is to produce improved conditions both of body and environment, so that the ultimate manifestation aimed at is always one of demonstration upon the plane of the visible and concrete. Therefore to afford conviction of an actual connection between the visible and the invisible, between the inner and the outer, is one of the most important points in the course of our studies.

That such a connection must exist is proved by metaphysical argument in answer to the question, "How did anything ever come into existence at all?" And the whole creation, ourselves included, stands as evidence to this great truth. But to many minds merely abstract argument is not completely convincing, or at any rate it becomes more convincing if it is supported by something of a more concrete nature; and for such readers I would give a few hints as to the correspondence between the physical and the mental. The subject covers a very wide area, and the limited space at my disposal will only allow me to touch on a few suggestive points, still these may be sufficient to show that the abstract argument has some corresponding facts at the back of it.

One of the most convincing proofs I have seen is that afforded by the "biometre," a little instrument invented by an eminent French scientist, the late Dr. Hippolyte Baraduc, which shows the action of what he calls the "vital current." His theory is that this force, whatever its actual nature may be, is universally present, and operates as a current of physical vitality perpetually, flowing with more or less energy through every physical organism, and which can, at any rate to some extent, be controlled by the power of the human will. The theory in all its minutiae is exceedingly elaborate, and has been described in detail in Dr. Baraduc's published works. In a conversation I had with him about a year ago, he told me he was writing another book which would throw further light on the subject, but a few months later he passed over before it was presented to the world. The fact, however, which I wish to put before the reader, is the ocular demonstration of the connection between mind and matter, which an experiment with the biometre affords.

The instrument consists of a bell glass, from the inside of which is suspended a copper needle by a fine silken thread. The glass stands on a wooden support, below which is a coil of copper wire, which, however, is not connected with any battery or other apparatus, and merely serves to condense the current. Below the needle, inside the glass, there is a circular card divided into degrees to mark the action of the needle. Two of these instruments are placed side by side, but in no way connected, and the experimenter then holds out the fingers of both hands to within about an inch of the glasses. According to the theory, the current enters at the left hand, circulates through the body, and passes out at the right hand, that is to say, there is an indrawing at the left and a giving-out at the right, thus agreeing with Reichenbach's experiments on the polarity of the human body.

I must confess that, although I had read Dr. Baraduc's book, "Les Vibrations Humaines," I approached the instrument in a very sceptical frame of mind; but I was soon convinced of my error. At first, holding a mental attitude of entire relaxation, I found that the left-hand needle was attracted through twenty degrees, while the right-hand needle, the one affected by the out-going current, was repelled through ten degrees. After allowing the instrument to return to its normal equilibrium I again approached it with the purpose of seeing whether a change of mental attitude would in the least modify the flow of current. This time I assumed the strongest mental attitude I could with the intention of sending out a flow through the right hand, and the result as compared with the previous one was remarkable. The left-hand needle was now attracted only through ten degrees, while the right-hand one was deflected through something over thirty, thus clearly indicating the influence of the mental faculties in modifying the action of the current. I may mention that the experiment was made in the presence of two medical men who noted the movement of the needles.

I will not here stop to discuss the question of what the actual constitution of this current of vital energy may be—it is sufficient for our present purpose that it is there, and the experiment I have described brings us face to face with the fact of a correspondence between our own mental attitude and the invisible forces of nature. Even if we say that this current is some form of electricity, and that the variation of its action is determined by changes in the polarization of the atoms of the body, then this change of polarity is the result of mental action; so that the quickening or retarding of the cosmic current is equally the result of the mental attitude whether we suppose our mental force to act directly upon the current itself or indirectly by inducing changes in the molecular structure of the body. Whichever hypothesis we adopt the conclusion is the same, namely, that the mind has power to open or close the door to invisible forces in such a way that the result of the mental action becomes apparent on the material plane.

Now, investigation shows that the physical body, is a mechanism specially adapted for the transmutation of the inner or mental power into modes of external activity. We know from medical science that the whole body is traversed by a network of nerves which serve as the channels of communication between the indwelling spiritual ego, which we call mind, and the functions of the external organism. This nervous system is dual. One system, known as the Sympathetic, is the channel for all those activities which are not consciously directed by our volition, such as the operation of the digestive organs, the repair of the daily wear and tear of the tissues, and the like. The other system, known as the Voluntary or Cerebro-spinal system, is the channel through which we receive conscious perception from the physical senses and exercise control over the movements of the body. This system has its centre in the brain, while the other has its centre in a ganglionic mass at the back of the stomach known as the solar plexus, and sometimes spoken of as the abdominal brain. The cerebro- spinal system is the channel of our

volitional or conscious mental action, and the sympathetic system is the
channel of that mental action which unconsciously supports the vital
functions of the body. Thus the cerebro- spinal system is the organ of
conscious mind and the sympathetic is that of sub-conscious mind.

But the interaction of conscious and subconscious mind requires a similar
interaction between the corresponding systems of nerves, and one
conspicuous connection by which this is provided is the "vagus" nerve. This
nerve passes out of the cerebral region as a portion of the voluntary system,
and through it we control the vocal organs; then it passes onwards to the
thorax sending out branches to the heart and lungs; and finally, passing
through the diaphragm, it loses the outer coating which distinguishes the
nerves of the voluntary system and becomes identified with those of the
sympathetic system, so forming a connecting link between the two and
making the man physically a single entity.

Similarly different areas of the brain indicate, their connection with the
objective and subjective activities of the mind respectively, and speaking in a
general way we may assign the frontal portion of the brain to the former and
the posterior portion to the latter, while the intermediate portion partakes of
the character of both.

The intuitional faculty has its correspondence in this upper area of the
brain situated between the frontal and posterior portions, and physiologically
speaking, it is here that intuitive ideas find entrance. These at first are more
or less unformed and generalized in character, but are nevertheless perceived
by the conscious mind, otherwise we should not be aware of them at all. Then
the effort of nature is to bring these ideas into more definite and usable shape,
so the conscious mind lays hold of them and induces a corresponding vibratory
current in the voluntary system of nerves, and this in turn induces a similar
current in the involuntary system, thus handing the idea over to the
subjective mind. The vibratory current which had first descended from the
apex of the brain to the frontal brain and thus through the voluntary system
to the solar plexus is now reversed and ascends from the solar plexus through
the sympathetic system to the posterior brain, this return current indicating
the action of the subjective mind.

If we were to remove the surface portion of the apex of the brain we
should find immediately below it the shining belt of brain substance called the
"corpus callosum." This is the point of union between the subjective and
objective, and as the current returns from the solar plexus to this point it is
restored to the objective portion of the brain in a fresh form which it has
acquired by the silent alchemy of the subjective mind. Thus the conception
which was at first only vaguely recognized is restored to the objective mind in
a definite and workable form, and then the objective mind, acting through the
frontal brain—the area of comparison and analysis—proceeds to work upon
a clearly perceived idea and to bring out the potentialities that are latent in
it.

It must of course be borne in mind that I am here speaking of the mental
ego in that, mode of its existence with which we are most familiar, that is as
clothed in flesh, though there may be much to say as to other modes of its
activity. But for our daily life we have to consider ourselves as we are in that

aspect of life, and from this point of view the physiological correspondence of the body to the action of the mind is an important item; and therefore, although we must always remember that the origin of ideas is purely mental, we must not forget that on the physical plane every mental action implies a corresponding molecular action in the brain and in the two-fold nervous system.

If, as the old Elizabethan poet says, "the soul is form, and doth the body make," then it is clear that the physical organism must be a mechanical arrangement as specially adapted for the use of the soul's powers as a steam-engine is for the power of steam; and it is the recognition of this reciprocity between the two that is the basis of all spiritual or mental healing, and therefore the study of this mechanical adaptation is an important branch of Mental Science. Only we must not forget that it is the effect and not the cause.

At the same time it is important to remember that such a thing as reversal of the relation between cause and effect is possible, just as the same apparatus may be made to generate mechanical power by the application of electricity, or to generate electricity by the application of mechanical power. And the importance of this principle consists in this. There is always a tendency for actions which were at first voluntary to become automatic, that is, to pass from the region of conscious mind into that of subconscious mind, and to acquire a permanent domicile there. Professor Elmer Gates, of Washington, has demonstrated this physiologically in his studies of brain formation. He tells us that every thought produces a slight molecular change in the substance of the brain, and the repetition of the same sort of thought causes a repetition of the same molecular action until at last a veritable channel is formed in the brain substance, which can only be eradicated by a reverse process of thought. In this way "grooves of thought" are very literal things, and when once established the vibrations of the cosmic currents flow automatically through them and thus react upon the mind by a process the reverse of that by which our voluntary and intentional in-drawing from the invisible is affected. In this way are formed what we call "habits," and hence the importance of controlling our thinking and guarding it against undesirable ideas.

But on the other hand this reactionary process may be used to confirm good and life-giving modes of thought, so that by a knowledge of its laws we may enlist even the physical body itself in the building up of that perfectly whole personality, the attainment of which is the aim and object of our studies.

THE SOUL

Having now obtained a glimpse of the adaptation of the physical organism to the action of the mind we must next realize that the mind itself is an organism which is in like manner adapted to the action of a still higher power, only here the adaptation is one of mental faculty. As with other invisible forces all we can know of the mind is by observing what it does, but with this difference, that since we ourselves *are* this mind, our observation is an interior observation of states of consciousness. In this way we recognize certain faculties of our mind, the working order of which I have considered at page 84; but the point to which I would now draw attention is that these faculties always work under the influence of something which stimulates them, and this stimulus may come either from without through the external senses, or from within by the consciousness of something not perceptible on the physical plane. Now the recognition of these interior sources of stimulus to our mental faculties, is an important branch of Mental Science, because the mental action thus set up works just as accurately through the physical correspondences as those which start from the recognition of external facts, and therefore the control and right direction of these inner perceptions is a matter of the first moment.

The faculties most immediately concerned are the intuition and the imagination, but it is at first difficult to see how the intuition, which is entirely spontaneous, can be brought under the control of the will. Of course, the spontaneousness of the intuition cannot in any way be interfered with, for if it ceased to act spontaneously it would cease to be the intuition. Its province is, as it were, to capture ideas from the infinite and present them to the mind to be dealt with at its discretion. In our mental constitution the intuition is the point of origination and, therefore, for it to cease to act spontaneously would be for it to cease to act at all. But the experience of a long succession of observers shows that the intuition can be trained so as to acquire increased sensitiveness in some, particular direction, and the choice of the *general direction* is determined by the will of the individual.

It will be found that the intuition works most readily in respect to those subjects which most habitually occupy our thought; and according to the physiological correspondences which we have been considering this might be accounted for on the physical plane by the formation of brain-channels specially adapted for the induction in the molecular system of vibrations corresponding to the particular class of ideas in question. But of course we must remember that the ideas themselves are not caused by the molecular changes but on the contrary are the cause of them; and it is in this translation of thought action into physical action that we are brought face to face with the eternal mystery of the descent of spirit into matter; and that though we may trace matter through successive degrees of refinement till it becomes what, in comparison with those denser modes that are most familiar, we might call a spiritual substance, yet at the end of it it is not the intelligent thinking principle itself. The criterion is in the word "vibrations." However delicately etheric the substance its movement commences by the vibration of its particles, and a vibration is a wave having a certain length, amplitude, and periodicity, that is to say, something which can exist only in terms of space and time; and as soon as we are dealing with anything capable of the conception of measurement we may be quite certain that we are not dealing with Spirit but only with one of its vehicles. Therefore although we may push our analysis of matter further and ever further back—and on this line there is a great deal of knowledge to be gained—we shall find that the point at which spiritual power or thought-force is translated into etheric or atomic vibration will always elude us. Therefore we must not attribute the origination of ideas to molecular displacement in the brain, though, by the reaction of the physical upon the mental which I have spoken of above, the formation of thought-channels in the grey matter of the brain may tend to facilitate the reception of certain ideas. Some people are actually conscious of the action of the upper portion of the brain during the influx of an intuition, the sensation being that of a sort of expansion in that brain area, which might be compared to the opening of a valve or door; but all attempts to induce the inflow of intuitive ideas by the physiological expedient of trying to open this valve by the exercise of the will should be discouraged as likely to prove injurious to the brain. I believe some Oriental systems advocate this method, but we may well trust the mind to regulate the action of its physical channels in a manner suitable to its own requirements, instead of trying to manipulate the mind by the unnatural forcing of its mechanical instrument. In all our studies on these lines we must remember that development is always by perfectly natural growth and is not brought about by unduly straining any portion of the system.

The fact, however, remains that the intuition works most freely in that direction in which we most habitually concentrate our thought; and in practice it will be found that the best way to cultivate the intuition in any particular direction is to meditate upon the *abstract principles* of that particular class of subjects rather than only to consider particular cases. Perhaps the reason is that particular cases have to do with specific phenomena, that is with the law working under certain limiting conditions, whereas the *principles* of the law are not limited by local conditions, and so habitual meditation on *them* sets our intuition free to range in an infinitude where the conception of antecedent conditions does not limit it. Anyway, whatever may be the theoretical explanation, you will find that the clear grasp of abstract principles in any direction has a wonderfully quickening effect upon the intuition in that particular direction.

The importance of recognizing our power of thus giving direction to the intuition cannot be exaggerated, for if the mind is attuned to sympathy with the highest phases of spirit this power opens the door to limitless possibilities of knowledge. In its highest workings intuition becomes inspiration, and certain great records of fundamental truths and supreme mysteries which have come down to us from thousands of generations bequeathed by deep thinkers of old can only be accounted for on the supposition that their earnest thought on the Originating Spirit, coupled with a reverent worship of It, opened the door, through their intuitive faculty, to the most sublime inspirations regarding the supreme truths of the universe both with respect to the evolution of the cosmos and to the evolution of the individual. Among such records explanatory of the supreme mysteries three stand out pre-eminent, all bearing witness to the same ONE Truth, and each throwing light upon the other; and these three are the Bible, the Great Pyramid, and the Pack of Cards—a curious combination some will think, but I hope in another volume of this series to be able to justify my present statement. I allude to these three records here because the unity of principle which they exhibit, notwithstanding their wide divergence of method, affords a standing proof that the direction taken by the intuition is largely determined by the will of the individual opening the mind in that particular direction.

Very closely allied to the intuition is the faculty of imagination. This does not mean mere fancies, which we dismiss without further consideration, but our power of forming mental images upon which we dwell. These, as I have said in the earlier part of this book, form a nucleus which, on its own plane, calls into action the universal Law of Attraction, thus giving rise to the principle of Growth. The relation of the intuition to the imagination is that the intuition grasps an idea from the Great Universal Mind, in which all things subsist as *potentials*, and presents it to the imagination in its essence rather than in a definite form, and then our image-building faculty gives it a clear and definite form which it presents before the mental vision, and which we then vivify by letting our thought dwell upon it, thus infusing our own personality into it, and so providing that personal element through which the specific action of the universal law relatively to the particular individual always takes place.[1] Whether our thought shall be allowed thus to dwell upon a particular mental image depends on our own will, and our exercise of our will depends on our belief in our power to use it so as to disperse or consolidate a given mental image; and finally our belief in our power to do this depends on our recognition of our relation to God, Who is the source of all power; for it is an invariable truth that our life will take its whole form, tone, and color from our conception of God, whether that conception be positive or negative, and the sequence by which it does so is that now given.

In this way, then, our intuition is related to our imagination, and this relation has its physiological correspondence in the circulus of molecular vibrations I have described above, which, having its commencement in the higher or "ideal" portion of the brain flows through the voluntary nervous system, the physical channel of objective mind, returning through the sympathetic system, the physical channel of subjective mind, thus completing the circuit and being then restored to the frontal brain, where it is consciously modelled into clear-cut forms suited to a specific purpose.

In all this the power of the will as regulating the action both of the intuition and the imagination must never be lost sight of, for without such a central controlling power we should lose all sense of individuality; and hence the ultimate aim of the evolutionary process is to evolve individual wills actuated by such beneficence and enlightenment as shall make them fitting vehicles for the outflowing of the Supreme Spirit, which has hitherto created cosmically, and can now carry on the creative process to its highest stages only through conscious union with the individual; for this is the only possible solution of the great problem, How can the Universal Mind act in all its fulness upon the plane of the individual and particular?

This is the ultimate of evolution, and the successful evolution of the individual depends on his recognizing this ultimate and working towards it; and therefore this should be the great end of our studies. There is a correspondence in the constitution of the body to the faculties of the soul, and there is a similar correspondence in the faculties of the soul to the power of the All-originating Spirit; and as in all other adaptations of specific vehicles so also here, we can never correctly understand the nature of the vehicle and use it rightly until we realize the nature of the power for the working of which it is specially adapted. Let us, then, in conclusion briefly consider the nature of that power.

THE SPIRIT

What must the Supreme All-originating Spirit be in itself? That is the question before us. Let us start with one fact regarding it about which we cannot have any possible doubt—it is *creative*. If it were not creative nothing could come into existence; therefore we know that its purpose, or Law of Tendency, must be to bring individual lives into existence and to surround them with a suitable environment. Now a power which has this for its inherent nature must be a kindly power. The Spirit of Life seeking expression in individual lives can have no other intention towards them than "that they might have life, and that they might have it more abundantly." To suppose the opposite would be a contradiction in terms. It would be to suppose the Eternal Principle of Life acting against itself, expressing itself as the reverse of what it is, in which case it would not be expressing itself but expressing its opposite; so that it is impossible to conceive of the Spirit of Life acting otherwise than to the increase of life. This is as yet only imperfectly apparent by reason of our imperfect apprehension of the position, and our consequent want of conscious unity with the *one* Eternal Life. As our consciousness of unity becomes more perfect so will the life-givingness of the Spirit become more apparent. But in the realm of principles the purely Affirmative and Life-giving nature of the All-originating Spirit is an unavoidable conclusion. Now by what name can we call such an inherent desire to add to the fulness of any individual life—that is, to make it stronger, brighter, and happier? If this is not Love, then I do not know what else it is; and so we are philosophically led to the conclusion that Love is the prime moving power of the Creating Spirit.

But expression is impossible without Form. What Form, then, should Love give to the vehicles of its expression? By the hypothesis of the case it could not find self-expression in forms that were hateful or repugnant to it—therefore the only logical correlative of Love is Beauty. Beauty is not yet universally manifested for the same reason that Life is not, namely, lack of recognition of its Principle; but, that the principle of Beauty is inherent in the Eternal Mind is demonstrated by all that is beautiful in the world in which we live.

These considerations show us that the inherent nature of the Spirit must consist in the eternal interaction of Love and Beauty as the Active and Passive polarity of Being. Then this is the Power for the working of which our soul faculties are specially adapted. And when this purpose of the adaptation is recognized we begin to get some insight into the way in which our intuition, imagination, and will should be exercized. By training our thought to habitually dwell upon this dual-unity of the Originating Forces of Love and Beauty the intuition is rendered more and more sensitive to ideas emanating from this supreme source, and the imagining faculty is trained in the formation of images corresponding to such ideas; while on the physical side the molecular structure of the brain and body becomes more and more perfectly adjusted to the generating of vibratory currents tending to the outward manifestation of the Originating Principle. Thus the whole man is brought into unison with himself and with the Supreme Source of Life, so that, in the words of St. Paul, he is being day by day renewed after the image of Him that created him.

Our more immediately personal recognition of the All-originating Love and Beauty will thus flow out as peace of mind, health of body, discretion in the management of our affairs, and power in the carrying out of our undertakings; and as we advance to a wider conception of the working of the Spirit of Love and Beauty in its infinite possibilities, so our intuition will find a wider scope and our field of activity will expand along with it—in a word we shall discover that our individuality is growing, and that we are becoming more truly ourselves than we ever were before.

The question of the specific lines on which the individual may be most perfectly trained into such recognition of his true relation to the All-embracing Spirit of Life is therefore of supreme importance, but it is also of such magnitude that even to briefly sketch its broad outlines would require a volume to itself, and I will therefore not attempt to enter upon it here, my present purpose being only to offer some hints of the principles underlying that wonderful three-fold unity of Body, Soul, and Spirit which we all know ourselves to be.

We are as yet only at the commencement of the path which leads to the realization of this unity in the full development of all its powers, but others have trodden the way before us, from whose experiences we may learn; and not least among these was the illustrious founder of the Most Christian Fraternity of the Rosicrucians. This master-mind, setting out in his youth with the intention of going to Jerusalem, changed the order of his journey and first sojourned for three years in the symbolical city of Damcar, in the mystical country of Arabia, then for about a year in the mystical country of Egypt, and then for two years in the mystical country of Fez. Then, having during these six years learned all that was to be acquired in those countries, he returned to his native land of Germany, where, on the basis of the knowledge he had thus gained, he founded the Fraternity R.C., for whose instruction he wrote the mystical books M. and T. Then, when he realized that his work in its present stage was accomplished, he of his own free will laid aside the physical body, not, it is recorded, by decay, or disease, or ordinary death, but by the express direction of the Spirit of Life, summing up all his knowledge in the words,

"Jesus mihi omnia."

And now his followers await the coming of "the Artist Elias," who shall bring the Magnum Opus to its completion.

"Let him that readeth understand."

FOOTNOTES

Footnote 1: See my "Doré Lectures."

Dore Lectures on Mental Science

TABLE OF CONTENTS

FOREWORD

The addresses contained in this volume were delivered by me at the Dore Gallery, Bond Street, London, on the Sundays of the first three months of the present year, and are now published at the kind request of many of my hearers, hence their title of "The Dore Lectures." A number of separate discourses on a variety of subjects necessarily labours under the disadvantage of want of continuity, and also under that of a liability to the frequent repetition of similar ideas and expressions, and the reader will, I trust, pardon these defects as inherent in the circumstances of the work. At the same time it will be found that, although not specially so designed, there is a certain progressive development of thought through the dozen lectures which compose this volume, the reason for which is that they all aim at expressing the same fundamental idea, namely that, though the laws of the universe can never be broken, they can be made to work under special conditions which will produce results that could not be produced under the conditions spontaneously provided by nature. This is a simple scientific principle and it shows us the place which is occupied by the personal factor, that, namely, of an intelligence which sees beyond the present limited manifestation of the Law into its real essence, and which thus constitutes the instru-mentality by which the infinite possibilities of the Law can be evoked into forms of power, usefulness, and beauty.

The more perfect, therefore, the working of the personal factor, the greater will be the results developed from the Universal Law; and hence our lines of study should be two-fold—on the one hand the theoretical study of the action of Universal Law, and on the other the practical fitting of ourselves to make use of it; and if the present volume should assist any reader in this two-fold quest, it will have answered its purpose.

The different subjects have necessarily been treated very briefly, and the addresses can only be considered as suggestions for lines of thought which the reader will be able to work out for himself, and he must therefore not expect that careful elabora-tion of detail which I would gladly have bestowed had I been writing on one of these subjects exclusively. This little book must be taken only for what it is, the record of somewhat fragmentary talks with a very indulgent audience, to whom I gratefully dedicate the volume.

June 5, 1909.

T.T.

ENTERING INTO THE SPIRIT OF IT

We all know the meaning of this phrase in our everyday life. The Spirit is that which gives life and movement to anything, in fact it is that which causes it to exist at all. The thought of the author, the impression of the painter, the feeling of the musician, is that without which their works could never have come into being, and so it is only as we enter into the IDEA which gives rise to the work, that we can derive all the enjoyment and benefit from it which it is able to bestow. If we cannot enter into the Spirit of it, the book, the picture, the music, are meaningless to us: to appreciate them we must share the mental attitude of their creator. This is a universal principle; if we do not enter into the Spirit of a thing, it is dead so far as we are concerned; but if we do enter into it we reproduce in ourselves the same quality of life which called that thing into existence.

Now if this is a general principle, why can we not carry it to a higher range of things? Why not to the highest point of all? May we not enter into the originating Spirit of Life itself, and so reproduce it in ourselves as a perennial spring of livingness? This, surely, is a question worthy of our careful consideration.

The spirit of a thing is that which is the source of its inherent movement, and therefore the question before us is, what is the nature of the primal moving power, which is at the back of the endless array of life which we see around us, our own life included? Science gives us ample ground for saying that it is not material, for science has now, at least theoretically, reduced all material things to a primary ether, universally distributed, whose innumerable particles are in absolute equilibrium; whence it follows on mathematical grounds alone that the initial movement which began to concentrate the world and all material substances out of the particles of the dispersed ether, could not have originated in the particles themselves. Thus by a necessary deduction from the conclusions of physical science, we are compelled to realize the presence of some immaterial power capable of separating off certain specific areas for the display of cosmic activity, and then building up a material universe with all its inhabitants by an orderly sequence of evolution, in which each stage lays the foundation for the development of the stage, which is to follow—in a word we find ourselves brought face to face with a power which exhibits on a stupendous scale, the faculties of selection and adaptation of means to ends, and thus distributes energy and life in accordance with a recognizable scheme of cosmic progression. It is therefore not only Life, but also Intelligence, and Life guided by Intelligence becomes Volition. It is this primary originating power which we mean when we speak of "The Spirit," and it is into this Spirit of the whole universe that we must enter if we would reproduce it as a spring of Original Life in ourselves.

Now in the case of the productions of artistic genius we know that we must enter into the movement of the creative mind of the artist, before we can realize the principle which gives rise to his work. We must learn to partake of the feeling, to find expression for which is the motive of his creative activity. May we not apply the same principle to the Greater Creative Mind with which we are seeking to deal? There is something in the work of the artist which is akin to that of original creation. His work, literary, musical, or graphic is original creation on a miniature scale, and in this it differs from that of the engineer, which is constructive, or that of the scientist which is analytical; for the artist in a sense creates something out of nothing, and therefore starts from the stand-point of simple feeling, and not from that of a pre-existing necessity. This, by the hypothesis of the case, is true also of the Parent Mind, for at the stage where the initial movement of creation takes place, there are no existing conditions to compel action in one direction more than another. Consequently the direction taken by the creative impulse is not dictated by outward circumstances, and the primary movement must therefore be entirely due to the action of the Original Mind upon itself; it is the reaching out of this Mind for realization of all that it feels itself to be.

The creative process thus in the first instance is purely a matter of feeling—exactly what we speak of as "motif" in a work of art.

Now it is this original feeling that we need to enter into, because it is the fons et origo of the whole chain of causation which subsequently follows. What then can this original feeling of the Spirit be? Since the Spirit is Life-in-itself, its feeling can only be for the fuller expression of Life—any other sort of feeling would be self-destructive and is therefore inconceivable. Then the full expression of Life implies Happiness, and Happiness implies Harmony, and Harmony implies Order, and Order implies Proportion, and Proportion implies Beauty; so that in recognizing the inherent tendency of the Spirit towards the production of Life, we can recognise a similar inherent tendency to the production of these other qualities also; and since the desire to bestow the greater fulness of joyous life can only be described as Love, we can sum up the whole of the feeling which is the original moving impulse in the Spirit as Love and Beauty—the Spirit finding expression through forms of beauty in centres of life, in harmonious reciprocal relation to itself. This is a generalized statement of the broad principle by which Spirit expands from the innermost to the outermost, in accordance with a Law of tendency inherent in itself.

It sees itself, as it were, reflected in various centres of life and energy, each with its appropriate form; but in the first instance these reflections can have no existence except within the originating Mind. They have their first beginning as mental images, so that in addition to the powers of Intelligence and Selection, we must also realise that of Imagination as belonging to the Divine Mind; and we must picture these powers as working from the initial motive of Love and Beauty.

Now this is the Spirit that we need to enter into, and the method of doing so is a perfectly logical one. It is the same method by which all scientific advance is made. It consists in first observing how a certain law works under the conditions spontaneously provided by nature, next in carefully considering what principle this spontaneous working indicates, and lastly deducing from this how the same principle would act under specially selected conditions, not spontaneously provided by nature.

The progress of shipbuilding affords a good example of what I mean. Formerly wood was employed instead of iron, because wood floats in water and iron sinks; yet now the navies of the world are built of iron; careful thought showed the law of floatation to be that anything could float which, bulk for bulk, is lighter than the mass of liquid displaced by it; and so we now make iron float by the very same law by which it sinks, because by the introduction of the *personal* factor, we provide conditions which do not occur spontaneously—according to the esoteric maxim that "Nature unaided fails." Now we want to apply the same process of specializing a generic Law to the first of all Laws, that of the generic life-giving tendency of Spirit itself. Without the element of *individual personality* the Spirit can only work cosmically by a *generic* law; but this law admits of far higher specialization, and this specialization can only be attained through the introduction of the personal factor. But to introduce this factor the individual must be fully aware of the *principle* which underlies the spontaneous or cosmic action of the law. Where, then, will he find this principle of Life? Certainly not by contemplating Death. In order to get a principle to work in the way we require it to, we must observe its action when it is working spon" taneously in this particular direction. We must ask why it goes in the right direction as far as it does—and having learnt this we shall then be able to make it go further. The law of floatation was not discovered by contemplating the sinking of things, but by contemplating the floating of things which floated naturally, and then intelligently asking why they did so.

The knowledge of a principle is to be gained by the study of its affirmative action; when we understand *that* we are in a position to correct the negative conditions which tend to prevent that action.

Now Death is the absence of Life, and disease is the absence of health, so to enter into the Spirit of Life we require to contemplate it, where it is to be found, and not where it is not- -we are met with the old question, "Why seek ye the living among the dead?" This is why we start our studies by considering the cosmic creation, for it is there that we find the Life Spirit working through untold ages, not merely as deathless energy, but with a perpetual advance into higher degrees of Life. If we could only so enter into the Spirit as to make it personally *in Ourselves* what it evidently is in *itself*, the magnum opus would be accomplished. This means realizing our life as drawn direct from the Originating Spirit; and if we now understand that the Thought or Imagination of the Spirit is the great reality of Being, and that all material facts are only correspondences, then it logically follows that what we have to do is to maintain our individual place in the Thought of the Parent Mind.

We have seen that the action of the Originating Mind must needs be *generic*, that is according to types which include multitudes of individuals. This type is the reflection of the Creative Mind at the level of that particular *genius*; and at the human level it is Man, not as associated with particular circumstances, but as existing in the absolute ideal.

In proportion then as we learn to dissociate our conception of ourselves from particular circumstances, and to rest upon our *Absolute* nature, as reflections of the Divine ideal, we, in our turn, reflect back into the Divine Imagination its original conception of itself as expressed in generic or typical Man, and so by a natural law of cause and effect, the individual who realizes this mental attitude enters permanently into the Spirit of Life, and it becomes a perennial fountain of Life springing up spontaneously within him.

He then finds himself to be as the Bible says, "the image and likeness of God." He has reached the level at which he affords a new starting point for the creative process, and the Spirit, finding a personal centre in him, begins its work de nova, having thus solved the great problem of how to enable the Universal to act directly upon the plane of the Particular.

It is in this sense, as affording the requisite centre for a new departure of the creative Spirit, that man is said to be a "microcosm," or universe in miniature; and this is also what is meant by the esoteric doctrine of the Octave, of which I may be able to speak more fully on some other occasion.

If the principles here stated are carefully considered, they will be found to throw light on much that would otherwise be obscure, and they will also afford the key to the succeeding essays.

The reader is therefore asked to think them out carefully for himself, and to note their connection with the subject of the next article.

INDIVIDUALITY

Individuality is the necessary complement of the Universal Spirit, which was the subject of our consideration last Sunday. The whole problem of life consists in finding the true relation of the individual to the Universal Originating Spirit; and the first step towards ascertaining this is to realize what the Universal Spirit must be in itself. We have already done this to some extent, and the conclusions we have arrived at are:—

That the essence of the Spirit is Life, Love, and Beauty.

That its Motive, or primary moving impulse, is to express the Life, Love and Beauty which it feels itself to be.

That the Universal cannot act on the plane of the Particular except by becoming the particular, that is by expression through the individual.

If these three axioms are clearly grasped, we have got a solid foundation from which to start our consideration of the subject for to-day.

The first question that naturally presents itself is,

If these things be so, why does not every individual express the life, love, and beauty of the Universal Spirit? The answer to this question is to be found in the Law of Consciousness. We cannot be conscious of anything except by realizing a certain relation between it and ourselves. It must affect us in some way, otherwise we are not conscious of its existence; and according to the way in which it affects us we recognize ourselves as standing related to it. It is this self-recognition on our own part carried out to the sum total of all our relations, whether spiritual, intellectual, or physical, that constitutes our realization of life. On this principle, then, for the *realization* of its own Livingness, the production of centres of life, through its relation to which this conscious realization can be attained, becomes a necessity for the Originating Mind. Then it follows that this realization can only be complete where the individual has perfect liberty to withhold it; for otherwise no true realization could have taken place. For instance, let us consider the working of Love. Love must be spontaneous, or it has no existence at all. We cannot imagine such a thing as mechanically induced love. But anything which is formed so as to automatically produce an effect without any volition of its own, is nothing but a piece of mechanism. Hence if the Originating Mind is to realize the reality of Love, it can Only be by relation to some being which has the power to withhold love. The same applies to the realization of all the other modes of livingness; so that it is only in proportion, as the individual life is an independent centre of action, with the option of acting either positively or negatively, that any real life has been produced at all. The further the created thing is from being a merely mechanical arrangement, the higher is the grade of creation. The solar system is a perfect work of mechanical creation, but to constitute centres which can reciprocate the highest nature of the Divine Mind, requires not a mechanism, however perfect, but a mental centre which is, in itself, an independent source of action. Hence by the requirements of the case man should be capable of placing himself either in a positive or a negative relation to the Parent Mind, from which he originates; otherwise he would be nothing more than a clockwork figure.

In this necessity of the case, then, we find the reason why the life, love, and beauty of the Spirit are not visibly reproduced in every human being. They *are* reproduced in the world of nature, so far as a mechanical and automatic action can represent them, but their perfect reproduction can only take place on the basis of a liberty akin to that of the Originating Spirit itself, which therefore implies the liberty of negation as well as of affirmation.

Why, then, does the individual make a negative choice? Because he does not understand the law of his own individuality, and believes it to be a law of limitation, instead of a Law of Liberty. He does not expect to find the starting point of the Creative Process reproduced within himself, and so he looks to the mechanical side of things for the basis of his reasoning about life. Consequently his reasoning lands him in the conclusion that life is limited, because he has assumed limitation in his premises, and so-logically cannot escape from it in his conclusion. Then he thinks that this is the law and so ridicules the idea of transcending it. He points to the sequence of cause and effect, by which death, disease, and disaster, hold their sway over the individual, and says that sequence is law. And he is perfectly right so far as he goes—it is a law; but not *The* Law. When we have only reached this stage of comprehension, we have yet to learn that a higher law can include a lower one so completely as entirely to swallow it up.

The fallacy involved in this negative argument, is the assumption that the law of limitation is essential in all grades of being. It is the fallacy of the old shipbuilders as to the impossibility of building iron ships. What is required is to get at the *Principle* which is at the back of the Law in its affirmative working, and specialize it under higher conditions than are spontaneously presented by nature, and this can only be done by the introduction of the personal element, that is to say an individual intelligence capable of comprehending the principle. The question, then, is, what is the principle by which we came into being? and this is only a personal application of the general question, How did anything come into being? Now, as I pointed out in the preceding article, the ultimate deduction from physical science is that the originating movement takes place in the Universal Mind, and is analogous to that of our own imagination; and as we have just seen, the perfect ideal can only be that of a being capable of reciprocating *all* the qualities of the Originating Mind. Consequently man, in his inmost nature, is the product of the Divine Mind imaging forth an image of itself on the plane of the relative as the complementary to its own sphere of the absolute.

If we will therefore go to the *Inmost* principle in ourselves, which philosophy and Scripture alike declare to be made in the image and likeness of God, instead of to the outer vehicles which it externalizes as instruments through which to function on the various planes of being, we shall find that we have reached a principle in ourselves which stands in loco dei towards all our vehicles and also towards our environment. It is above them all, and creates them, however unaware we may be of the fact, and relatively to them it occupies the place of first cause. The recognition of this is the discovery of our own relation to the whole world of the relative. On the other hand this must not lead us into the mistake of supposing that there is nothing higher, for, as we have already seen, this inmost principle or ego is itself the effect of an antecedent cause, for it proceeds from the imaging process in the Divine Mind.

We thus find ourselves holding an intermediate position between true First Cause, on the one hand, and the world of secondary causes on the other, and in order to understand the nature of this position, we must fall back on the axiom that the Universal can only work on the plane of the Particular through the individual. Then we see that the function of the individual is to *differentiate* the undistributed flow of the Universal into suitable directions for starting different trains of secondary causation.

Man's place in the cosmic order is that of a distributor of the Divine power, subject, however, to the inherent Law of the power which he distributes. We see one instance of this in ordinary science, in the fact that we never create force; all we can do is to distribute it. The very word Man means distributor or measurer, as in common with all words derived from the Sanderit root MN., it implies the idea of measurement, just as in the words moon, month, mens, mind, and "man," the Indian weight of 80 1bs.; and it is for this reason that man is spoken of in Scripture as a "steward," or dispenser of the Divine gifts. As our minds become open to the full meaning of this position, the immense possibilities and also the responsibility contained in it will become apparent.

It means that the individual is the creative centre of his own world. Our past experience affords no evidence against this, but on the contrary, is evidence for it. Our true nature is always present, only we have hitherto taken the lower and mechanical side of things for our starting point, and so have created limitation instead of expansion. And even with the knowledge of the Creative Law which we have now attained, we shall continue to do this, if we seek our starting point in the things which are below us and not in the only thing which is above us, namely the Divine Mind, because it is only there that we can find illimitable Creative Power. Life is *being*, it is the experience of states of consciousness, and there is an unfailing correspondence between these inner states and our outward conditions. Now we see from the Original Creation that the state of consciousness must be the cause, and the corresponding conditions the effect, because at the starting of the creation no conditions existed, and the working of the Creative Mind upon itself can only have been a state of consciousness. This, then, is clearly the Creative Order—from states to conditions. But we invert this order, and seek to create from conditions to states. We say, If I had such and such conditions they would produce the state of feeling which I desire; and in so saying we run the risk of making a mistake as to the correspondence, for it may turn out that the particular conditions which we fixed on are not such as would produce the desired state. Or, again, though they might produce it in a certain degree, other conditions might produce it in a still greater degree, while at the same time opening the way to the attainment of still higher states and still better conditions. Therefore our wisest plan is to follow the pattern of the Parent Mind and make mental self-recognition our starting point, knowing that by the inherent Law of Spirit the corelated conditions will come by a natural process of growth. Then the great self-recognition is that of our relation to the Supreme Mind. That is the generating centre and we are distributing centres; just as electricity is generated at the central station and delivered in different forms of power by reason of passing through appropriate centres of distribution, so that in one place it lights a room, in another conveys a message, and in a third drives a tram car. In like manner the power of the Universal Mind takes particular forms through the particular mind of the individual. It does not interfere with the lines of his individuality, but works along them, thus making him, not less, but more himself. It is thus, not a compelling power, but an expanding and illuminating one; so that the more the individual recognizes the reciprocal action between it and himself, the more full of life he must become.

Then also we need not be troubled about future conditions because we know that the All-originating Power is working through us and for us, and that according to the Law proved by the whole existing creation, it produces all the conditions required for the expression of the Life, Love and Beauty which it is, so that we can fully trust it to open the way as we go along. The Great Teacher's words, "Take no thought for the morrow"—and note that the correct translation is "Take no anxious thought"— are the practical application of the soundest philosophy. This does not, of course, mean that we are not to exert ourselves. We must do our share in the work, and not expect God to do *for* us what He can only do *through* us. We are to use our common sense and natural faculties in working upon the conditions now present. We must make use of them, *as far as they go*, but we must not try and go further than the present things require; we must not try to force things, but allow them to grow naturally, knowing that they are doing so under the guidance of the All-Creating Wisdom.

Following this method we shall grow more and more into the habit of looking to mental attitude as the Key to our progress in Life, knowing that everything else must come out of that; and we shall further discover that our mental attitude is eventually determined by the way in which we regard the Divine Mind. Then the final result will be that we shall see the Divine Mind to be nothing else than Life, Love and Beauty—Beauty being identical with Wisdom or the perfect adjustment of parts to whole—and we shall see ourselves to be distributing centres of these primary energies and so in our turn subordinate centres of creative power. And as we advance in this knowledge we shall find that we transcend one law of limitation after another by finding the higher law, of which the lower is but a partial expression, until we shall see clearly before us, as our ultimate goal, nothing less than the Perfect Law of Liberty—not liberty without Law which is anarchy, but Liberty according to Law. In this way we shall find that the Apostle spoke the literal truth, when he said, that we shall become like Him when we see Him *as he is*, because the whole process by which our individuality is produced is one of reflection of the image existing in the Divine Mind. When we thus learn the Law of our own being we shall be able to specialize it in ways of which we have hitherto but little conception, but as in the case of all natural laws the specialization cannot take place until the fundamental principle of the generic law has been fully realized. For these reasons the student should endeavour to realize more and more perfectly, both in theory and practice, the law of the relation between the Universal and the Individual Minds. It is that of *reciprocal* action. If this fact of reciprocity is grasped, it will be found to explain both why the individual falls short of expressing the fulness of Life, which the Spirit is, and why he can attain to the fulness of that expression; just as the same law explains why iron sinks in water, and how it can be made to float. It is the individualizing of the Universal Spirit, by recognizing its reciprocity to ourselves, that is the secret of the perpetuation and growth of our own individuality.

THE NEW THOUGHT AND THE NEW ORDER

In the two preceding lectures I have endeavoured to reach some conception of what the All-originating Spirit is in itself, and of the relation of the individual to it. So far as we can form any conception of these things at all we see that they are universal principles applicable to all nature, and, at the human level, applicable to all men: they are general laws the recognition of which is an essential preliminary to any further advance, because progress is made, not by setting aside the inherent law of things, which is impossible, but by specializing it through presenting conditions which will enable the same principle to act in a less limited manner. Having therefore got a general idea of these two ultimates, the universal and the individual, and of their relation to one another, let us now consider the process of specialization. In what does the specialization of a natural law consist? It consists in making that law or principle produce an effect which it could not produce under the simply generic conditions spontaneously provided by nature. This selection of suitable conditions is the work of Intelligence, it is a process of consciously arranging things in a new order, so as to produce a new result. The principle is never new, for principles are eternal and universal; but the knowledge that the same principle will produce new results when working under new conditions is the key to the unfoldment of infinite possibilities. What we have therefore to consider is the working of Intelligence in providing specific conditions for the operation of universal principles, so as to bring about new results which will transcend our past experiences. The process does not consist in the introduction of new elements, but in making new combinations of elements which are always present; just as our ancestors had no conception of carriages that could go without horses, and yet by a suitable combination of elements which were always in existence, such vehicles are common objects in our streets today. How, then, is the power of Intelligence to be brought to bear upon the generic law of the relation between the Individual and the Universal so as to specialize it into the production of greater results than those which we have hitherto obtained?

All the practical attainments of science, which place the civilized world of to-day in advance of the times of King Alfred or Charlemagne, have been gained by a uniform method, and that a very simple one. It is by always enquiring what is the affirmative factor in any existing combination, and asking ourselves why, in that particular combination, it does not act beyond certain limits. What makes the thing a success, so far as it goes, and what prevents it going further? Then, by carefully considering the nature of the affirmative factor, we see what sort of conditions to provide to enable it to express itself more fully. This is the scientific method; it has proved itself true in respect of material things, and there is no reason why it should not be equally reliable in respect of spiritual things also.

Taking this as our method, we ask, What is the affirmative factor in the whole creation, and in ourselves as included in the creation, and, as we found in the first lecture, this factor is Spirit—that invisible power which concentrates-the primordial ether into forms, and endows those forms with various modes of motion, from the simply mechanical motion of the planet up to the volitional motion in man. And, since this is so, the primary affirmative factor can only be the Feeling and the Thought of the Universal Spirit.* Now, by the hypothesis of the case, the Universal Spirit must be the Pure Essence of Life, and therefore its feeling and thought can only be towards the continually increasing expression of the livingness which it is; and accordingly the specialization, of which we are in search, must be along the line of affording it a centre from which it may more perfectly realize this feeling and express this thought: in other words the way to specialize the generic principle of Spirit is by providing new mental conditions in consonance with its own original nature.

The scientific method of enquiry therefore brings us to the conclusion that the required conditions for translating the racial or generic operation of the Spirit into a specialized individual operation is a new way of *thinking* mode of thought concurring with, and not in opposition to, the essential forward movement of the Creative Spirit itself. This implies an entire reversal of our old conceptions. Hitherto we have taken forms and conditions as the starting point of our thought and inferred that they are the causes of mental states; now we have learnt that the true order of the creative process is exactly the reverse, and that thought and feeling are the causes, and forms and conditions the effects. When we have learnt this lesson we have grasped the foundation principle on which individual specialization of the generic law of the creative process becomes a practical possibility.

New Thought, then, is not the name of a particular sect, but is the essential factor by which our own future development is to be carried on; and its essence consists in seeing the relation of things in a New Order. Hitherto we have inverted the true order of cause and effect; now, by carefully considering the real nature of the Principle of Causation in itself—causa causans as distinguished from cause causata—we return to the true order and adopt a new method of thinking in accordance with it.

In themselves this order and this method of thinking are not new. They are older than the foundation of the world, for they are those of the Creative Spirit itself; and all through the ages this teaching has been handed down under various forms, the true meaning of which has been perceived only by a few in each generation. But as the light breaks in upon any individual it is a new light to him, and so to each one in succession it becomes the New Thought. And when anyone reaches it, he finds himself in a New Order. He continues indeed to be included in the universal order of the cosmos, but in a perfectly different way to what he had previously supposed; for, from his new standpoint, he finds that he is included, not so much as a part of the general effect, but as a part of the general cause; and when he perceives this he then sees that the method of his further advance must be by letting the General Cause flow more and more freely into his own specific centre, and he therefore seeks to provide thought conditions which will enable him to do so.

Then, still employing the scientific method of following up the affirmative factor, he realizes that this universal causative power, by whatever name he may call it, manifests as Supreme Intelligence in the adaptation of means to ends. It does so in the mechanism of the planet, in the production of supply for the support of physical life, and in the maintenance of the race as a whole. True, the investigator is met at every turn with individual failure; but his answer to this is that there is no cosmic failure, and that the apparent individual failure is itself a part of the cosmic process, and will diminish in proportion as the individual attains to the recognition of the Moving Principle of that process, and provides the necessary conditions to enable it to take a new starting point in his own individuality. Now, one of these conditions is to recognize it as Intelligence, and to remember that when working through our own mentality it in no way changes its essential nature, just as electricity loses none of its essential qualities in passing through the special apparatus which enables it to manifest as light.

When we see this, our line of thought will run something as follows:—"My mind is a centre of Divine operation. The Divine operation is always for expansion and fuller expression, and this means the production of something beyond what has gone before, something entirely new, not included in past experience, though proceeding out of it by an orderly sequence of growth. Therefore, since the Divine cannot change its inherent nature, it must operate in the same manner in me; consequently in my own special world, of which I am the centre, it will move forward to produce new conditions, always in advance of any that have gone before." This is a legitimate line of argument, from the premises established in the recognition of the relation between the individual and the Universal Mind; and it results in our looking to the Divine Mind, not only as creative, but also as directive— that is as determining the actual forms which the conditions for its manifestation will take in our own particular world, as well as supplying the energy for their production. We miss the point of the relation between the individual and the universal, if we do not see that the Originating Spirit is a FORMING power. It is the forming power throughout nature, and if we would specialize it we must learn to trust its formative quality when operating from its new starting point in ourselves.

But the question naturally arises, If this is so, what part is taken by the individual? Our part is to provide a concrete centre round which the Divine energies can play. In the generic order of being we exercise upon it a force of attraction in accordance with the innate pattern of our particular individuality; and as we begin to realize the Law of this relation, we, in our turn, are attracted towards the Divine along the lines of least resistance, that is on those lines which are most natural to our special bent of mind. In this way we throw out certain aspirations with the result that we intensify our attraction of the Divine forces in a certain specific manner, and they then begin to act both through us and around us in accordance with our aspirations. This is the rationale of the reciprocal action be tween the Universal Mind and the individual mind, and this shows us that our desires should not be directed so much to the acquisition of particular *things* as to the reproduction in ourselves of particular phases of the Spirit's activity; and this, being in its very nature creative, is bound to externalize as corresponding things and circumstances. Then, when these external facts appear in the circle of our objective life, we must work upon them from the objective stand-point. This is where many fall short of completed work. They realize the subjective or creative process, but do not see that it must be followed by an objective or constructive process, and consequently they are unpractical dreamers and never reach the stage of completed work. The creative process brings the materials and conditions for the work to our hands; then we must make use of them with diligence and common-sense—God will provide the food, but He will not cook the dinner.

This, then, is the part taken by the individual, and it is thus that he becomes a distributing centre of the Divine energy, neither on the one hand trying to lead it like a blind force, nor on the other being himself under a blind unreasoning impulse from it. He receives guidance because he seeks guidance; and he both seeks and receives according to a Law which he is able to recognize; so that he no more sacrifices his liberty or dwarfs his powers, than does an engineer who submits to the generic laws of electricity, in order to apply them to some specific purpose. The more intimate his knowledge of this Law of Reciprocity becomes, the more he finds that it leads on to Liberty, on the same principle by which we find in physical science that nature obeys us precisely in the same degree to which we first obey nature. As the esoteric maxim has it "What is a truth on one plane is a truth on all." But the key to this enfranchisement of body, mind, and circumstances is in that new thought which becomes creative of new conditions, because it realizes the true order of the creative process. Therefore it is that, if we would bring a new order of Life, Light, and Liberty into our lives we must commence by bringing a new order into our thought, and find in ourselves the starting point of a new creative series, not by the force of personal will, but by union with the Divine Spirit, which in the expression of its inherent Love and Beauty, makes all things new.

THE LIFE OF THE SPIRIT

The three preceding lectures have touched upon certain fundamental truths in a definite order—first the nature of the Originating Spirit itself, next the generic relation of the individual to this All-embracing Spirit, and lastly the way to specialize this relation so as to obtain greater results from it than spontaneously arise by its merely generic action, and we have found that this can only be done through a new order of thought. This sequence is logical because it implies a Power, an Individual who understands the Power, and a Method of applying the power deduced from understanding its nature. These are general principles without realizing which it is impossible to proceed further, but assuming that the reader has grasped their significance, we may now go on to consider their application in greater detail.

Now this application must be a personal one, for it is only through the individual that the higher specialization of the power can take place, but at the same time this must not lead us to suppose that the individual, himself, brings the creative force into being. To suppose this is inversion; and we cannot impress upon ourselves too deeply that the relation of the individual to the Divine Spirit is that of a distributor, and not that of the original creator. If this is steadily borne in mind the way will become clear, otherwise we shall be led into confusion.

What, then, is the Power which we are to distribute? It is the Originating Spirit itself. We are sure that it is this because the new order of thought always begins at the beginning of any series which it contemplates bringing into manifestation, and it is based upon the fact that the origin of everything is Spirit. It is in this that its creative power resides; hence the person who is in the true new order of thought assumes as an axiomatic fact that what he has to distribute, or differentiate into manifestation is nothing else than the Originating Spirit. This being the case, it is evident that the *purpose* of the distribution must be the more perfect expression of the Originating Spirit as that which it is in itself, and what it is in itself is emphatically Life. What is seeking for expression, then, is the perfect Livingness of the Spirit; and this expression is to be found, through ourselves, by means of our renewed mode of thought. Let us see, then, how our new order of thought, with regard to the Principle of Life, is likely to operate In our old order of thought we have always associated Life with the physical body—life has been for us the supreme physical fact. Now, however, we know that Life is much more than this; but, as the greater includes the less, it includes physical life as one mode of its manifestation. The true order does not require us to deny the reality of physical life or to call it an illusion; on the contrary it sees in physical life the completion of a great creative series, but it assigns it the proper place in that series, which is what the old mode of thought did not.

When we realize the truth about the Creative Process, we see that the originating life is not physical: its livingness consists in thought and feeling.

By this inner movement it throws out vehicles through which to function, and these become living forms because of the inner-principle which is sustaining them; so that the Life with which we are primarily concerned in the new order is the life of thought and feeling in ourselves as the vehicle, or distributing medium, of the Life of the Spirit.

Then, if we have grasped the idea of the Spirit as the great *Forming* Power, as stated in the last lecture, we shall seek in it the fountain-head of Form as well as of Power: and as a logical deduction from this we shall look to it to give form to our thoughts and feelings. If the principle is once recognised the sequence is obvious. The form taken by our outward conditions, whether of body or circumstance, depends on the form taken by our thoughts and feelings, and our thoughts and feelings will take form from that source from which we allow them to receive suggestion. Accordingly if we allow them to accept their fundamental suggestions from the relative and limited, they will assume a corresponding form and transmit them to our external environment, thus repeating the old order of limitation in a ceaselessly recurring round. Now our object is to get out of this circle of limitation, and the only way to do so is to get our thoughts and feelings moulded into new forms continually advancing to greater and greater perfection. To meet this requirement, therefore, there must be a forming power greater than that of our own unaided conceptions, and this is to be found in our realization of the Spirit as the Supreme Beauty, or Wisdom, moulding our thoughts and feelings into shapes harmoniously adjusted to the fullest expression, in and through us, of the Livingness which Spirit is in itself.

Now this is nothing more than transferring to the innermost plane of origination, a principle with which all readers who are "in the thought" may be presumed to be quite familiar—the principle of Receptiveness. We all know what is meant by a receptive mental attitude when applied to healing or telepathy; and does it not logically follow that the same principle may be applied to the receiving of life itself from the Supreme Source? What is wanted, therefore, is to place ourselves in a receptive mental attitude towards the Universal Spirit with the intention of receiving its forming influence into our mental substance. It is always the presence of a definite intention that distinguishes the intelligent receptive attitude of mind from a merely sponge-like absorbency, which sucks in any and every influence that may happen to be floating round: for we must not shut our eyes to the fact that there are various influences in the mental atmosphere by which we are surrounded, and some of them of the most undesirable kind. Clear and definite intention is therefore as necessary in our receptive attitude as in our active and creative one; and if our intention is to have our own thoughts and feelings moulded into such forms as to express those of the Spirit, then we establish that relation to the Spirit which, by the conditions of the case, must necessarily lead us to the conception of new ideals vitalised by a power which will enable us to bring them into concrete manifestation. It is in this way that we become differentiating centres of the Divine Thought giving it expression in form in the world of space and time, and thus is solved the great problem of enabling the Universal to act upon the plane of the particular without being hampered by those limitations which the merely generic law of manifestation imposes upon it. It is just here that subconscious mind performs the function of a "bridge" between the finite and the infinite as noted in my "Edinburgh Lectures on Mental Science" (page 31), and it is for this reason that a recognition of its susceptibility to impression is so important.

By establishing, then, a personal relation to the life of the Spirit, the sphere of the individual becomes enlarged. The reason is that he allows a greater intelligence than his own to take the initiative; and since he knows that this Intelligence is also the very Principle of Life itself, he cannot have any fear that it will act in any way to the diminution of his individual life, for that would be to stultify its own operation—it would be self-destructive action which is a contradiction in terms to the conception of Creative Spirit. Knowing, then, that by its inherent nature this Intelligence can only work to the expansion of the individual life, we can rest upon it with the utmost confidence and trust it to take an initiative which will lead to far greater results than any we could forecast from the stand-point of our own knowledge. So long as we insist on dictating the particular form which the action of the Spirit is to take, we limit it, and so close against ourselves avenues of expansion which might otherwise have been open to us; and if we ask ourselves why we do this we shall find that in the last resort it is because we do not believe in the Spirit as a *forming* power. We have, indeed, advanced to the conception of it as executive power, which will work to a prescribed pattern, but we have yet to grasp the conception of it as versed in the art of design, and capable of elaborating schemes of construction, which will not only be complete in themselves, but also in perfect harmony with one another. When we advance to the conception of the Spirit as containing in itself the ideal of Form as well as of Power, we shall cease from the effort of trying to force things into a particular shape, whether on the inner or the outer plane, and shall be content to trust the inherent harmoniousness or Beauty of the Spirit to produce combinations far in advance of anything that we could have conceived ourselves. This does not mean that we shall reduce ourselves to a condition of apathy, in which all desire, expectation and enthusiasm have been quenched, for these are the mainspring of our mental machinery; but on the contrary their action will be quickened by the knowledge that there is working at the back of them a Formative Principle so infallible that it cannot miss its mark; so that however good and beautiful the existing forms may be, we may always rest in the happy expectation of something still better to come. And it will come by a natural law of growth, because the Spirit is in itself the Principle of Increase. They will grow out of present conditions for the simple reason that if you are to reach some further point it can only be by starting from where you are now. Therefore it is written, "Despise not the day of small things." There is only one proviso attached to this forward movement of the Spirit in the world of our own surroundings, and that is that we shall co-operate with it; and this co-operation consists in making the best use of existing conditions in cheerful reliance on the Spirit of Increase to express itself through us, and for us, because we are in harmony with it. This mental attitude will be found of immense value in setting us free from worry and anxiety, and as a consequence our work will be done in a much more efficient manner. We shall do the present work *for its own* sake, knowing that herein is the principle of unfoldment; and doing it simply for its own sake we shall bring to bear upon it a power of concentration which cannot fail of good results—and this quite naturally and without any toilsome effort. We shall then find that the secret of co-operation is to have faith in ourselves because we first have faith in God; and we shall discover that this Divine self-confidence is something very different from a boastful egotism which assumes a personal superiority over others. It is simply the assurance of a man who knows that he is working in accordance with a law of nature. He does not claim as a personal achievement what the Law does *for* him: but on the other hand he does not trouble himself about outcries against his presumptuous audacity raised by persons who are ignorant of the Law which he is employing. He is therefore neither boastful nor timorous, but simply works on in cheerful expectancy because he knows that his reliance is upon a Law which cannot be broken.

In this way, then, we must realize the Life of the Spirit as being also the Law of the Spirit. The two are identical, and cannot deny themselves. Our recognition of them gives them a new starting point through our own mentality, but they still continue to be the same in their nature, and unless limited or inverted by our mental affirmation of limited or inverted conditions, they are bound to work out into fuller and continually fuller expression of the Life, Love, and Beauty which the Spirit is in itself. Our path, therefore, is plain; it is simply to contemplate the Life, Love, and Beauty of the Originating Spirit and affirm that we are already giving expression to it in our thoughts and in our actions however insignificant they may at present appear. This path may be very narrow and humble in its beginning, but it ever grows wider and mounts higher, for it is the continually expanding expression of the Life of the Spirit which is infinite and knows no limits.

ALPHA AND OMEGA

Alpha and Omega, the First and the Last. What does this mean? It means the entire series of causation from the first originating movement to the final and completed result. We may take this on any scale from the creation of a cosmos to the creation of a lady's robe. Everything has its origin in an idea, a thought; and it has its completion in the manifestation of that thought in form. Many intermediate stages are necessary, but the Alpha and Omega of the series are the thought and the thing. This shows us that in essence the thing already existed in the thought. Omega is already potential in Alpha, just as in the Pythagorean system all numbers are said to proceed from unity and to be resolvable back again into it. Now it is this general principle of the already existence of the thing in the thought that we have to lay hold of, and as we find it true in an architect's design of the house that is to be, so we find it true in the great work of the Architect of the Universe. When we see this we have realized a general principle, which we find at work everywhere. That is the meaning of a general principle: it can be applied to any sort of subject; and the use of studying general principles is to give them particular application to anything we may have to deal with. Now what we have to deal with most of all is ourselves, and so we come to the consideration of Alpha and Omega in the human being. In the vision of St. John, the speaker of the words, "I am Alpha and Omega, the First and the Last," is described as "Like unto a son of man"—that is, however transcendent the appearance in the vision, it is essentially human, and thus suggests to us the presence of the universal principle at the human level. But the figure in the apocalyptic vision is not that of man as we ordinarily know him. It is that of Omega as it subsists enshrined in Alpha: it is the ideal of humanity as it subsists in the Divine Mind which was manifested in objective form to the eyes of the seer, and therefore presented the Alpha and Omega of that idea in all the majesty of Divine glory.

But if we grasp the truth that the thing is already existent in the thought, do we not see that this transcendent Omega must be already existent in the Divine ideal of every one of us? If on the plane of the absolute time is not, then does it not follow that this glorified humanity is a present fact in the Divine Mind? And if this is so, then this fact is eternally true regarding every human being. But if it is true that the thing exists in the thought, it is equally true that the thought finds form in the thing; and since things exist under the relative conditions of time and space, they are necessarily subject to a law of Growth, so that while the subsistence of the thing in the thought is perfect ab initio, the expression of the thought in the thing is a matter of gradual development. This is a point which we must never lose sight of in our studies; and we must never lose sight of the perfection of the thing in the thought because we do not yet see the perfection of the thought in the thing. Therefore we must remember that man, as we know him now, has by no means reached the ultimate of his evolution. We are only yet in the making, but we have now reached a point where we can facilitate the evolutionary process by conscious co-operation with the Creative Spirit. Our share in this work commences with the recognition of the Divine ideal of man, and thus finding the pattern by which we are to be guided. For since the person to be created after this pattern is ourself, it follows that, by whatever processes the Divine ideal transforms itself into concrete reality, the place where those processes are to work must be within ourselves; in other words, the creative action of the Spirit takes place through the laws of our own mentality. If it is a true maxim that the thing must take form in the thought before the thought can take form in the thing, then it is plain that the Divine Ideal can only be externalized in our objective life in proportion as it is first formed in our thought; and it takes form in our thought only to the extent to which we apprehend its existence in the Divine Mind. By the nature of the relation between the individual mind and the Universal Mind it is strictly a case of reflection; and in proportion as the mirror of our own mind blurs or clearly reflects the image of the Divine ideal, so will it give rise to a correspondingly feeble or vigorous reproduction of it in our external life.

This being the rationale of the matter, why should we limit our conception of the Divine ideal of ourselves? Why should we say, "I am too mean a creature ever to reflect so glorious an image"— or "God never intended such a limitless ideal to be reproduced in human beings." In saying such things we expose our ignorance of the whole Law of the Creative Process. We shut our eyes to the fact that the Omega of completion already subsists in the Alpha of conception, and that the Alpha of conception would be nothing but a lying illusion if it was not capable of expression in the Omega of completion. The creative process in us is that we become the individual reflection of what we realize God to be relatively to ourselves, and therefore if we realize the Divine Spirit as the *infinite* potential of all that can constitute a perfected human being, this conception must, by the Law of the Creative Process, gradually build up a corresponding image in our mind, which in turn will act upon our external conditions.

This, by the laws of mind, is the nature of the process and it shows us what St. Paul means when he speaks of Christ being formed in us (Gal. iv. 19) and what in another place he calls being renewed in knowledge after the image of Him that created us (Col. iii. 10). It is a thoroughly logical sequence of cause and effect, and what we require is to see more clearly the Law of this sequence and use it intelligently—that is why St. Paul says it is being "renewed in knowledge": it is a New Knowledge, the recognition of principles which we had not previously apprehended. Now the fact which, in our past experience, we have not grasped is that the human mind forms a new point of departure for the work of the Creative Spirit; and in proportion as we see this more and more clearly, the more we shall find ourselves entering into a new order of life in which we become less and less subject to the old limitations. This is not a reward arbitrarily bestowed upon us for holding dogmatically to certain mere verbal statements, but it is the natural result of understanding the supreme law of our own being. On its own plane it is as purely scientific as the law of chemical reaction; only here we are not dealing with the interaction of secondary causes but with the Self-originating action of Spirit. Hence a new force has to be taken into account which does not occur in physical science, the power of Feeling. Thought creates form, but it is feeling that gives vitality to thought. Thought without feeling may be constructive as in some great engineering work, but it can never be creative as in the work of the artist or musician; and that which originates within itself a new order of causation is, so far as all pre-existing forms are concerned, a creation ex nihilo, and is therefore Thought expressive of Feeling. It is this indissoluble union of Thought and Feeling that distinguishes creative thought from merely analytical thought and places it in a different category; and therefore if we are to afford a new starting-point for carrying on the work of creation it must be by assimilating the feeling of the Originating Spirit as part and parcel of its thought—it is that entering into the Mind of the Spirit of which I spoke in the first address.

Now the images in the Mind of the Spirit must necessarily be GENERIC. The reason for this is that by its very nature the Principle of Life must be prolific, that is, tending to Multiplicity, and therefore the original Thought-image must be fundamental to whole races, and not exclusive to particular individuals. Consequently the images in the Mind of the Spirit must be absolute types of the true essentials of the perfect development of the race, just what Plato meant by architypal ideas. This is the perfect subsistence of the thing in the thought. Therefore it is that our evolution as centres of *Creative* activity, the exponents of new laws, and through them of new conditions, depends on our realizing in the Divine Mind the architype of mental perfection, at once as thought and feeling. But when we find all this in the Divine Mind, do we not meet with an infinite and glorious Personality? There is nothing lacking of all that we can understand by Personality, excepting outward form; and since the very essence of telepathy is that it dispenses with the physical presence, we find ourselves in a position of interior communion with a Personality at once Divine and Human. This is that Personality of the Spirit which St. John saw in the apocalyptic vision, and which by the very conditions of the case is the Alpha and Omega of Humanity.

But, as I have said, it is simply *generic* in itself, and it becomes active and specific only by a purely personal relation to the individual. But once more we must realize that nothing can take place except according to Law, and therefore this specific relation is nothing arbitrary, but arises out of the generic Law applied under specific conditions. And since what makes a law generic is precisely the fact that it does not supply the specific conditions, it follows that the conditions for the specializing of the Law must be provided by the individual. Then it is that his recognition of the originating creative movement, as arising from combined Thought and Feeling, becomes a practical working asset. He realizes that there is a Heart and Mind of the Spirit reciprocal to his own heart and mind, that he is not dealing with a filmy abstraction, nor yet with a mere mathematical sequence, but with something that is pulsating with a Life as warm and vivid and full of interest as his own—nay, more so, for it is the Infinite of all that he himself is. And his recognition goes even further than this, for since this specialization can only take place through the individual himself, it logically follows that the Life, which he thus specializes, become *his own* life. Quoad the individual it does not know itself apart from him. But this self-recognition through the individual cannot in any way change the inherent nature of the Creative Spirit, and therefore to the extent to which the individual perceives its identification with himself, he places himself under its guidance, and so he becomes one of those who are "led by the Spirit." Thus he begins to find the Alpha and Omega of the Divine ideal reproduced in himself—in a very small degree at present, but containing the principle of perpetual growth into an infinite expansion of which we can as yet form no conception.

St. John sums up the whole of this position in his memorable words:—"Beloved now are we the Sons of God, and it doth not yet appear what we *shall* be; but we know that when He shall appear (i.e., become clear to us) we shall be like Him; for (i.e., the reason of all this) we shall see Him as He is" (I. John iii. 2).

THE CREATIVE POWER OF THOUGHT

One of the great axioms in the new order of ideas, of which I have spoken, is that our Thought possesses creative power, and since the whole superstructure depends on this foundation, it is well to examine it carefully. Now the starting point is to see that Thought, or purely mental action, is the only possible source from which the existing creation could ever have come into manifestation at all, and it is on this account that in the preceding addresses I have laid stress on the origin of the cosmos. It is therefore not necessary to go over this ground again, and we will start this morning's enquiry on the assumption that every manifestation is in essence the expression of a Divine Thought. This being so, our own mind is the expression of a Divine Thought. The Divine Thought has produced something which itself is capable of thinking; but the question is whether its thinking has the same creative quality as that of the Parent Mind.

Now by the very hypothesis of the case the whole Creative Process consists in the continual pressing so forward of the Universal Spirit for expression through the individual and particular, and Spirit in its different modes is therefore the Life and Substance of the universe. Hence it follows that if there is to be an expression of thinking power it can only be by expressing the same thinking power which subsists latent in the Originating Spirit. If it were less than this it would only be some sort of mechanism and would not be thinking power, so that to be thinking power at all it must be identical in kind with that of the Originating Spirit. It is for this reason that man is said to be created in the image and likeness of God; and if we realize that it is impossible for him to be otherwise, we shall find a firm foundation from which to draw many important deductions.

But if our thought possesses this creative power, why are we hampered by adverse conditions? The answer is, because hitherto we have used our power invertedly. We have taken the starting point of our thought from external facts and consequently created a repetition of facts of a similar nature, and so long as we do this we must needs go on perpetuating the old circle of limitation. And, owing to the sensitiveness of the subconscious mind to suggestion—(See Edinburgh Lectures, chapter V.)—we are subject to a very powerful negative influence from those who are unacquainted with affirmative principles, and thus race-beliefs and the thought-currents of our more immediate environment tend to consolidate our own inverted thinking. It is therefore not surprising that the creative power of our thought, thus used in a wrong direction, has produced the limitations of which we complain. The remedy, then, is by reversing our method of thinking, and instead of taking external facts as our starting point, taking the inherent nature of mental power as our starting point. We have already gained two great steps in this direction, first by seeing that the whole manifested cosmos could have had its origin nowhere but in mental power, and secondly by realizing that our own mental power must be the same in kind with that of the Originating Mind.

Now we can go a step further and see how this power in ourselves can be perpetuated and intensified. By the nature of the creative process your mind is itself a thought of the Parent Mind; so, as long as this thought of the Universal Mind subsists, you will subsist, for you are it. But so long as you think this thought it continues to subsist, and necessarily remains present in the Divine Mind, thus fulfilling the logical conditions required for the perpetuation of the individual life. A poor analogy of the process may be found in a self-influencing dynamo where the magnetism generates the current and the current intensifies the magnetism with the result of producing a still stronger current until the limit of saturation is reached; only in the substantive infinitude of the Universal Mind and the potential infinitude of the Individual Mind there is no limit of saturation. Or we may compare the interaction of the two minds to two mirrors, a great and a small one, opposite each other, with the word "Life" engraved on the large one. Then, by the law of reflection, the word "Life" will also appear on the image of the smaller mirror reflected in the greater. Of course these are only very imperfect analogies; but if you car once grasp the idea of your own individuality as a thought in the Divine Mind which is able to perpetuate itself by thinking of itself as the thought which it is, you have got at the root of the whole matter, and by the same process you will not only perpetuate your life but will also expand it.

When we realize this on the one hand, and on the other that all external conditions, including the body, are produced by thought, we find ourselves standing between two infinites, the infinite of Mind and the infinite of Substance—from both of which we can draw what we will, and mould specific conditions out of the Universal Substance by the Creative Power which we draw in from the Universal Mind. But we must recollect that this is not by the force of personal will upon the substance, which is an error that will land us in all sorts of inversion, but by realizing our mind as a channel through which the Universal Mind operates upon substances in a particular way, according to the mode of thought which we are seeking to embody. If, then, our thought is habitually concentrated upon principles rather than on particular things, realizing that principles are nothing else than the Divine Mind in operation, we shall find that they will necessarily germinate to produce their own expression in corresponding facts, thus verifying the words of the Great Teacher, "Seek ye first the Kingdom of God and His righteousness and all these things shall be added unto you."

But we must never lose sight of the reason for the creative power of our thought, that it is because our mind is itself a thought of the Divine Mind, and that consequently our increase in livingness and creative power must be in exact proportion to our perception of our relation to the Parent Mind. In such considerations as these is to be found the philosophical basis of the Bible doctrine of "Sonship," with its culmination in the conception of the Christ. These are not mere fancies but the expression of strictly scientific principles, in their application to the deepest problems of the individual life; and their basis is that each one's world, whether in or out of the flesh, must necessarily be created by his own consciousness, and, in its turn, his mode of consciousness will necessarily take its colour front his conception of his relation to the Divine Mind— to the exclusion of light and colour, if he realizes no Divine Mind, and to their building up into forms of beauty in proportion as he realizes his identity of being with that All-Originating Spirit which is Light, Love, and Beauty in itself. Thus the great creative work of Thought in each of us is to make us consciously "sons and daughters of the Almighty," realizing that by our divine origin we can never be really separated from the Parent Mind which is continually seeking expression through us, and that any apparent separation is due to our own misconception of the true nature of the inherent relation between the Universal and the Individual. This is the lesson which the Great Teacher has so luminously out before us in the parable of the Prodigal Son.

THE GREAT AFFIRMATIVE

The Great Affirmative appears in two modes, the cosmic and the individual. In its essence it is the same in both, but in each it works from a different standpoint. It is always the principle of Being—that which is, as distinguished from that which is not; but to grasp the true significance of this saying we must understand what is meant by "that which is not." It is something more than mere non-existence, for obviously we should not trouble ourselves about what is non-existent. It is that which bath is and is not at the same time, and the thing that answers to this description is "Conditions." The little affirmative is that which affirms particular conditions as all that it can grasp, while the great affirmative grasps a wider conception, the conception of that which gives rise to conditions. Cosmically it is that power of Spirit which sends forth the whole creation as its expression of itself, and it is for this reason that I have drawn attention in the preceding lectures to the idea of the creation ex nihilo of the whole visible universe. As Eastern and Western Scriptures alike tell us it is the breathing-forth of Original Spirit; and if you have followed what I have said regarding the reproduction of this Spirit in the individual—that by the very nature of the creative process the human mind must be of the same quality with the Divine Mind—then we find that a second mode of the Originating Spirit becomes possible, namely that of operation through the individual mind. But whether acting cosmically or personally it is always the same Spirit and therefore cannot lose its inherent character which is-that of the Power which creates ex nihilo. It is the direct contradiction of the maxim "ex nihilo nihil fit"—nothing can be made out of nothing; and it is the recognition of the presence in ourselves of this power, which can make something out of nothing, that is the key to our further progress. As the logical outcome of the cosmic creative process, the evolutionary work reaches a point where the Originating Power creates an image of itself; and thus affords a fresh point of departure from which it can work specifically, just as in the cosmic process it works generically. From this new standpoint it does not in any way contradict the laws of the cosmic order, but proceeds to specialize them, and thus to bring out results through the individual which could not be otherwise attained.

Now the Spirit does this by the same method as in the Original Creation, namely by creating em nihilo; for otherwise it would be bound by the limitations necessarily inherent in the cosmic form of things, and so no fresh creative starting point would have been attained. This is why the Bible lays such stress on the principle of Monogenesis, or creation from a single power instead of from a pair or syzygy; and it is on this account that we are told that this One-ness of God is the foundation of all the commandments, and that the "Son of God" is declared to be "monogenes" or one-begotten, for that is the correct translation of the Greek word. The immense importance of this principle of creation from a single power will become apparent as we realize more fully the results proceeding from the assumption of the opposite principle, or the dualism of the creative power; but as the discussion of this great subject would require a volume to itself, I must, at present, content myself with saying that this insistence of the Bible upon the singleness of the Creative Power is based upon a knowledge which goes to the very root of esoteric principles, and is therefore not to be set aside in favour of dualistic systems, though superficially the latter may appear more consonant to reason.

If, then, it is possible to put the Great Affirmation into words it is that God is *One* and that this *One* finds centre in ourselves; and if the full meaning of this statement is realized, the logical result will be found to be a new creation both in and from ourselves. We shall realize in ourselves the working of a new principle whose distinguishing feature is its simplicity. It is *one*-ness and is not troubled about any second. Hence what it contemplates is not how its action will be modified by that of some second principle, something which will compel it to work in a particular manner and so limit it; but what it contemplates is its own Unity. Then it perceives that its Unity consists in a greater and a lesser movement, just as the rotation of the earth on its axis does not interfere with its rotation round the sun but are both motions of the same unit, and are definitely related to each other. In like manner we find that the Spirit is moving simultaneously in the macrocosm of the universe and in the microcosm of the individual, and the two movements harmonize because they are that of the same Spirit, and the latter is included in the former and pre-supposes it. The Great Affirmation, therefore, is the perception that the "I *am*" is *One*, always harmonious with itself, and including all things in this harmony for the simple reason that there is no second creative power; and when the individual realizes that this always-single power is the root of his own being, and therefore has centre in himself and finds expression through him, he learns to trust its singleness and the consequent harmony of its action in him with what it is doing AROUND him. Then he sees that the affirmation "I and my Father are *One*" is a necessary deduction from a correct apprehension of the fundamental principles of being; and then, on the principle that the less must be included in the greater, he desires that harmonious unity of action be maintained by the adaptation of his own particular movement to the larger movement of the Spirit working as the Creative Principle through the great whole. In this way we become centres through which the creative forces find specialization by the development of that personal factor on which the specific application of general laws must always depend. A specific sort of individuality is formed, capable of being the link between the great Spiritual Power of the universal and the manifestation of the relative in time and space because it consciously partakes of both; and because the individual of this class recognizes the singleness of the Spirit as the starting point of all things, he endeavours to withdraw his mind from all arguments derived from external conditions, whether past or present, and to fix it upon the forward movement of the Spirit which he knows to be always identical both in the universe and in himself. He ceases the attempt to dictate to the Spirit, because he does not see in it a mere blind force, but reveres it as the Supreme Intelligence: and on the other hand he does not grovel before it in doubt and fear, because he knows it is one with himself and is realizing itself through him, and therefore cannot have any purpose antagonistic to his own individual welfare. Realizing this he deliberately places his thoughts under the guidance of the Divine Spirit, knowing that his outward acts and conditions must thereby be brought into harmony with the great forward movement of the Spirit, not only at the stage he has now reached, but at all future stages. He does not at all deny the power of his own thought as the creative agent in his own personal world,—on the contrary it is precisely on the knowledge of this fact that his perception of the true adjustment between the principles of Life is based; but for this very reason he is the more solicitous to be led by that Wisdom which can see what he cannot see, so that his personal control over the conditions of his own life may be employed to its continual increase and development.

In this way our affirmation of the "I am" ceases to be the petulant assertion of our limited personality and becomes the affirmation that the Great I *am* affirms its own I *am*-ness both in us and through us, and thus our use of the words becomes in very truth the Great Affirmative, or that which is the root of all being as distinguished from that which has no being in itself but is merely externalized by being as the vehicle for its expression. We shall realize our true place as subordinate creative centres, perfectly independent of existing conditions because the creative process is that of monogenesis and requires no other factor than the Spirit for its exercise, but at the same time subordinate to the Divine Spirit in the greatness of its inherent forward movement because there is only *One* Spirit and it cannot from one centre antagonize what it is doing from another. Thus the Great Affirmation makes us children of the Great King, at once living in obedience to that Power which is above us, and exercising this same power over all that world of secondary causation which is below us.

Thus in our measure and station each one of us will receive the mission of the I *am*.

CHRIST THE FULFILLING OF THE LAW

"Think not that I am come to destroy the law or the proph.ets: I am not come to destroy but to fulfil." (Matt. v. 17.)

"Christ is the end of the law for righteousness to everyone that believeth." (Rom. x. 4.)

If these words are the utterance of a mere sectarian superstition they are worthless; but if they are the statement of a great principle, then it is worth our while to enquire what that principle is. The fulfilling of anything is the bringing into complete realization of all that it potentially contains, and so the filling of any law to its fulness means bringing out all the possibilities which are hidden in it. This is precisely the method which has brought forth all the advances of material civilization. The laws of nature are the same now that they were in the days of our rugged Anglo-Saxon ancestors, but they brought out only an infinitesimal fraction of the possibilities which those laws contain: now we have brought out a good deal more, but we have by no means exhausted them, and so we continue to advance, not by contradicting natural laws, but by more fully realizing their capacity. Why should we not, then, apply the same method to ourselves and see whether there are no potentialities hidden away in the law of our own being which we have not as yet by any means brought to their fulfilment? We talk of a good time coming and of the ameliorating of the race; but do we reflect that the race is composed of individuals and that therefore real advance is to be made only by individual improvement, and not by Act of Parliament? and if so, then the individual with whom to begin is ourself.

The complete manifestation of the Law of Individuality is the end or purpose of the Bible teaching concerning Christ. It is a teaching based upon Law, spiritual and mental, fully recognizing that no effect can be produced except by the operation of an adequate cause, and Christ is set before us both as explaining the causes and exhibiting the full measure of the effects. All this is according to Law; and the importance of its being according to Law is that Law is universal, and the potentialities of the Law are therefore inherent in everyone there is no special law for anybody, but anybody can specialize the law by using it with a fuller understanding of how much can be got out of it; and the purpose of the Scripture teaching regarding Christ is to help us to do this.

The preceding lectures have led us step by step to see that the Originating Spirit, which first brought the world into existence, is also the root of our own individuality, and is therefore always ready, by its inherent nature, to continue the creative process from this individual stand-point as soon as the necessary conditions are provided, and these conditions are thought-conditions. Then by realizing the relation of Christ to the Originating Mind, the Parent Spirit or "Father," we receive a Standard of thought which is bound to act creatively bringing out all the potentialities of our hidden being. Now the relation of Christ to the "Father" is that of the Architypal Idea in the All-creating Mind of which I have previously spoken, and so we arrive at the conception of the Christ-idea as a universal principle, and as being an idea therefore capable of reproduction in the individual Mind, thus explaining St. Paul's meaning when he speaks of Christ being formed in us. It is here that the principle of monogenesis comes in, that principle which I have endeavoured to describe in the earlier part of the present series as originating the whole manifested creation by an internal action of the Spirit upon itself; and it is the entire absence of control by any second power that renders the realization in external actuality of a purely mental ideal possible. For this reason systematic spiritual study commences with the contemplation of the existing cosmos, and we then transfer the conception of the monogenetic power of the Spirit from the cosmos to the individual and realize that the same Spirit is able to do the same thing in ourselves. This is the New Thought which in time will fulfil itself in the New Order, and we thus provide new thought-conditions which enable the Spirit to carry on its creative work from a new stand-point, that of our own individuality. This attainment by the Spirit of a new starting-point is what is meant by the esoteric doctrine of the Octave. The Octave is the starting-point of a new series reduplicating the starting-point of the previous series at a different level, just as does the octave note in music. We find this principle constantly referred to in Scripture—the completion of a prior series in the number Seven, and the starting of a new series by the number Eight, which takes the same place in the second series that the number One did in the first. The second series comes out of the first by natural growth and could not come into existence without it, hence the First or Originating number of the second series is the Eighth if we regard the second series as the prolongation of the first. Seven is the numerical correspondence of complete manifestation because it is the combination of three and four, which respectively represent the complete working of the spiritual and material factors—involution and evolution—and thus together constitute the finished whole. Students of the Tarot will here realize the process by which the Yod of Yod becomes the Yod of He. It is for this reason that the primary or cosmic creation terminates in the rest of the Seventh Day, for it can proceed no further until a fresh starting-point is found; But when this fresh starting-point is found in Man realizing his relation to the "Father," we start a new series and strike the Creative Octave and therefore the Resurrection takes place, not on the Sabbath or Seventh Day, but on the Eighth day which then becomes the First day of the new creak five week. The principle of the Resurrection is the realization by man of his individualization of the Spirit and his recognition of the fact that, since the Spirit is always the same Spirit, it becomes the Alpha of a new creation from his own centre of being.

Now all this is necessarily an interior process taking place on the mental plane; but if we realize that the creative process is always primarily one of involution, or formation in the spiritual world, we shall grasp something of the meaning of Christ as "The Son of God"—the concentration of the Universal Spirit into a Personality on the spiritual plane correlatively to the individuality of each one who affords the necessary thought-conditions. To all who apprehend it there is then discovered in the Universal Spirit the presence of a Divine Individuality reciprocal to that of the individual man, the recognition of which is the practical solution of all metaphysical problems regarding the emanation of the individual soul from the Universal Spirit and the relations arising therefrom; for it takes these matters out of the region of intellectual speculation, which is never creative but only analytical, and transfers it to the region of feeling and spiritual sensation which is the abode of the creative forces. This personal recognition of the Divine then affords us a new basis of Affirmation, and we need no longer trouble to go further back in order to analyze it, because we know experimentally that it is there; so now we find the starting-point of the new creation ready-made for us according to the architypal pattern in the Divine Mind itself and therefore perfectly correctly formed. When once this truth is clearly apprehended, whether we reach it by an intellectual process or by simple intuition, we can make it our starting-point and claim to have our thought permeated by the creative power of the Spirit on this basis.

But vast as is the conception thus reached we must remember that it is still a starting-point. It, indeed, transcends our previous range of ideas and so presents a culmination of the cosmic creative series which passes beyond that series and thus brings us to number Eight or the Octave; but on this very account it is the number One of a new creative series which is personal to the individual.

Then, because the Spirit is always the same, we may look for a repetition of the creative process at a higher level, and, as we all know, that process consists first of the involution of Spirit into Substance, and consequently of the subsequent evolution of Substance into forms continually increasing in fitness as vehicles for Spirit: so now we may look for a repetition of this universal process from its new starting-point in the individual mind and expect a corresponding externalization in accordance with our familiar axiom that thoughts are things.

Now it is as such an external manifestation of the Divine ideal that the Christ of the Gospels is set before us. I do not wish to dogmatize, but I will only say that the more clearly we realize the nature of the creative process on the spiritual side the more the current objections to the Gospel narrative lose their force; and it appears to me that to deny that narrative as a point-blank impossibility is to make a similar affirmation with regard to the power of the Spirit in ourselves. You cannot affirm a principle and deny it in the same breath; and if we affirm the externalizing power of the Spirit in our own case, I do not see how we can logically lay down a limit for its action and say that under highly specialized conditions it could not produce highly specialized effects. It is for this reason that St. John puts the question of Christ manifest in the flesh as the criterion of the whole matter (I. John iv., 2). If the Spirit can create at all then you cannot logically limit the extent or method of its working; and since the basis of our expectation of individual expansion is the limitless creative power of the Spirit, to reject the Christ of the Gospels as an impossibility is to cut away the ground from under our own feet. It is one thing to say "I do not understand why the Spirit should have worked in that way"—that is merely an honest statement of our present stage of knowledge, or we may even go the length of saying that we do not feel convinced that it did work in that way—that is a true confession of our intellectual difficulty—but certainly those who are professedly relying on the power of the Spirit to produce external results cannot say that it does not possess that power, or possesses it only in a limited degree: the position is logically self-destructive. What we should do therefore, is to suspend judgment and follow the light as far as we can see it, and bye-and-bye it will become clearer to us. There are, it appears to me, occult heights in the doctrine of Christ designed by the Supreme Wisdom to counteract corresponding occult depths in the Mystery of Darkness. I do not think it is at all necessary, or even possible, for us to scale these heights or fathom those depths, with our present infantile intelligence, but if we realize how completely the law of our being receives its fulfilment in Christ as far as we know that law, may we not well conceive that there are yet deeper phases of that law the existence of which we can only faintly surmise by intuition? Occasionally just the fringe of the veil is lifted for some of us, but that momentary glance is enough to show us that there are powers and mysteries beyond our present conception. But even there Law reigns supreme, and therefore taking Christ as our basis and starting-point, we start with the Law already fulfilled, whether in those things which are familiar to us or in those realms which are beyond our thought, and so we need have nc fear of evil. Our starting-point is that of a divinely ordained security from which we may quietly grow into that higher evolution which is the fulfilment of the law of our own being.

THE STORY OF EDEN

The whole Bible and the whole history of the world, past, present and future, are contained in embryo in the story of Eden, for they are nothing else than the continuous unfolding of certain great principles which are there allegorically stated. That this is by no means a new notion is shown by the following quotation from Origen:—"Who is there so foolish and without common-sense as to believe that God planted trees in the Garden of Eden like a husbandman; and planted therein the tree of life perceptible to the eyes and to the senses, which gave life to the eater; and another tree which gave to the eater a knowledge of good and evil? I believe that everybody must regard these as figures under which a recondite sense is concealed." Let us, then, follow up the suggestion of this early Father of the Church, and enquire what may be the "recondite sense" concealed under this figure of the two trees. On the face of the story there are two roots, one of Life and the other of Death, two fundamental principles bringing about diametrically opposite results. The distinctive mark of the latter is that it is the knowledge of good and evil, that is to say, the recognition of two antagonistic principles, and so requiring a knowledge of the relations between them to enable us to continually make the needful adjustments to keep ourselves going. Now, in appearance this is exceedingly specious. It looks so entirely reasonable that we do not see its ultimate destructiveness; and so we are told that Eve ate the fruit because she "saw that the tree was pleasant to the eyes." But careful consideration will show us in what the destructive nature of this principle consists. It is based on the fallacy that good is limited by evil, and that you cannot receive any good except through eliminating the corresponding evil by realizing it and beating it back. In this view life becomes a continual combat against every imaginable form of evil, and after we have racked our brains to devise precautions against all possible evil happenings, there remains the chance, and much more than the chance, that we have by no means exhausted the category of negative possibilities, and that others may arise which no amount of foresight on our part could have imagined. The more we see into this position the more intolerable it becomes, because from this stand-point we can never attain any certain basis of action, and the forces of possible evil multiply as we contemplate them. To set forth to out-wit all evil by our own knowledge of its nature is to attempt a task the hopelessness of which becomes apparent when we see it in its true light.

The mistake is in supposing that Life can be generated in ourselves by an intellectual process; but, as we have seen in the preceding lectures, Life is the primary movement of the Spirit, whether in the cosmos or in the individual. In its proper order intellectual knowledge is exceedingly important and useful, but its place in the order of the whole is not that of the Originator. It is not Life in itself, but is a function of life; it is an effect and not the cause. The reason why this is so is because intellectual study is always the study of the various laws which arise from the different *relations* of things to one another; and it therefore presupposes that these things together with their laws are already in existence. Consequently it does not start from the truly creative stand-point, that of creating something entirely new, creation ex nihilo as distinguished from *Construction*, or the laying-together of existing materials, which is what the word literally means. To recognize evil as a force to be reckoned with is therefore to give up the creative stand-point altogether. It is to quit the plane of First Cause and descend into the realm of secondary causation and lose ourselves amid the confusion of a multiplicity of relative causes and effects without grasping any unifying principle behind them.

Now the only thing that can release us from the inextricable confusion of an infinite multiplicity is the realization of an underlying unity, and at the back of all things we find the presence of one Great Affirmative principle without which nothing could have existence. This, then, is the Root of Life; and if we credit it with being able, not only to supply the power, but also the form for its manifestation we shall see that we need not go beyond this *Single* Power for the production of anything. It is Spirit producing Substance out of its own essence, and the Substance taking Form in accordance with the movement of the Spirit. What we have to realize is, not only that this is the way in which the cosmos is brought into existence, but also that, because the Spirit finds a new centre in ourselves, the same process is repeated in our own mentality, and therefore we are continually creating ex nihilo whether we know it or not. Consequently, if we look upon evil as a force to be reckoned with, and therefore requiring to be studied, we are in effect creating it; while on the other hand if we realize that there is only *One* force to be considered, and that absolutely good, we are by the law of the creative process bringing that good into manifestation. No doubt for this affirmative use of our creative power it is necessary that we start from the basic conception of a *single* originating power which is absolutely good and life-giving; but if there were a self-originating power which was destructive then no creation could ever have come into existence at all, for the positive and negative self-originating powers would cancel each other and the result would be zero. The fact, therefore, of our own existence is a sufficient proof of the singleness and goodness of the Originating Power, and from this starting-point there is no second power to be taken into consideration, and consequently we do not have to study the evil that may arise out of existing or future circumstances, but require to keep our minds fixed only upon the good which we intend to create. There is a very simple reason for this. It is that every new creation necessarily carries its own law with it and by that law produces new conditions of its own. A balloon affords a familiar illustration of my meaning. The balloon with its freight weighs several hundredweight, yet the introduction of a new factor, the gas, brings with it a law of its own which entirely alters the conditions, and the force of gravity is so completely overcome that the whole mass rises into the air. The Law itself is never altered, but we have previously known it only under limiting conditions. These conditions, however, are no part of the Law itself; and a clearer realization of the Law shows us that it contains in itself the power of transcending them. The law which every new creation carries with it is therefore not a contradiction of the old law but its specialization into a higher mode of action.

Now the ultimate Law is that of production ex nihilo by the movement of the Spirit within itself, and all subordinate laws are merely the measurements of the relations which spontaneously arise between different things when they are brought into manifestation, arid therefore, if an entirely new thing is created it must necessarily establish entirely new relations and so produce entirely new laws. This is the reason why, if we take the action of pure unmanifested Spirit as our starting-point, we may confidently trust it to produce manifestations of law which, though perfectly new from the stand-point of our past experience, are quite as natural in their own way as any that have gone before. It is on this account that in these addresses I lay so much stress on the fact that Spirit creates ex nihilo, that is, out of no pre-existing forms, but simply by its own movement within itself. If, then, this idea is clearly grasped, it logically follows from it that the Root of Life is not to be found in the comparison of good and evil, but in the simple affirmation of the Spirit as the All-creating power of Good. And since, as we have already seen, this same all-creating Spirit finds a centre and fresh starting-point of operation in our own minds, we can trust it to follow the Law of its own being there as much as in the creation of the cosmos.

Only we must not forget that it is working through our own minds. It thinks through our mind, and our mind must be made a suitable channel for this mode of its operation by conforming itself to the broad generic lines of the Spirit's thinking. The reason for this is one which I have sought to impress throughout these lectures, namely, that the specialization of a law is never the denial of it, but on the contrary the fuller recognition of its basic principles; and if this is the case in ordinary physical science it must be equally so when we come to specialize the great Law of Life itself. The Spirit can never change its essential nature as the essence of Life, Love, and Beauty; and if we adopt these characteristics, which constitute the Law of the Spirit, as the basis of our own thinking, and reject all that is contrary to them, then we afford the broad generic conditions for the specialized thinking of the Spirit through our own minds: and the thinking of the Spirit is that *involution*, or passing of spirit into form, which is the whole being of the creative process.

The mind which is all the time being thus formed is our own. It is not a case of control by an external individuality, but the fuller expression of the Universal through an organized mentality which has all along been a less perfect expression of the Universal; and therefore the process is one of growth. We are not losing our individuality, but are coming into fuller possession of ourselves by the conscious recognition of our personal share in the great work of creation. We begin in some slight measure to understand what the Bible means when it speaks of our-being "partakers of the Divine nature" (II. Peter i. 4) and we realize the significance of the "unity of the Spirit" (Ephesians iv. 3). Doubtless this will imply changes in our old mode of thinking; but these changes are not forced upon us, they are brought about naturally by the new stand-point from which we now see things. Almost imperceptibly to ourselves we grow into a New Order of Thought which proceeds, not from a knowledge of good and evil, but from the Principle of Life itself. That is what makes the difference between our old thought and our new thought. Our old thought was based upon a comparison of limited facts: our new thought is based upon a comprehension of principles. The difference is like that between the mathematics of the infant, who cannot count beyond the number of apples or marbles put before him, and that of the senior wrangler who is not dependent upon visible objects for his calculations, but plunges boldly into the unknown because he knows that he is working by indubitable principles. In like manner when we realize the infallible Principle of the Creative Law we no longer find we need to see everything cut and dried beforehand, for if so, we could never get beyond the range of our old experiences; but we can move steadily forward because we know the certainty of the creative principle by which we are working, or rather, which is working through us, and that our life, in all its minutes" details, is its harmonious expression. Thus the Spirit thinks through our thought only its thought is greater than ours. It is the paradox of the less containing the greater. Our thought will not be objectless or unintelligible to ourselves. It will be quite clear as far as it goes. We shall know exactly what we want to do and why we want to do it, and so will act in a reasonable and intelligent manner. But what we do not know is the greater thought that is all the time giving rise to our smaller thought, and which will open out from it as our lesser thought progresses into form. Then we gradually see the greater thought which prompted our smaller one and we find ourselves working along its lines, guided by the invisible hand of the Creative Spirit into continually increasing degrees of livingness to which we need assign no limits, for it is the expansion of the Infinite within ourselves.

This, as it appears to me, is the hidden meaning of the two trees in Eden, the Garden of the Soul. It is the distinction between a knowledge which is merely that of comparisons between different sorts of conditions, and a knowledge which is that of the Life which gives rise to and therefore controls conditions. Only we must remember that the control of conditions is not to be attained by violent self-assertion which is only recognizing them as substantive entities to be battled with, but by conscious unity with that All-creating Spirit which works silently, but surely, on its own lines of Life, Love, and Beauty.

"Not by might, nor by power, but by My Spirit, saith the Lord of Hosts."

THE WORSHIP OF ISHI

In Hosea ii. 16 we find this remarkable statement:—"And it shall be at that day, saith the Lord, that thou shalt call Me Ishi, and shalt no more call Me Baali"; and with this we may couple the statement in Isaiah lxii. 4:—"Thou shalt be called Hephzibah, and thy land Beulah; for the Lord delighteth in thee, and thy land shall be married."

In both these passages we find a change of name; and since a name stands for something which corresponds to it, and in truth only amounts to a succinct description, the fact indicated in these texts is a change of condition answering to the change of name.

Now the change from Baali to Ishi indicates an important alteration in the relation between the Divine Being and the worshipper; but since the Divine Being cannot change, the altered relation must result from a change in the stand-point of the worshipper: and this can only come from a new mode of looking at the Divine, that is, from a new order of thought regarding it. Baali means Lord, and Ishi means husband, and so the change in relation is that of a female slave who is liberated and married to her former master. We could not have a more perfect analogy. Relatively to the Universal Spirit the individual soul is esoterically feminine, as I have pointed out in "Bible Mystery and Bible Meaning," because its function is that of the receptive and formative. This is necessarily inherent in the nature of the creative process. But the individual's development as the specializing medium of the Universal Spirit will depend entirely upon his own conception of his relation to it. So long as he only regards it as an arbitrary power, a sort of slave owner, he will find himself in the position of a slave driven by an inscrutable force, he knows not whither or for what purpose. He may worship such a God, but his worship is only the worship of fear and ignorance, and there is no personal interest in the matter except to escape some dreaded punishment. Such a worshipper would gladly escape from his divinity, and his worship, when analyzed, will be found to be little else than disguised hatred. This is the natural result of a worship based upon *unexplained* traditions instead of intelligible principles, and is the very opposite of that worship in Spirit and in truth which Jesus speaks of as the true worship.

But when the light begins to break in upon us, all this becomes changed. We see that a system of terrorism cannot give expression to the Divine Spirit, and we realize the truth of St. Paul's words, "He hath not given us the spirit of fear, but of power, and of love, and of a sound mind." As the true nature of the relation between the individual mind and the Universal Mind becomes clearer, we find it to be one of mutual action and re-action, a perfect reciprocity which cannot be better symbolized than by the relation between an affectionate husband and wife. Everything is done from love and nothing from compulsion, there is perfect confidence on both sides, and both are equally indispensable to each other. It is simply the carrying out of the fundamental maxim that the Universal cannot act on the plane of the Particular except through the Particular; only this philosophical axiom develops into a warm living intercourse.

Now this is the position of the soul which is indicated by the name Hephzibah. In common with all other words derived from the Semitic root "hafz" it implies the idea of guarding, just as in the East a hasfiz is one who guards the letter of the Koran by having the whole book by heart, and in many similar expressions. Hephzibah may therefore be translated as "a guarded one," thus recalling the New Testament description of those who are "guarded into salvation." It is precisely this conception of being guarded by a superior power that distinguishes the worship of Ishi from that of Baali. A special relation has been established between the Divine Spirit and the individual soul, one of absolute confidence and personal intercourse. This does not require any departure from the general law of the universe, but is due to that specializing of the law through the presentation of special conditions personal to the individual, of which I have spoken before. But all the time there has been no change in the Universal Spirit, the only change has been in the mental attitude of the individual—he has come into a new thought, a clearer perception of God. He has faced the questions, What is God? Where is God? How does God work? and he has found the answer in the apostolic statement that God is "over all, through all, and in all," and he realises that "God" is the root of his (the individual's) own being, ever present IN him, ever working *through* him, and universally present around him.

This realization of the true relation between the Originating Spirit and the individual mind is what is esoterically spoken of as the Mystical Marriage in which the two have ceased to be separate and have become one. As a matter of fact they always were one, but since we can apprehend things only from the stand-point of our own consciousness, it is our recognition of the fact that makes it a practical reality for ourselves. But an intelligent recognition will never make a confusion of the two parts of which the whole consists, and will never lead the individual to suppose that he is handling a blind force or that a blind force is handling him. He will neither dethrone God, nor lose himself by absorption in deity, but he will recognize the reciprocity of the Divine and the human as the natural and logical outcome of the essential conditions of the creative process.

And what is the Whole which is thus created? It is our conscious *personality*; and therefore whatever we draw from the Universal Spirit acquires in us the quality of personality. It is that process of differentiation of the universal into the particular of which I have so often spoken, which, by a rude analogy, we may compare to the differentiation of the universal electric fluid into specific sorts of power by its passage through suitable apparatus. It is for this reason that relatively to ourselves the Universal Spirit must necessarily assume a personal aspect, and that the aspect which it will assume will be in exact correspondence with our own conception of it. This is in accordance with mental and spiritual laws inherent in our own being, and it is on this account that the Bible seeks to build up our conception of God on such lines as will set us free from all fear of evil, and thus leave us at liberty to use the creative power of our thought affirmatively from the stand-point of a calm and untroubled mind. This stand-point can only be reached by passing beyond the range of the happenings of the moment, and this can only be done by the discovery of our immediate relation to the undifferentiated source of all good. I lay stress on these words "immediate" and "undifferentiated" because in them is contained the secret of the whole position. If we could not draw immediately from the Universal Spirit our receiving would be subject to the limitations of the channel through which it reached us; and if the force which we receive were not undifferentiated in itself it could not take appropriate form in our own minds and become to each of us just what we require it to be. It is this power of the human soul to differentiate limitlessly from the Infinite that we are apt to overlook, but as we come to realize that the soul is itself a reflection and image of the Infinite Spirit—and a clear recognition of the cosmic creative process shows that it cannot be anything else—we find that it must possess this power, and that-in fact it is our possession of this power which is the whole raison d'etre of the creative process: if the human soul did not possess an unlimited power of differentiation from the Infinite, then the Infinite would not be reflected in it, and consequently the Infinite Spirit would find no outlet for its *conscious* recognition of itself as the Life, Love, and Beauty which it is. We can never too deeply ponder the old esoteric definition of Spirit as "the Power which knows itself": the secret of all things, past, present, and future is contained in these few words. The self -recognition or self-contemplation of Spirit is the primary movement out of which all creation proceeds, and the attainment in the individual of a fresh centre for self-recognition is what the Spirit *gains* in the process—this *gain* accruing to the Spirit is what is referred to in the parables where the lord is represented as receiving increase from his servants.

When the individual perceives this relation between himself and Infinite Spirit, he finds that he has been raised from a position of slavery to one of reciprocity. The Spirit cannot do without him any more than he can do without the Spirit: the two are as necessary to each other as the two poles of an electric battery. The Spirit is the unlimited essence of Love, Wisdom, and Power, all three in one undifferentiated and waiting to be differentiated by *appropriation*, that is, by the individual *Claiming* to be the channel of their differentiation. It only requires the claim to be made with the recognition that by the Law of Being it is bound to be answered, and the right feeling, the right seeing, and the right working for the particular matter we have in hand will flow in quite naturally. Our old enemies, doubt and fear, may seek to bring us back under bondage to Baali, but our new stand-point for the recognition of the All-originating Spirit as being absolutely unified with ourselves must always be kept resolutely in mind; for, short of this, we are not working on the creative level—we are creating, indeed, for we can never divest ourselves of our creative power, but we are creating in the image of the old limiting and destructive conditions, and this is merely perpetuating the cosmic Law of Averages, which is just what the individual has to rise superior to. The creative level is where new laws begin to manifest themselves in a new order of conditions, something transcending our past experiences and thus bringing about a real advance; for it is no advance only to go on in the same old round even if we kept at it for centuries: it is the steady go-ahead nature of the Spirit that has made the world of to-day an improvement upon the world of the pterodactyl and the icthiosaurus, and we must look for the same forward movement of the Spirit from its new starting-point in ourselves.

Now it is this special, personal, and individual relation of the Spirit to ourselves which is typified by the names Ishi and Hephzibah. From this stand-point we may say that as the individual wakes up to the oneness with the Spirit, the Spirit wakes up to the same thing. It becomes conscious of itself through the consciousness of the individual, and thus is solved the paradox of individual self-recognition by the Universal Spirit, without which no new-creative power could be exercised and all things would continue to proceed in the old merely cosmic order. It is of course true that in the merely generic order the Spirit must be present in every form of Life, as the Master pointed out when He said that not a sparrow falls to the ground without "the Father." But as the sparrows He alluded to had been shot and were on sale at a price which shows that this was the fate of a good many of them, we see here precisely that stage of manifestation where the Spirit has not woke up to individual self-recognition, and remains at the lower level of self-recognition, that of the generic or race-spirit. The Master's comment, "Ye are of more value than many sparrows" points out this difference: in us the generic creation has reached the level which affords the conditions for the waking up of the Spirit to self-recognition in the Individual.

And we must bear in mind that all this is perfectly natural. There is no posing or straining after effect about it. If *you* have to pump up the Life, who is going to put the Life into you to pump it? Therefore it is spontaneous or nothing. That is why the Bible speaks of it as the free gift of God. It cannot be anything else. You cannot originate the originating force; it must originate you: but what you can do is to distribute it. Therefore immediately you experience any sense of friction be sure there is something wrong somewhere; and since God can never change, you may be sure that the friction is being caused by some error in your own thinking—you are limiting the Spirit in some way: set to work to find out what it is. It is always *limiting* the Spirit that does this. You are tying it down to conditions somewhere, saying it is bound by reason of some existing forms. The remedy is to go back to the original starting point of the Cosmic Creation and ask, Where were the pre-existing forms that dictated to the Spirit then? Then because the Spirit never changes it is *still the same*, and is just as independent of existing conditions now as it was in the beginning; and so we must pass over all existing conditions, however apparently adverse, and go straight to the Spirit as the originator of new forms and new conditions. This is real New Thought, for it does not trouble about the old things, but is going straight ahead from where we are now. When we do this, just trusting the Spirit, and not laying down the particular details of its action—just telling it what we want without dictating *how* we are to get it— we shall find that things will open out more and more clearly day by day both on the inner and the outer plane. Remember that the Spirit is alive and working here and now, for if ever the Spirit is to get from the past into the future it must be by passing through the present; therefore what you have to do is to acquire the habit of living direct -from the Spirit here and now. You will soon find that this is a matter of personal intercourse, perfectly natural and not requiring any abnormal conditions for its production. You just treat the Spirit as you would any other kind-hearted sensible person, remembering that it is always there—"closer than hands and feet," as Tennyson says—and you will gradually begin to appreciate its reciprocity as a very practical fact indeed.

This is the relation of Hephzibah to Ishi, and is that worship in Spirit and in truth which needs neither the temple in Jerusalem nor yet in Samaria for its acceptance, for the whole world is the temple of the Spirit and you yourself its sanctuary. Bear this in mind, and remember that nothing is too great or too small, too interior or too external, for the Spirit's recognition and operation, for the Spirit is itself both the Life and the Substance of all things and it is also Self-recognition from the stand-point of your own individuality; and therefore, because the Self-recognition of Spirit is the Life of the creative process, you will, by simply trusting the Spirit to work according to its own nature, pass more and more completely into that New Order which proceeds from the thought of Him who says, "Behold I make all things new."

THE SHEPHERD AND THE STONE

The metaphor of the Shepherd and the Sheep is of constant occurrence throughout the Bible and naturally suggests the idea of the guiding, guarding, and feeding both of the individual sheep and of the whole flock and it is not difficult to see the spiritual correspondence of these things in a general sort of way. But we find that the Bible combines the metaphor of the Shepherd with another metaphor that of "the Stone," and at first sight the two seem rather incongruous.

"From thence is the Shepherd the Stone of Israel," says the Old Testament (Genesis xlix. 24), and Jesus calls himself both "The Good Shepherd" and "The Stone which the builders rejected." The Shepherd and the Stone are thus identified and we must therefore seek the interpretation in some conception which combines the two. A shepherd suggests Personal care for the welfare of the sheep, and an intelligence greater than theirs. A stone suggests the idea of Building, and consequently of measurement, adaptation of parts to whole, and progressive construction according to plan. Combining these two conceptions we get the idea of the building of an edifice whose stones are persons, each taking their more or less conscious part in the construction—thus a building, not constructed from without, but self-forming by a principle of growth from within under the guidance of a Supreme Wisdom permeating the whole and conducting it stage by stage to ultimate completeness. This points to a Divine Order in human affairs with which we may more or less consciously co-operate: both to our personal advantage and also to the furtherance of the great scheme of human evolution as a whole; the ultimate purpose being to establish in *all* men that principle of "The Octave" to which I have already alluded; and in proportion as some adumbration of this principle is realized by individuals and by groups of individuals they specialize the law of race-development, even though they may not be aware of the fact, and so come under a *specialized* working of the fundamental Law, which thus differentiates them from other individuals and nationalities, as by a peculiar guidance, producing higher developments which the merely generic operation of the Law could not.

Now if we keep steadily in mind that, though the purpose, or Law of Tendency, or the Originating Spirit must always be universal in its nature, it must necessarily be individual in its operation, we shall see that this universal purpose can only be accomplished through the instrumentality of specific means. This results from the fundamental proposition that the Universal can only work on the plane of the Particular by becoming the individual and particular; and when we grasp the conception that the merely generic operation of the Creative Law has now brought the human race as far as it can, that is to say it has completely evolved the merely natural *genus* home, it follows that if any further development is to take place it can only be by the co-operation of the individual himself. Now it is the spread of this individual co-operation that the forward movement of the Spirit is leading us to, and it is the gradual extension of this universal principle that is alluded to in the prophecy of Daniel regarding the Stone cut out without hands that spreads until it fills the whole earth (Daniel ii. 34 and 44). According to the interpretation given by Daniel, this Stone is the emblem of a spiritual Kingdom, and the identity of the Stone and the Shepherd indicates that the Kingdom of the Stone must be also the Kingdom of the Shepherd; and the Master, who identified himself with both the Stone and the Shepherd, emphatically declared that this Kingdom was, in its essence, an interior Kingdom—"the Kingdom of Heaven is within you." We must look for its foundation therefore, in a spiritual principle or mental law inherent in the constitution of all men but waiting to be brought into fuller development by more accurate compliance with its essential requirements; which is precisely the method by which science has evoked powers from the laws of nature which were undreamt of in former ages; and in like manner the recognition of our true relation to the Universal Spirit, which is the source of all individual being, must lead to an advance both for the race and for the individual such as we can at present scarcely form the faintest idea of, but which we dimly apprehend through the intuition and speak of as the New Order. The approach of this New Order is everywhere making itself vaguely felt; it is, as the French say, in the air, and the very vagueness and mystery attending it is causing a feeling of unrest as to what form it may assume. But to the student of Spiritual Law this should not be the case. He knows that the Form is always the expression of the Spirit, and therefore, since he is in touch with the forward movement of the Spirit, he knows that he himself will always be harmoniously included in any form of development which the Great Forward Movement may take. This is the practical and personal benefit arising from the realization of the Principle which is symbolized under the two-fold metaphor of the Shepherd and the Stone. and in all those new developments which are perhaps even now within measurable distance, we can rest on the knowledge that we are under the care of a kind Shepherd, and under the formation of a wise Master Builder.

But the principle of the Shepherd and the Stone is not something hitherto unheard of which is only to conne into existence in the future. If there were no manifestations of this principle in the past, we might question whether there were any such principle at all; but a careful study of the subject will show us that it has been at work all through the ages, sometimes in modes more immediately bearing the aspect of the Shepherd, and sometimes in modes more immediately bearing the aspect of the Stone, though the one always implies the other, for they are the same thing seen from different points of view. The subject is one of immense interest, but covering such a wide range of study that all I can do here is to point out that such a field of investigation exists and is worth exploration; and the exploration brings its reward with it, not only by putting us in possession of the key to the history of the past, but by showing us that it is the key to the history of the future also, and furthermore by making evident on a large scale the working of the same principle of Spiritual Law by cooperation with which we may facilitate the process of our own individual evolution. It thus adds a vivid interest to life, giving us something worth looking forward to and introducing us to a personal future which is not limited by the proverbial three-score years and ten.

Now, we have seen that the first stage in the Creative Process is always that of Feeling—a reaching-out by the Spirit in a particular direction, and therefore we may look for something of the same kind in the development of the great principle which we are now considering. And we find this first vague movement of this great principle in the intuitions of a particular race which appears from time immemorial to have combined the two characteristics of nomad wandering with their flocks and herds and the symbolization of their religious beliefs in monuments of stone. The monuments themselves have taken different forms in different countries and ages, but the identity of their symbolism becomes clear under careful investigation. Together with this symbolism we always find the nomad character of the builders and that they are invested with an aura of mystery and romance such as we find nowhere else, though we always find it surrounding these builders, even in countries so far apart as India and Ireland. Then, as we pass beyond the merely monumental stage, we find threads of historical evidence connecting the different branches of this race, increasing in their complexity and strengthening in their cumulative force as we go on, until at last we are brought to the history of the age in which we live; and finally most remarkable affinities of language put the finishing touch to the mass of proofs which can be gathered along all these different lines. In this magic circle countries so remote from one another as Ireland and Greece, Egypt and India, Palestine and Persia, are brought into close contiguity—a similar tradition, and even a similar nomenclature, unite the mysterious builders of the Great Pyramid with the equally mysterious builders of the Round Towers of Ireland—and the Great Pyramid itself, perhaps antedating the call of Abraham, re-appears as the official seal of the United States; while tradition traces the crowning-stone in Westminster Abbey back to the time of Solomon's temple and even earlier. For the most part the erewhile wanderers are now settled in their destined homes, but the Anglo-Saxon race—the People of the Corner-Stone—are still the pioneers among the nations, and there is something esoteric in the old joke that when the North Pole is reached a Scotchman will be found there. And not least in the chain of evidence is the link afforded by a tribe who are wanderers still, the Gipsies with their duplicate of the Pyramid in the pack of cards—a volume which has been called "The Devil's Picture Book" by those who know it only in its misuse and inversion, but which when interpreted in the light of the knowledge we are now gaining, affords a signal instance of that divine policy by which as St. Paul says, God employs the foolish things of this world to confute the wise; while a truer apprehension of the Gipsies themselves indicates their unmistakable connection with that race who through all its wanderings has ever been the guardian of the Stone.

In these few paragraphs I have only been able to point out very briefly the broad lines of enquiry into a subject of national importance to the British and American peoples, and which interests us personally, not only as members of these nations, but as affording proof on the largest scale of the same specialization of universal laws which each of us has to effect individually for ourself. But whether the process be individual or national it is always the same, and is the translation to the very highest plane—that of the All-originating Life itself—of the old maxim that "Nature will obey us exactly in proportion as we first obey Nature"; it is the old parable of the lord who, finding his servants girt and awaiting him, then girds himself and serves them (Luke xii. 35 to 37). The nation or the individual who thus realizes the true principle of the Shepherd and the Stone, comes under a special Divine guidance and protection, not by a favouritism incompatible with the conception of universal Law, but by the very operation of the Law itself. They have come into touch with its higher possibilities, and to recur to an analogy which I have already employed, they learn to make their iron float by the very same law by which it sinks; and so they become the flock of the Great Shepherd and the building of the Great Architect, and each one, however insignificant his or her sphere may appear, becomes a sharer in the great work, and by a logical consequence begins to grow on new lines of development for the simple reason that a new principle necessarily produces new modes of manifestation. If the reader will think over these things he will see that the promises contained in the Bible whether national or personal, are nothing else than statements of the universal law of Cause and Effect applied to the inmost principles of our being, and that therefore it is not mere rhapsody, but the figurative expression of a great truth when the Psalmist says `"The Lord is my Shepherd," and "Thou art my God and the Rock of my salvation."

SALVATION IS OF THE JEWS

What does this saying of the Master's mean? Certainly not a mere arrogant assumption in favour of His own nationality—such an idea is negatived, not only by the universality of all His other teaching, but also by the very instruction in which these words occur, for He declared that the Jewish temple was equally with the Samaritan of no account in the matter. He said that the true worship was purely spiritual and entirely independent of places and ceremonies, while at the same time He emphasized the Jewish expectation of a Messiah, so that in this teaching we are met by the paradox of a universal principle combined with what at first sight appears like a tribal tradition quite incompatible with any recognition of the universal reign of law. How to reconcile these apparent opposites, therefore, seems to be the problem which He here sets before us. Its solution is to be found in that principle which I have endeavoured to elucidate throughout these lectures, the specializing of universal law. Opinions may differ as to whether the Bible narrative of the birth of Christ is to be taken literally or symbolically, but as to the spiritual principle involved there can, I think, be no difference of opinion. It is that of the specialization by the individual of the generic relation of the soul to the Infinite Spirit from which it proceeds. The relation itself is universal and results from the very nature of the creative process, but the law of the universal relation admits of particular specialization exactly in the same way as all other natural laws—it is simply applying to the supreme Law of Life the same method by which we have learnt to make iron float, that is to say by a fuller recognition of what the Law is in itself. Whatever other meanings we may apply to the name Messiah, it undoubtedly stands for the absolutely perfect manifestation in the individual of all the infinite possibilities of the Principle of Life.

Now it was because this grand ideal is the basis on which the Hebrew nationality was founded that Jesus made this statement. This foundation had been lamentably misconceived by the Jewish people; but nevertheless, however imperfectly, they still held by it, and from them this ideal has spread throughout the Christian world. Here also it continues to be lamentably misconceived, nevertheless it is still retained, and only needs to be recognized in its true light as a universal principle, instead of an unintelligible dogma, to become the salvation of the world. Hence, as affording the medium through which this supreme ideal has been preserved and spread, it is true that "Salvation is of the Jews."

Their fundamental idea was right but their apprehension of it was wrong—that is why the Master at the same time sweeps away the national worship of the temple and preserves the national idea of the Messiah; and this is equally true of the Christian world at the present day. If salvation is anything real it must have its cause in some law, and if there is a law it must be founded upon some universal principle: therefore it is this principle which we must seek if we would understand this teaching of the Master's.

Now whether we take the Bible story of the birth of Christ literally or symbolically, it teaches one great lesson. It teaches that the All-originating Spirit is the true Parent of the individual both in soul and body. This is nothing else than realizing from the stand-point of the individual what we cannot help realizing in regard to the original creation of the cosmos— it is the realization that the All-originating Spirit is at once the Life and the Substance in each individual here and now, just as it must have been in the origin of all things. Human parentage counts for nothing—it is only the channel through which Universal Spirit has acted for the concentration of an individual centre; but the ultimate cause of that centre, both in life and substance, continues at every moment to be the One same Originating Spirit.

This recognition cuts away the root of all the power of the negative, and so in principle it delivers us from all evil, for the root of evil is the denial of the power of the Spirit to produce good. When we realize that the Spirit is finding its own individualization in us in its two-fold essence as Life and Substance, then we see that it must be both able and willing to create for us all good. The only limit is that which we ourselves impose by denying its operation, and when we realize the inherent creativeness of Spirit we find that there is no reason why we should stop short at any point and say that it can go no further. Our error is in looking on the life of the body as separate from the life of the Spirit, and this error is met by the consideration that, in its ultimate nature, Substance must emanate from Spirit and is nothing else than the record of Spirit's conception of itself as finding expression in space and time. And when this becomes clear it follows that Substance need not be taken into calculation at all. The material form stands in the same relation to Spirit that the image projected on the screen stands to the slide in the lantern. If we wish to change the exhibited subject we do not manipulate the reflection on the screen, but we alter the slide; and in like manner, when we come to realize the true nature of the creative process, we learn that the exterior things are to be changed by a change of the interior spiritual attitude. Our spiritual attitude will always be determined by our conception of our relation to God or Infinite Spirit; and so when we begin to see that this relation is one of absolute reciprocity—that it is the self-recognition of Infinite Spirit from our own centre of consciousness—then we find that the whole Secret of Life consists in simple reliance upon the Allcreating Spirit as consciously identifying itself with us. It has, so to say, awakened to a new mode of self-recognition peculiar to ourselves, in which we individually form the centre of its creative energy. To realize this is to specialize the Principle of Life. The logic of it is simple. We have found that the originating movement of Spirit from which all creation proceeds can only be Self-contemplation. Then, since the Original Spirit cannot change its nature its self-contemplation through our own minds must be as creative in, for, and through us as it ever was in the beginning; and consequently we find the original creative process repeated in ourselves and directed by the conscious thought of our own minds.

In all this there is no place for the consideration of outward conditions, whether of body or circumstances; for they are only effects and not the cause;

and therefore when we reach this stand-point we cease to take them into our calculations. Instead we employ the method of self-contemplation knowing that this is the creative method, and so we contemplate ourselves as allied to the infinite Love and Wisdom of the Divine Spirit which will take form through our conscious thought, and so act creatively as a Special Providence entirely devoted to guarding, guiding, providing for, and illuminating us. The whole thing is perfectly natural when seen from a clear recognition of what the creative working of Spirit must be in itself; and when it is realized in this perfectly natural manner all strain and effort to compel its action ceases—we are at one with the All-creating Power which has now found a new centre in ourselves from which to continue its creative work to more perfect manifestation than could be attained through the unspecialized generic conditions of the merely cosmic order.

Now this is what Messiah stands for, and therefore it is written that "to them gave He power to become sons of God, even to as many as believe on His Name." This "belief" is the recognition of a universal principle and personal reliance upon it as a law which cannot be broken; for it is the Law of the whole creative process specialized in our own individuality. Then, too, however great may be the mystery, the removal and cleansing away of all sin follows as an essential part of this realization of new life; and it is in this sense that we may read all that the Bible tells us on this aspect of the subject. The *principle* of it is Love; for when we are reunited to the Parent Spirit in mutual confidence and love, what room is there on either side for any remembrance of our past failures?

This, then is what Messiah stands for to the individual; but if we can conceive a nation based upon such a recognition of its special relation to the Directing Power of the Universe, such a people must of necessity become the leader of the nations, and those who oppose it must fail by a self-destructive principle inherent in the very nature of the position they take up. The leadership resulting from such a national self-recognition, will not be based upon conquest and compulsion, but will come naturally. Other nations will enquire the reason for the phenomenal success and prosperity of the favoured people, and finding this reason in a universal Law, they will begin to apply the same law in the same manner, and thus the same results will spread from country to country until at last the whole earth will be full of the glory of the Lord. And such a nation, and rather company of nations, exists. To trace its present development from its ancient beginnings is far beyond the scope of this volume, and still more to speculate upon its further growth; but to my readers on both sides of the Atlantic I may say that this people is the Anglo-Saxon race throughout the world. I write these lines upon the historic Hill of Tara; this will convey a hint to many of my readers. At some future time I may enlarge upon this subject; but at present my aim is merely to suggest some lines of thought arising from the Master's saying that "Salvation is of the Jews."

The Law and the Word

Late Divisional Judge, Punjab. Honorary member of the Medico-Legal Society of New York. First Vice-President International New Thought Alliance

TABLE OF CONTENTS

FOREWORD: THOMAS TROWARD AN APPRECIATION

How is one to know a friend? Certainly not by the duration of acquaintance. Neither can friendship be bought or sold by service rendered. Nor can it be coined into acts of gallantry or phrases of flattery. It has no part in the small change of courtesy. It is outside all these, containing them all and superior to them all.

To some is given the great privilege of a day set apart to mark the arrival of a total stranger panoplied with all the insignia of friendship. He comes unannounced. He bears no letter of introduction. No mutual friend can vouch for him. Suddenly and silently he steps unexpectedly out of the shadow of material concern and spiritual obscurity, into the radiance of intimate friendship, as a picture is projected upon a lighted screen. But unlike the phantom picture he is an instant reality that one's whole being immediately recognizes, and the radiance of fellowship that pervades his word, thought and action holds all the essence of long companionship.

Unfortunately there are too few of these bright messengers of God to be met with in life's pilgrimage, but that Judge Troward was one of them will never be doubted by the thousands who are now mourning his departure from among us. Those whose closest touch with him has been the reading of his books will mourn him as a friend only less than those who listened to him on the platform. For no books ever written more clearly expressed the author. The same simple lucidity and gentle humanity, the same effort to discard complicated non-essentials, mark both the man and his books.

Although the spirit of benign friendliness pervades his writings and illuminated his public life, yet much of his capacity for friendship was denied those who were not privileged to clasp hands with him and to sit beside him in familiar confidence. Only in the intimacy of the fireside did he wholly reveal his innate modesty and simplicity of character. Here alone, glamoured with his radiating friendship, was shown the wealth of his richly-stored mind equipped by nature and long training to deal logically with the most profound and abstruse questions of life. Here indeed was proof of his greatness, his unassuming superiority, his humanity, his keen sense of honour, his wit and humour, his generosity and all the characteristics of a rare gentleman, a kindly philosopher and a true friend.

To Judge Troward was given the logician's power to strip a subject bare of all superfluous and concealing verbiage, and to exhibit the gleaming jewels of truth and reality in splendid simplicity. This supreme quality, this ability to make the complex simple, the power to subordinate the non-essential, gave to his conversation, to his lectures, to his writings, and in no less degree to his personality, a direct and charming naïveté that at once challenged attention and compelled confidence and affection.

His sincerity was beyond question. However much one might differ from
him in opinion, at least one never doubted his profound faith and complete
devotion to truth. His guileless nature was beyond ungenerous suspicions and
selfish ambitions. He walked calmly upon his way wrapped in the majesty of
his great thoughts, oblivious to the vexations of the world's cynicism. Charity
and reverence for the indwelling spirit marked all his human relations.
Tolerance of the opinions of others, benevolence and tenderness dwelt in his
every word and act. Yet his careful consideration of others did not paralyze
the strength of his firm will or his power to strike hard blows at wrong and
error. The search for truth, to which his life was devoted, was to him a holy
quest. That he could and would lay a lance in defence of his opinions is
evidenced in his writings, and has many times been demonstrated to the
discomfiture of assailing critics. But his urbanity was a part of himself and
never departed from him.

Not to destroy but to create was his part in the world. In developing his
philosophy he built upon the foundation of his predecessors. No good and true
stone to be found among the ruins of the past, but was carefully worked into
his superstructure of modern thought, radiant with spirituality, to the
building of which the enthusiasm of his life was devoted.

To one who has studied Judge Troward, and grasped the significance of
his theory of the "Universal Sub-conscious Mind," and who also has attained
to an appreciation of Henri Bergson's theory of a "Universal Livingness,"
superior to and outside the material Universe, there must appear a distinct
correlation of ideas. That intricate and ponderously irrefutable argument that
Bergson has so patiently built up by deep scientific research and unsurpassed
profundity of thought and crystal-clear reason, that leads to the substantial
conclusion that man has leapt the barrier of materiality only by the urge of
some external pressure superior to himself, but which, by reason of infinite
effort, he alone of all terrestrial beings has succeeded in utilizing in a superior
manner and to his advantage: this well-rounded and exhaustively
demonstrated argument in favour of a super-livingness in the universe, which
finds its highest terrestrial expression in man, appears to be the scientific
demonstration of Judge Troward's basic principle of the "Universal
Sub-conscious Mind." This universal and infinite God-consciousness which
Judge Troward postulates as man's sub-consciousness, and from which man
was created and is maintained, and of which all physical, mental and
spiritual manifestation is a form of expression, appears to be a corollary of
Bergson's demonstrated "Universal Livingness." What Bergson has so
brilliantly proven by patient and exhaustive processes of science, Judge
Troward arrived at by intuition, and postulated as the basis of his argument,
which he proceeded to develop by deductive reasoning.

The writer was struck by the apparent parallelism of these two distinctly
dissimilar philosophies, and mentioned the discovery to Judge Troward who
naturally expressed a wish to read Bergson, with whose writings he was
wholly unacquainted. A loan of Bergson's "Creative Evolution" produced no
comment for several weeks, when it was returned with the characteristic
remark, "I've tried my best to get hold of him, but I don't know what he is

talking about." I mention the remark as being characteristic only because it indicates his extreme modesty and disregard of exhaustive scientific research.

The Bergson method of scientific expression was unintelligible to his mind, trained to intuitive reasoning. The very elaborateness and microscopic detail that makes Bergson great is opposed to Judge Troward's method of simplicity. He cared not for complexities, and the intricate minutiæ of the process of creation, but was only concerned with its motive power—the spiritual principles upon which it was organized and upon which it proceeds.

Although the conservator of truth of every form and degree wherever found, Judge Troward was a ruthless destroyer of sham and pretence. To those submissive minds that placidly accept everything indiscriminately, and also those who prefer to follow along paths of well-beaten opinion, because the beaten path is popular, to all such he would perhaps appear to be an irreverent iconoclast seeking to uproot long accepted dogma and to overturn existing faiths. Such an opinion of Judge Troward's work could not prevail with any one who has studied his teachings.

His reverence for the fundamental truths of religious faith was profound, and every student of his writings will testify to the great constructive value of his work. He built upon an ancient foundation a new and nobler structure of human destiny, solid in its simplicity and beautiful in its innate grandeur.

But to the wide circle of Judge Troward's friends he will best and most gloriously be remembered as a teacher. In his magic mind the unfathomable revealed its depths and the illimitable its boundaries; metaphysics took on the simplicity of the ponderable, and man himself occupied a new and more dignified place in the Cosmos. Not only did he perceive clearly, but he also possessed that quality of mind even more rare than deep and clear perception, that clarity of expression and exposition that can carry another and less-informed mind along with it, on the current of its understanding, to a logical and comprehended conclusion.

In his books, his lectures and his personality he was always ready to take the student by the hand, and in perfect simplicity and friendliness to walk and talk with him about the deeper mysteries of life—the life that includes death—and to shed the brilliant light of his wisdom upon the obscure and difficult problems that torment sincere but rebellious minds.

His artistic nature found expression in brush and canvas and his great love for the sea is reflected in many beautiful marine sketches. But if painting was his recreation, his work was the pursuit of Truth wherever to be found, and in whatever disguise.

His life has enriched and enlarged the lives of many, and all those who knew him will understand that in helping others he was accomplishing exactly what he most desired. Knowledge, to him, was worth only what it yielded in uplifting humanity to a higher spiritual appreciation, and to a deeper understanding of God's purpose and man's destiny.

A man, indeed! He strove not for a place, Nor rest, nor rule. He daily walked with God. His willing feet with service swift were shod— An eager soul to serve the human race, Illume the mind, and fill the heart with grace— Hope blooms afresh where'er those feet have trod.

Paul Derrick

SOME FACTS IN NATURE

If I were asked what, in my opinion, distinguishes the thought of the present day from that of a previous generation, I should feel inclined to say, it is the fact that people are beginning to realize that Thought is a power in itself, one of the great forces of the Universe, and ultimately the greatest of forces, directing all the others. This idea seems to be, as the French say, "in the air," and this very well expresses the state of the case—the idea is rapidly spreading through many countries and through all classes, but it is still very much "in the air." It is to a great extent as yet only in a gaseous condition, vague and nebulous, and so not leading to the practical results, both individual and collective, which might be expected of it, if it were consolidated into a more workable form. We are like some amateurs who want to paint finished pictures before they have studied the elements of Art, and when they see an artist do without difficulty what they vainly attempt, they look upon him as a being specially favoured by Providence, instead of putting it down to their own want of knowledge. The idea is true. Thought *is* the great power of the Universe. But to make it practically available we must know something of the principles by which it works—that it is not a mere vaporous indefinable influence floating around and subject to no known laws, but that on the contrary, it follows laws as uncompromising as those of mathematics, while at the same time allowing unlimited freedom to the individual.

Now the purpose of the following pages, is to suggest to the reader the lines on which to find his way out of this nebulous sort of thought into something more solid and reliable. I do not profess, like a certain Negro preacher, to "unscrew the inscrutable," for we can never reach a point where we shall not find the inscrutable still ahead of us; but if I can indicate the use of a screw-driver instead of a hatchet, and that the screws should be turned from left to right, instead of from right to left, it may enable us to unscrew some things which would otherwise remain screwed down tight. We are all beginners, and indeed the hopefulness of life is in realizing that there are such vistas of unending possibilities before us, that however far we may advance, we shall always be on the threshold of something greater. We must be like Peter Pan, the boy who never grew up—heaven defend me from ever feeling quite grown up, for then I should come to a standstill; so the reader must take what I have to say simply as the talk of one boy to another in the Great School, and not expect too much.

The first question then is, where to begin. Descartes commenced his book with the words "Cogito, ergo sum." "I think, therefore I am," and we cannot do better than follow his example. There are two things about which we cannot have any doubt—our own existence, and that of the world around us. But what is it in us that is aware of these two things, that hopes and fears and plans regarding them? Certainly not our flesh and bones. A man whose leg has been amputated is able to think just the same. Therefore it is obvious that there is something in us which receives impressions and forms ideas, that reasons upon facts and determines upon courses of action and carries them out, which is not the physical body. This is the real "I Myself." This is the Person we are really concerned with; and it is the betterment of this "I Myself" that makes it worth while to enquire what our Thought has to do in the matter.

Equally true it is on the other hand that the forces of Nature around us do not think. Steam, electricity, gravitation, and chemical affinity do not think. They follow certain fixed laws which we have no power to alter. Therefore we are confronted at the outset by a broad distinction between two modes of Motion—the Movement of Thought and the Movement of Cosmic Energy—the one based upon the exercise of Consciousness and Will, and the other based upon Mathematical Sequence. This is why that system of instruction known as Free Masonry starts by erecting the two symbolic pillars Jachin and Boaz—Jachin so called from the root "Yak" meaning "One," indicating the Mathematical element of Law; and Boaz, from the root "Awáz" meaning "Voice" indicating Personal element of Free Will. These names are taken from the description in I Kings vii, 21 and II Chron. iii, 17 of the building of Solomon's Temple, where these two pillars stood before the entrance, the meaning being that the Temple of Truth can only be entered by passing between them, that is, by giving each of these factors their due relation to the other, and by realizing that they are the two Pillars of the Universe, and that no real progress can be made except by finding the true balance between them. Law and Personality—these are the two great principles with which we have to deal, and the problem is to square the one with the other.

Let me start, then, by considering some well established facts in the physical world which show how the known Law acts under certain known conditions, and this will lead us on in an intelligible manner to see how the same Law is likely to work under as yet unknown conditions. If we had to deal with unknown laws as well as unknown conditions we should, indeed, be up a gum tree. Fancy a mathematician having to solve an equation, both sides of which were entirely made up of unknown quantities—where would he be? Happily this is not the case. The Law is *One* throughout, and the apparent variety of its working results from the infinite variety of the conditions under which it may work. Let us lay a foundation, then, by seeing how it works in what we call the common course of Nature. A few examples will suffice.

Hardly more than a generation ago it was supposed that the analysis of matter could not be carried further than its reduction to some seventy primary chemical elements, which in various combinations produced all material substances; but there was no explanation how all these different elements came into existence. Each appeared to be an original creation, and there was no accounting for them. But now-a-days, as the rustic physician says in Molière's play of the "Médecin Malgré Lui," "nous avons changé tout cela." Modern science has shown conclusively that every kind of chemical atom is composed of particles of one original substance which appears to pervade all space, and to which the name of Ether has been given. Some of these particles carry a positive charge of electricity and some a negative, and the chemical atom is formed by the grouping of a certain number of negatively charged particles round a centre composed of positive electricity around which they revolve; and it is the number of these particles and the rate of their motion that determines the nature of the atom, whether, for instance, it will be an atom of iron or an atom of hydrogen, and thus we are brought back to Plato's old aphorism that the Universe consists of Number and Motion.

The size of these etheric particles is small beyond anything but abstract mathematical conception. Sir Oliver Lodge is reported to have made the following comparison in a lecture delivered at Birmingham. "The chemical atom," he said, "is as small in comparison to a drop of water as a cricket-ball is compared to the globe of the earth; and yet this atom is as large in comparison to one of its constituent particles as Birmingham town-hall is to a pin's head." Again, it has been said that in proportion to the size of the particles the distance at which they revolve round the centre of the atom is as great as the distance from the earth to the sun. I must leave the realization of such infinite minuteness to the reader's imagination—it is beyond mine.

Modern science thus shows us all material substance, whether that of inanimate matter or that of our own bodies, as proceeding out of one primary etheric substance occupying all space and homogeneous, that is being of a uniform substance—and having no qualities to distinguish one part from another. Now this conclusion of science is important because it is precisely the fact that out of this homogeneous substance particles are produced which differ from the original substance in that they possess positive and negative energy and of these particles the atom is built up. So then comes the question: What started this differentiation?

The electronic theory which I have just mentioned takes us as far as a universal homogeneous ether as the source from which all matter is evolved, but it does not account for how motion originated in it; but perhaps another closely allied scientific theory will help us. Let us, then, turn to the question of Vibrations or Waves in Ether. In scientific language the length of a wave is the distance from the crest of one wave to that of the wave immediately following it. Now modern science recognizes a long series of waves in ether, commencing with the smallest yet known measuring 0.1 micron, or about 1/254,000 of an inch, in length, measured by Professor Schumann in 1893, and extending to waves of many miles in length used in wireless telegraphy—for instance those employed between Clifden in Galway and Glace Bay in Nova Scotia are estimated to have a length of nearly four miles. These infinitesimally small ultra-violet or actinic waves, as they are called, are the principal agents in photography, and the great waves of wireless telegraphy are able to carry a force across the Atlantic which can sensibly affect the apparatus on the other side; therefore we see that the ether of space affords a medium through which energy can be transmitted by means of vibrations.

But what starts the vibrations? Hertz announced his discovery of the electro-magnetic waves, now known by his name, in 1888; but, following up the labours of various other investigators, Lodge, Marconi and others finally developed their practical application after Hertz's death which occurred in 1894. To Hertz, however, belongs the honour of discovering how to generate these waves by means of sudden, sharply defined, electrical discharges. The principle may be illustrated by dropping a stone in smooth water. The sudden impact sets up a series of ripples all round the centre of disturbance, and the electrical impulse acts similarly in the ether. Indeed the fact that the waves flow in all directions from the central impulse is one of the difficulties of wireless telegraphy, because the message may be picked up in any direction by a receiver tuned to the same rate of vibration, and the interest for us consists in the hypothesis that thought-waves act in an analogous manner.

That vibrations are excited by sound is beautifully exemplified by the eidophone, an instrument invented, I believe, by Mrs. Watts-Hughes, and with which I have seen that lady experiment. Dry sand is scattered on a diaphragm on which the eidophone concentrates the vibrations from music played near it. The sand, as it were, dances in time to the music, and when the music stops is found to settle into definite forms, sometimes like a tree or a flower, or else some geometrical figure, but never a confused jumble. Perhaps in this we may find the origin of the legends regarding the creative power of Orpheus' lyre, and also the sacred dances of the ancients—who knows!

Perhaps some critical reader may object that sound travels by means of atmospheric and not etheric waves; but is he prepared to say that it cannot produce etheric waves also. The very recent discovery of transatlantic telephoning tends to show that etheric waves can be generated by sound, for on the 20th of October, 1915, words spoken in New York were immediately heard in Paris, and could therefore only have been transmitted through the ether, for sound travels through the atmosphere only at the rate of about 750 miles an hour, while the speed of impulses through ether can only be compared to that of light or 186,000 miles in a second. It is therefore a fair inference that etheric vibrations can be inaugurated by sound.

Perhaps the reader may feel inclined to say with the Irishman that all this is "as dry as ditch-water," but he will see before long that it has a good deal to do with ourselves. For the present what I want him to realize by a few examples is the mathematical accuracy of Law. The value of these examples lies in their illustration of the fact that the Law can always be trusted to lead us on to further knowledge. We see it working under known conditions, and relying on its unchangeableness, we can then logically infer what it will do under other hypothetical conditions, and in this way many important discoveries have been made. For instance it was in this way that Mendeléef, the Russian chemist, assumed the existence of three then unknown chemical elements, now called Scandium, Gallium and Germanium. There was a gap in the orderly sequence of the chemical elements, and relying on the old maxim—"Natura nihil facit per saltum"—Nature nowhere leaves a gap to jump over—he argued that if such elements did not exist they ought to, and so he calculated what these elements ought to be like, giving their atomic weight, chemical affinities, and the like; and when they were discovered many years later they were found to answer exactly to his description. He prophesied, not by guesswork, but by knowledge of the Law; and in much the same way radium was discovered by Professor and Madame Curie. In like manner Hertz was led to the discovery of the electro-magnetic waves. The celebrated mathematician Clerk-Maxwell had calculated all particulars of these waves twenty-five years before Hertz, on the basis of these calculations, worked out his discovery. Again, Neptune, the outermost known planet of our system was discovered by the astronomer Galle in consequence of calculations made by Leverrier. Certain variations in the movements of the planets were mathematically unaccountable except on the hypothesis that some more remote planet existed. Astronomers had faith in mathematics and the hypothetical planet was found to be a reality. Instances of this kind might be multiplied, but as the French say "à quoi bon?" I think these will be sufficient to convince the reader that the invariable sequence of Law is a factor to be relied upon, and that by studying its working under known conditions we may get at least some measure of light on conditions which are as yet unknown to us.

Let us now pass on to the human subject and consider a few examples of what is usually called the psychic side of our nature. Walt Whitman was quite right when he said that we are not all included between our hat and our boots; we shall find that our modes of consciousness and powers of action are not entirely restricted to our physical body. The importance of this line of enquiry lies in the fact that if we do possess extra-physical powers, these also form part of our personality and must be included in our estimate of our relation to our environment, and it is therefore worth our while to consider them.

Some very interesting experiments have been made by De Rochas, an eminent French scientist, which go to show that under certain magnetic conditions the sensation of physical touch can be experienced at some distance from the body. He found that under these conditions the person experimented on is insensible to the prick of a needle run into his skin, but if the prick is made about an inch-and-a-half away from the surface of the skin he feels it. Again at about three inches from this point he feels the prick of the needle, but is insensible to it in the space between these two points. Then there comes another interval in which no sensation is conveyed, but at about three inches still further away he again feels the sensation, and so on; so that he appears to be surrounded by successive zones of sensation, the first about an inch-and-a-half from the body, and the others at intervals of about three inches each. The number of these zones seems to vary in different cases, but in some there are as many as six or seven, thus giving a radius of sensation, extending to more than twenty inches beyond the body.

Now to explain this we must have recourse to what I have already said about waves. The heart and the lungs are the two centres of automatic rhythmic movement in the body, and each projects its own series of vibrations into the etheric envelope. Those projected by the lungs are estimated to be three times the length of those projected by the heart, while those projected by the heart are three times as rapid as those projected by the lungs. Consequently if the two sets of waves start together the crest of every third wave of the rapid series of short waves will coincide with the crest of one of the long waves of the slower series, while the intermediate short waves will coincide with the depression of one of the long waves. Now the effect of the crest of one wave overtaking that of another going in the same direction, is to raise the two together at that point into a single wave of greater amplitude or height than the original waves had by themselves; if the reader has the opportunity of studying the inflowing of waves on the seabeach he can verify this for himself. Consequently when the more rapid etheric waves overtake the slower ones they combine to form a larger wave, and it is at these points that the zones of sensation occur. If the reader will draw a diagram of two waved lines travelling along the same horizontal line and so proportioned that the crest of each of the large waves coincides with the crest of every third wave of the small ones, he will see what I mean: and if he then recollects that the fall in the larger waves neutralizes the rise in the smaller ones, and that because this double series starts from the interior of the body the surface of the body comes just at one of these neutralized points, he will see why sensation is neutralized there; and he will also see why the succeeding zones of sensation are double the distance from each other that the first one is from the surface of the body; it is simply because the surface of the body cuts the first long wave exactly in the middle, and therefore only half that wave occurs outside the body. This is the explanation given by De Rochas, and it affords another example of that principle of mathematical sequence of which I have spoken. It would appear that under normal conditions the double series of vibrations is spread all over the body, and so all parts are alike sensitive to touch.

I think, then, we may assume on the basis of De Rochas' experiments and others that there are such things as etheric vibrations proceeding from human personality, and in the next chapter I will give some examples showing that the psychic personality extends still further than these experiments, taken by themselves, would indicate—in fact that we possess an additional range of faculties far exceeding those which we ordinarily exercise through the physical body, and which must therefore be included in our conception of ourselves if we are to have an adequate idea of what we really are.

SOME PSYCHIC EXPERIENCES

The preceding chapter has introduced the reader to the general subject of etheric vibration as one of the natural forces of the Universe, both as the foundation of all matter and as the medium for the transmission of energy to immense distances, and also as something continually emanating from human beings. In the present chapter I shall consider it more particularly in this last aspect, which, as included in our own personality, very immediately concerns ourselves. I will commence with an instance of the practical application of this fact. Some years ago I was lunching at the house of Lady —— in company of a well-known mental healer whom I will call Mr. Y. and a well-known London physician whom I will call Dr. W. Mr. Y. mentioned the case of a lady whose leg had been amputated above the knee some years previously to her coming under his care, yet she frequently felt pains in the (amputated) knee and lower part of the left leg and foot. Dr. W. said this was to be attributed to the nerves which convey to the brain the sensation of the extremities, much as a telegraph line might be tapped in the middle, and Mr. Y. agreed that this was perfectly true on the purely physical side. But he went on to say, that accidentally putting his hand where the amputated foot should have been he felt it there. Then it occurred to him that since there was no material foot to be touched, it must be through the medium of his own psychic body that the sensation of touch was conveyed to him, and accordingly he asked the lady to imagine that she was making various movements with the amputated limb, all of which he felt, and was able to tell her what each movement was, which she said he did correctly. Then, to carry the experiment further, he reversed the process and with his hand moved the invisible leg and foot in various ways, all of which the lady felt and described. He then determined to treat the invisible leg as though it were a real one, and joined up the circuit by taking her left foot in his right hand and her right foot (the amputated one) in his left, with the result that she immediately felt relief; and after successive treatments in this way was entirely cured.

A well authenticated case like this opens up a good many interesting questions regarding the Psychic Body, but the most important point appears to me to be that we are able to experience sensation by means of it. In this case, however, and those mentioned in the preceding chapter, the physical body was actually present, and if we stopped at this point, we might question whether its presence was not a *sine qua non* for the action of the etheric vibrations. I will therefore pass on to a class of examples which show that very curious phenomena can take place without the physical body being on the spot. There are numerous well verified cases of the kind to be found in the records of the Society for Psychical Research and in other books by trustworthy writers; but it may perhaps interest the present reader to hear one or two instances of my personal experience which, though they may not

be so striking as some of those recorded by others, still point in the same
direction.

My first introduction to Scotland was when I delivered the course of
lectures in Edinburgh which led to the publication of my first book, the
"Edinburgh Lectures on Mental Science." The following years I gave a second
course of lectures in Edinburgh, but the friends who had kindly entertained
me on the former occasion had in the meanwhile gone to live elsewhere.
However, a certain Mr. S., whose acquaintance I had made on my previous
visit, invited me to stay with him for a day or two while I could look round for
other accommodation, though, as it turned out, I remained at his house during
the whole month I was in Edinburgh. I had, however, never seen his house,
which was on the opposite side of the town to where I had stayed before. I
arrived there on a Tuesday, and Mr. S. and his family at once met me with the
question:

"What were you thinking of at ten o'clock on Sunday evening?"

I could not immediately recall this, and also wanted to know the reason
of their question.

"We have something curious to tell you," they replied, "but first try to
remember what you were thinking of at ten o'clock on Sunday evening—were
you thinking about us?"

Then I recollected that about that time I was saying my usual prayers
before going to bed and had asked that, if I could stay only a day or two with
Mr. S., I should be directed to a suitable place for the remainder of the time.

"That explains it," they replied; and then they went on to tell me that at
the hour in question Mr. S. and his son, a young man of about twenty, had
entered their dining-room together and seen me standing leaning against the
mantel-shelf. They were both hard-headed Scotchmen engaged in business in
Edinburgh, and certainly not the sort of people to conjure up fanciful
imaginings, nor is it likely that the same fancy should have occurred to both
of them; and therefore I can only suppose that they actually saw what they
said they did. Now I myself was in London at the time of this appearance in
Edinburgh, of which I had no consciousness whatever; at the same time the
fact of my being seen in Edinburgh exactly at the time when my thought, in
prayer, was centred upon Mr. S.'s house (which I had not then seen) is a
coincidence suggesting that in some way my Thought had made itself visible
there in the image of my external personality.

In this case, as I have said, I was not conscious of my psychic visit to
Edinburgh, but I will now relate a converse instance, which occurred in
connection with my first visit there. At that time I had never been in
Scotland, and so far as I knew was never likely to go there. I was wide awake,
writing in my study at Norwood, where I then lived, when I suddenly found
myself in a place totally unknown to me, where stood the ruins of an ancient
abbey, part of which, however, was still roofed over and used as a place of
worship. I felt much interested, and among other things I noted a Latin
inscription on a tablet in one of the walls. There seemed to be an invisible
guide showing me over the place, who then pointed out a long low house
opposite the abbey, and said: "This is the house of the clergyman of the abbey";
and I was then taken inside the house and shown a number of antique-looking

rooms. Then I came to myself, and found I was sitting at my writing-table in Norwood. I had, however, a clear recollection of the place I had seen, but no idea where it was, or indeed whether any such place really existed. I also remembered a portion of the Latin inscription, which I at once wrote down in a note-book, as my curiosity was aroused.

As I have said, I had no reason at that time to suppose I should ever go to Scotland, but some weeks later I was invited to lecture in Edinburgh. Another visitor in the house where I was a guest there, was the wife of the County Court Judge of Cumberland, and I showed her and our hostess the part of the Latin inscription I had retained, and suggested that perhaps it might exist somewhere in Edinburgh. However nothing answering to what I had seen was to be found, so we relegated the whole thing to the region of unaccountable fancies, and thought no more about it. The Judge's wife took her departure before me, and kindly invited me to spend a few days at their residence near Carlisle on my return journey, which I did. One day she drove me out to see Lanercost Abbey, one of the show-places of the neighbourhood, and walking round the building I found in one of the walls the Latin inscription in question. I called Mrs. ——, who was a little way off, and said: "Look at this inscription."

She at once replied: "Why! that is the very inscription we were all puzzling over in Edinburgh!"

It turned out to be an inscription in memory of the founder of the abbey, dating from somewhere in the eleven-hundreds. The whole place answered exactly to what I had seen, and the long low parsonage was there also.

"I should have liked you to see it inside," said Mrs. ——, "but I have never met the vicar, though I know his mother-in-law, so we must give it up."

We were just entering our carriage when the garden-gate opened, and who should come out but the mother-in-law.

"Oh, Mrs. ——," she said, addressing the Judge's wife, "I am here on a visit and you must come in and take tea." So we went in and were shown over the house, much as I had been in my vision, and some portions were so old that, among other rooms, we were shown the one occupied by King Edward I on his march against Scotland in the year 1296, when the Scottish regalia was captured, and the celebrated Crowning-Stone was brought to England and placed in Westminster Abbey, where it has ever since remained—a stone having an occult relation to the history of the British and American peoples of the highest interest to both, but as there is already an extensive literature on this subject I will not enter upon it here.

I will now relate another curious experience. We had only recently taken up our residence at Norwood, when one day I was seated in the dining-room, but suddenly found myself in the hall, and saw two ladies going up the stairs. They passed close to me, and turning round the landing at the top of the stairs passed out of sight in a perfectly natural manner. They looked as solid as any one I have ever seen in my life. One of them was a stout lady with a rather florid complexion, apparently between forty-five and fifty, wearing a silk blouse with thin purple and white stripes. Leaning on her arm was a slightly-built old lady with white ringlets, dressed all in black and wearing a lace mantilla. I noticed their appearance particularly. The next moment I found I was really sitting in the dining-room, and that the ladies I had seen were nothing but visionary figures. I wondered what it could mean, but as we had only recently taken the house, thought it better not to mention it to any of my family, for fear of causing them alarm. But a few days later I mentioned it to a Mrs. F. who I knew had had some experience in such matters, and she said: "You have seen either some one who has lived in the house or who is going to live there." Then the matter dropped.

About a month later my wife arranged by correspondence for a certain Miss B. to come as governess to our children. When she arrived there was no mistaking her identity. She was the stout lady I had seen, and the next morning she came down to breakfast dressed in the identical blouse with purple and white stripes. There was no mistaking her, but I was puzzled as to who the other figure could be whom I had seen along with her. I resolved, however, to say nothing about the matter until we became better acquainted, lest she should think that my mind was not quite balanced. I therefore held my peace for six months, at the end of which time I concluded that we knew enough of each other to allow one another credit for being fairly level-headed. Then I thought, now if I tell her what I saw she may perhaps be acted upon by suggestion and imagine a resemblance between the unknown figure and some acquaintance of hers, so I will not begin by telling her of the vision, but will first ask if she knows any one answering to the description, and give her the reason afterwards. I therefore took a suitable opportunity of asking her if she knew any such person, describing the figure to her as accurately as I could.

Her look of surprise grew as I went on, and when I had finished she explained with astonishment: "Why, Mr. Troward, where *could* you have seen my mother? She is an invalid, and I am certain you have never seen her, and yet you have described her most accurately."

Then I told her what I had seen. She asked what I thought was the explanation of the appearance, and the only explanation I could give was, that I supposed she was on the look-out for a post and paid us a preliminary visit to see whether ours would suit her, and that, being naturally interested in her welfare, her mother had accompanied her. Perhaps you will say: "What came of it?" Well, nothing "came of it," nor did anything "come" of my psychic visits to Edinburgh and Lanercost Abbey. Such occurrences seem to be simple facts in Nature which, though on some occasions connected with premonitions of more or less importance, are by no means necessarily so. They are the functioning of certain faculties which we all possess, but of the nature of which we as yet know very little.

It will be noticed that in the first of these three cases I myself was the person seen, though unaware of the fact. In the last I was the percipient, but the persons seen by me were unconscious of their visit; and in the second case I was conscious of my presence at a place which I had never heard of, and which I visited some time after. In two of these cases, therefore, the persons, making the psychic visit, were not aware of having done so, while in the third, a memory of what had been seen was retained. But all three cases have this in common, that the psychic visit was not the result of an act of conscious volition, and also, that the psychic action took place at a long distance from the physical body.

From these personal experiences, as well as from many well authenticated cases recorded by other writers, I should be inclined to infer that the psychic action is entirely independent of the physical body, and in support of this view I will cite yet another experience.

It was about the year 1875, when I was a young Assistant Commissioner in the Punjab, that I was ordered to the small up-country station of Akalpur,[1] and took possession of the Assistant Commissioner's bungalow there. On the night of our arrival in the bungalow, my wife and I had our charpoys—light Indian bedsteads—placed side by side in a certain room and went to bed. The last thing I remembered before falling asleep, was seeing my wife sitting up in bed, reading with a lamp on a small table beside her. Suddenly I was awakened by the sound of a shot, and starting up, found the room in darkness. I immediately lit a candle which was on a chair by my bedside, and found my wife still sitting up with the book on her knee, but the lamp had gone out.

"Take me away, take me into another room," she exclaimed.

"Why, what is the matter?" I said.

"Did you not see it?" she replied.

"See what?" I asked.

"Don't stop to ask any questions," she replied; "get me out of this room at once; I can't stop here another minute."

I saw she was very frightened, so I called up the servants, and had our beds removed to a room on the other side of the house, and then she told me what she had seen. She said: "I was sitting reading as you saw me, when looking round, I saw the figure of an Englishman standing close by my bedside, a fine-looking man with a large fair moustache and dressed in a grey suit. I was so surprised that I could not speak, and we remained looking at each other for about a minute. Then he bent over me and whispered: 'Don't be afraid,' and with that there was the sound of a shot, and everything was in darkness."

"My dear girl, you must have fallen asleep over your book and been dreaming," I said.

"No, I was wide awake," she insisted; "you were asleep, but I was awake all the time. But you heard the shot, did you not?"

"Yes," I replied, "that is what woke me—some one must have fired a shot outside."

"But why should any one be shooting in our garden at nearly midnight?" my wife objected.

It certain seemed strange, but it was the only explanation that suggested itself; so we had to agree to differ, she being convinced that she had seen a ghost, and that the shot had been inside the room, and I being equally convinced that she had been dreaming, and that the shot had been fired outside the house.

The next morning the owner of the bungalow, an old widow lady, Mrs. La Chaire, called to make kindly enquiries as to whether she could be of any service to us on our arrival. After thanking her, my wife said: "I expect you will laugh at me, but I cannot help telling you there is something strange about the bungalow"; and she then went on to narrate what she had seen.

Instead of laughing the old lady looked more and more serious as she went on, and when she had done asked to be shown exactly where the apparition had appeared. My wife took her to the spot, and on being shown it old Mrs. La Chaire exclaimed: "This is the most wonderful thing I have ever heard of. Eighteen years ago my bed was on the very spot where yours was last night, and I was lying in it too ill to move, when my husband, whom you have described most accurately, stood where you saw him and shot himself dead."

This statement of the widow convinced me that my wife had really seen what she said she had, and had not dreamed it; and this experience has led me to make further enquiries into the nature of happenings of this kind, with the result, that after carefully eliminating all cases which could be accounted for in any other manner, I have found myself compelled to admit a considerable number of instances of what are called "ghosts," on the word of persons whose veracity and soundness of judgment I should not doubt on any other subject. It is often said that you never meet any one who has himself seen a ghost, but only those who have heard of somebody else seeing one. This I can entirely contradict, for I have met with many trustworthy persons of both sexes, who have given me accounts of such appearances having been actually witnessed by themselves. In conclusion, I may mention that I was telling this story some twenty years later to a Colonel Fox, who had known the unfortunate man who committed suicide, and he said to me: "Do you know what were the last words he said to his wife?"

"No," I replied.

"The very same words he spoke to your wife," said Colonel Fox.

This is the story I refer to in my book "Bible Mystery and Bible Meaning" as that of "the Ghost that I did not see." I do not attempt to offer any explanation of it, but merely give the facts as they occurred, and the reader must form his own theory on the subject; but the reason I bring in this story in the present connection is, that in this instance there could be no question of the physical body contributing to the psychic phenomenon, since the person seen had been dead for nearly twenty years; and coupling this fact with the distance from the physical body at which the psychic action took place in the other cases I have mentioned, I think there is a very strong presumption that the psychic powers can, and do, act independently of the physical body; though of course it does not follow from this that they cannot also act in conjunction with it.

On the other hand, a comparison of the present case with those previously mentioned, fails to throw any light on the important question whether the deceased feels any consciousness of the action which the percipient sees, or whether what is seen is like a sort of photograph impressed upon the atmosphere of a particular locality, and visible only to certain persons, who are able to sense etheric wave-lengths which are outside the range of the single octave forming the solar spectrum. It throws no light on this question, because, in the case of my being seen by Mr. S. in Edinburgh and that of Miss B. and her mother being seen by me at Norwood, none of us were conscious of having been at those places; while in the case of my psychic visit to

Lanercost Abbey, and other similar experiences I have had, I have been fully aware of seeing the places in question. The evidence tells both ways, and I can therefore only infer that there are two modes of psychic action, in one of which the person projecting that action, whether voluntarily or involuntarily, experiences corresponding sensations, and the other in which he does not; but I am unable to offer any criterion by which the observer can, with certainty, distinguish between the two.

It appears to me, that such instances as those I have mentioned, point to ranges of etheric action beyond those ordinarily recognized by physical science, but the principle seems to be the same, and it is for this reason that I have taken the modern scientific theory of etheric vibration as our starting-point. The universe is one great whole, and the laws of one part cannot contradict those of another; therefore the explanation of such queer happenings is not to be found by denying the well-ascertained laws of Nature on the physical plane, but by considering whether these laws do not extend further. It is on this account that I would lay stress on the Mathematical side of things, and have adduced instances where various discoveries have been made by following up the sequence indicated by the laws already known, and which have thus enabled us to fill up gaps in our knowledge, which would otherwise stop, or at least seriously hinder, our further progress. It is in this way that Jachin helps Boaz, and that the undeviating nature of Law, so far from limiting us, becomes our faithful ally if we will only allow it to do so.

I think, then, that the scientific idea of the ether, as a universal medium pervading all space, and permeating all substance, will help us to see that many things which are popularly called supernatural, are to be attributed to the action of known laws working under, as yet, unknown conditions, and therefore, when we are confronted with strange phenomena, a knowledge of the general principles involved, will show us in what direction to look for an explanation. Now applying this to the present subject, we may reasonably argue, that since all physical matter is scientifically proved to consist of the universal ether in various degrees of condensation, there may be other degrees of condensation, forming other modes of matter, which are beyond the scope of physical vision and of our laboratory apparatus. And similarly, we may argue, that just as various effects can be produced on the physical plane, by the action of etheric waves of various lengths, so other effects might be produced on these finer modes of matter, by etheric waves of other lengths. And in this connection we must not forget that a gap occurs between the "dark heat" groups and the Hertzian group, consisting of five octaves of waves, the lengths of which have been theoretically calculated, but whose action has not yet been discovered. Here we admittedly have a wide field for the working of known laws under as yet unknown conditions; and again, how can we say that there are not ranges of unknown waves, yet smaller than the minute ultra-violet ones, which commence the present known scale, or transcending those largest ones, which bear our messages across the Atlantic? Mathematically, there is no limit to the scale in either direction; and so, taking our stand on the demonstrated facts of science, we find, that the known laws of Nature point to their continuation in modes of matter and of force, of which we have as yet no conception. It is therefore not at all necessary to spurn the ground of established science to spread the wings of our fancy; rather it affords us the requisite basis from which to start, just as the aeronaut cannot rise without a solid surface from which to spring.

Now if we realize that the ether is an infinitely subtle fluid, pervading all space, we see that it must constitute a connecting link between all modes of substance, whether visible or invisible, in all worlds, and may therefore be called the Universal Medium; and following up our conception of the Continuity of Law, we may suppose that trains of waves, inconceivably smaller or greater than any known to modern science, are set up in this medium, in the same way as the electro-magnetic waves with which we are acquainted; that is, by an impulse which generates them from some particular point. In the region of finer forces we are now prospecting, this impulse might well be the Desire or Will of the spiritual entity which we ourselves are—that thinking, feeling, inmost essence of ourself, which is the "noumenon" of our individuality, and which, for the sake of brevity we call our "Ego," a Latin word which simply means "I myself." This idea of spiritual impulse is quite familiar to us in our every-day talk. We speak of an impulsive person, meaning one who acts on a sudden thought without giving due heed to consequences; so in our ordinary speech we look upon thought as the initial impulse, only we restrict this to the case of unregulated thought. But if unregulated thought acts as a centre of impulse, why should not regulated thought do the same? Therefore we may accept the idea of Thought as the initial impulse, which starts trains of waves in the Universal Medium, whether with or without due consideration, and having thus recognized its dynamic power, we must learn to make the impulses we thus send forth intelligent, well defined, and directed to some useful purpose. The operator at some wireless station does not use his instruments to send out a lot of jumbled-up waves into the ether, but controls the impulses into a definite and intelligible order, and we must do the same.

On some such lines as these, then, we may picture the desire of the Ego as starting a train of waves in the Universal Medium, which are reproduced in corresponding *form* on reaching their destination. As with the electro-magnetic waves, they may spread all round, just as ripples do if we throw a stone into a pond; but they will only take form where there is a correspondence able to receive them. This is what in the language of electrical engineers is called "Syntony," which means being tuned to the same rate of vibration, and no doubt it is from some such cause, that we sometimes experience what seem inexplicable feelings of attraction or repulsion towards different persons. This also appears to furnish a key to thought-transference, hypnotism, and other allied phenomena.

If the reader questions whether thought is capable of generating impulses in the etheric medium I would refer him to the experiment mentioned in Chapter XIV of my "Edinburgh Lectures on Mental Science," where I describe how, when operating with Dr. Baraduc's biometer, I found that the needle revolved through a smaller or large arc of the circle, in response to my mental intention of concentrating a smaller or larger degree of force upon it. Perhaps you will say that the difference in the movement of the needle depended on the quantity of magnetism that was flowing from me, to say nothing of other known forces, such as heat, light, electricity, etc. Well, that is precisely the proposition I am putting forward. What caused the difference in the intensity of the magnetic flow was my intention of varying it, so that we come back to mental action as the centre of impulsion from which the etheric waves were generated. If, then, such a demonstration can be obtained on the plane of purely physical matter, why need we doubt that the same Law will work in the same way, in respect of those finer modes of substance, and wider ranges of etheric vibrations, which, starting from the basis of recognized physical science, the Law of Continuity would lead to by an orderly sequence, and which the occurrence of what, for want of a better name, we call occult phenomena require for their explanation?

Before passing on to the more practical generalizations to be drawn from the suggestions contained in this chapter, I may advert to an objection sometimes brought by the sceptical in this matter. They say: "How is it that apparitions are always seen in the dark?" and then they answer their own question by saying, it is because superstitious people are nervous in the dark and imagine all sorts of things. Then they laugh and think they have disposed of the whole subject. But it is not disposed of quite so easily, for not only are there many well attested cases of such appearances in broad daylight, but there are also scientific facts, showing that if we are right in explaining such happenings by etheric action, such action is more readily produced at night than in the presence of sunlight.

In the early part of 1902 Marconi made some experiments on board the American liner *Philadelphia*, which brought out the remarkable fact that, while it was possible to transmit signals to a distance of fifteen hundred miles during the night, they could not be transmitted further than seven hundred miles during the day. The same was found to be the case by Lieutenant Solari of the Italian Navy, at whose disposal the ship *Carlo Alberta* was placed by the King of Italy in 1902, for the purpose of making investigations into wireless telegraphy; and summing up the points which he considered to have been fully established by his experiments on board that ship, he mentions among them the fact, that sunlight has the effect of reducing the power of the electro-magnetic waves, and that consequently a greater force is required to produce a given result by day than by night. Here, then, is a reason why we might expect to see more supernatural appearances, as we call them, at night than in the day—they require a smaller amount of force to produce them. At the same time, it is found that the great magnetic waves which cover immense distances, work even more powerfully in the light than in the dark. May it not be that these things show, that there is more than a merely metaphorical use of words, when the Bible tells us of the power of Light to dissipate, and bring to naught, the powers of Darkness, while the Light itself is the Great Power, using the forces of the universe on the widest scale? Perhaps it is none other than the continuity of unchanging universal principles extending into the mysterious realms of the spiritual world.

MAN'S PLACE IN THE CREATIVE ORDER

In the preceding chapters we have found certain definite facts,—that all known matter is formed out of one primordial Universal Substance,—that the ether spreading throughout limitless space is a Universal Medium, through which it is possible to convey force by means of vibrations,—and that vibrations can be started by the power of Sound. These we have found to be well established facts of ordinary science, and taking them as our starting-point, we may now begin to speculate as to the possible workings of the known laws under unknown conditions.

One of the first things that naturally attract our attention is the question,—How did Life originate? On this point I may quote two leading men of science. Tyndall says: "I affirm that no shred of trustworthy experimental testimony exists, to prove that life in our day has ever appeared independently of antecedent life"; and Huxley says: "The doctrine of biogenesis, or life only from life, is victorious along the whole line at the present time." Such is the testimony of modern science to the old maxim "Omne vivum exvivo." "All life proceeds from antecedent life." Think it out for yourself and you will see that it could not possibly be otherwise.

Whatever may be our theory of the origin of life on the physical plane, whether we regard it as commencing in a vivified slime at the bottom of the sea, which we call protoplasm, or in any other way, the question of how life got there still remains unanswered. The protoplasm being material substance, must have its origin like all other material substances, in the undifferentiated etheric Universal Substance, no particle of which has any power of operating upon any other particle until some initial vibration starts the movement; so that, on any theory whatever, we are always brought back to the same question: What started the condensation of the ether into the beginnings of a world-system? So whether we consider the life which characterizes organized matter, or the energy which characterizes inorganic matter, we cannot avoid the conclusion, that both must have their source in some Original Power to which we can assign no antecedent. This is the conclusion which has been reached by all philosophic and religious systems that have really tried to get at the root of the matter, simply because it is impossible to form any other conception.

This Living Power is what we mean when we speak of the All-Originating Spirit. The existence of this Spirit is not a theological invention, but a logical and scientific ultimate, without predicating which, nothing else can be accounted for. The word "Spirit" comes from the Latin "spiro" "I breathe," and so means "The Breath," as in Job xxxiii, 4,—"The Spirit of God hath made me, and the breath of the Almighty hath given me life"; and again in Ps. xxxiii, 6—"By the word of the Lord were the heavens made, and all the host of them by the breath of his mouth."

In the opening chapter of Genesis, we are told that "the Spirit of God moved upon the face of the waters." The words rendered "the Spirit of God" are, in the original Hebrew "rouah Ælohim," which is literally "the Breathing of God"; and similarly, the ancient religious books of India, make the "Swára" or Great Breath the commencement of all life and energy. The word "rouah" in Genesis is remarkable. According to rabbinical teaching, each letter of the Hebrew alphabet has a certain symbolic significance, and when examined in this manner, the root from which this word is derived conveys the idea of Expansive Movement. It is the opposite of the word "hoshech," translated "darkness" in the same passage of our Bible, which is similarly derived from a root conveying the idea of Hardening and Compressing. It is the same idea that is personified in the Zendavesta, the sacred book of the ancient Persians, under the names of Ormuzd, the Spirit of Light; and Ahriman, the Spirit of Darkness; and similarly in the old Assyrian myth of the struggle between the Sun-God and Tiámat, the goddess of darkness.

This conception of conflict between two opposite principles, Light and Darkness, Compression and Expansion, will be found to underlie all the ancient religions of the world, and it is conspicuous throughout our own Scriptures. But it should be borne in mind that the oppositeness of their nature does not necessarily mean conflict. The two principles of Expansion and Contraction are not necessarily destructive; on the contrary they are necessary correlatives to one another. Expansion alone cannot produce form; cohesion must also be present. It is the regulated balance between them that results in Creation. In the old legend, if I remember rightly, the conflict is ended by Tiámat marrying her former opponent. They were never really enemies, but there was a misunderstanding between them, or rather there was a misunderstanding on the part of Tiámat so long as she did not perceive the true character of the Spirit of Light, and that their relation to one another was that of co-operation and not of opposition. Thus also St. John tells us that "the light shineth in darkness and the darkness comprehended it not" (John i, 5). It is this want of comprehension that is at the root of all the trouble.

The reader should note, however, that I am here speaking of that Primeval Substance, which necessarily has no light in itself, because there is as yet no vibration in it, for there can be no light without vibration. We must not make the mistake of supposing that Matter is evil in itself: it is our misconception of it that makes it the vehicle of evil; and we must distinguish between the darkness of Matter and moral darkness, though there is a spiritual correspondence between them. The true development of Man consists in the self-expansion of the Divine Spirit working through his mind, and thence upon his psychic and physical organisms, but this can only be by the individual's *willingness to receive* that Spirit. Where the hindrance to this working is only caused by ignorance of the true relation between ourselves and the Divine Spirit, and the desire for truth is present, the True Light will in due course disperse the darkness. But on the other hand, if the hindrance is caused by *unwillingness* to be led by the Divine Spirit, then the Light cannot be *forced* upon any one, and for this reason Jesus said: "This is the condemnation, that light is come into the World, and men loved darkness rather than light, because their deeds were evil. For every one that doeth evil hateth the light, neither cometh to the light, lest his deeds should be reproved. But he that doeth truth cometh to the light, that his deeds may be made manifest, that they are wrought in God" (John iii: 19-21). In physical science these things have an exact parallel in "Ohm's Law" regarding the resistance offered by the conductor to the flow of the electric current. The correspondence is very remarkable and will be found more fully explained in a later chapter. The Primary Darkness, both of Substance and of Mind, has to be taken into account, if we would form an intelligent conception of the twofold process of Involution and Evolution continually at work in ourselves, which, by their combined action, are able to lead to the limitless development both of the individual and of the race.

According to all teaching, then, both ancient and modern, all life and energy have their source in a Primary Life and Energy, of which we can only say that IT IS. We cannot conceive of any time when it was not, for, if there was a time when no such Primary Energizing Life existed, what was there to energize it? So we are landed in a *reductio ad absurdum* which leaves no alternative but to predicate the Eternal Existence of an All-Originating Living Spirit.

Let us stop for a moment to consider what we mean by "Eternal." When, do you suppose, twice two began to make four? And when, do you suppose, twice two will cease to make four? It is an eternal principle, quite independent of time or conditions. Similarly with the Originating Life. It is above time and above conditions—in a word it is *undifferentiated* and contains in itself the *potential* of infinite differentiation. This is what the Eternal Life is, and what we want for the expansion of our own life is a truer comprehension of it. We are like Tiámat, and must enter into intelligent and loving union with the Spirit of Light, in order to realize the infinite possibilities that lie before us. This is the ultimate meaning of the maxim "Omne vivum ex vivo."

We see, then, that the material universe, including our own bodies, has its origin in the undifferentiated Universal Substance, and that the first movement towards differentiation must be started by some initial impulse, analogous to those which start vibrations in the ether known to science; and that therefore this impulse must, in the first instance, proceed from some Living Power eternal in itself, and independent of time and conditions. Now all the ancient religions of the world concur, in attributing this initial impulse to the power of Sound; and we have seen, that as a matter of fact, sound has the power of starting vibrations, and that these vibrations have an exact correspondence with the quality of the sound, what we now call synchronous vibration.

At this point, however, we are met by another fact. Cosmic activity takes place only in certain definite areas. Solar systems do not jostle each other in space. In a word the Sound, which thus starts the initial impulse of creation, is guided by Intelligent Selection. Now sounds, directed by purposeful intention, amount to Words, whether the words of some spoken language or the tapping of the Morse code—it is the meaning at the back of the sound that gives it verbal significance. It is for this reason, that the concentration of creative energy in particular areas, has from time immemorial been attributed to "The Word." The old Sanskrit books call this selective concentrative power "Vach," which means "Voice," and is the root of the Latin word "Vox," having the same meaning. Philo, and the Neo-Platonists of Alexandria who follow him, call it "Logos," which means the same; and we are all familiar with the opening verses of St. John's Gospel and First Epistle in which he attributes Creation to "The Word."

Now we know, as a scientific fact, that solar systems have a definite beginning in the gyration of nebulous matter, circling through vast fields of interstellar space, as the great nebula in Andromeda does at the present day. Æons upon æons elapse, before the primary nebula consolidates into a solar system such as ours is now; but science shows, that from the time when the nebula first spreads its spiral across the heavens, the mathematical element of Law asserts itself, and it is by means of our recognition of the mathematical relations between the forces of attraction and repulsion, that we have been able to acquire any knowledge on the subject. I do not for an instant wish to suggest that the Spiritual Power has not continued to be in operation also, but a centre for the working of a Cosmic Law being once established, the Spiritual Power works through that Law and not in opposition to it. On the other hand, the selection of particular portions of space for the manifestation of cosmic activity, indicates the action of free volition, not determined by any law except the obvious consideration of allowing room for the future solar system to move in. Similarly also with regard to time. Spectroscopic analysis of the light from the stars, which are suns many of them much greater than our own, shows that they are of various ages—some quite young, some arrived at maturity, and some passing into old age. Their creation must therefore be assigned to different epochs, and we thus see the Originating Spirit exercising the powers of Selection and Volition as to the time when, as well as to the place where, a new world-system shall be inaugurated.

Now it is this power of inauguration that all the ancient systems of teaching attribute to the Divine Word. It is the passing of the undifferentiated into differentiation, of the unmanifested into manifestation, of the unlocalized into localization. It is the ushering in of what the Brahminical books call a "Manvantara" or world-period, and in like manner our Bible says that "In the beginning was the Word." The English word "word" is closely allied to the Latin word "verbum" which signifies both *word* and *verb*. Grammarians tell us that the verb "to be" is a verb-substantive, that is, it does not indicate any action passing from the subject to the object. Now this exactly describes the Spirit in its Eternity. We cannot conceive of It except as always *Being*; but the distribution of world-systems both in time and space shows that it is not always cosmically active. In itself, apart from manifestation, it is Pure Beingness, if I may coin such a word; and it is for this reason that the Divine Name announced to Moses was "I *am*." But the fact that Creation exists, shows that from this Substantive Pure Being there flows out a Verb Active, which reproduces in action, what the I *Am* is in essence. It is just the same with ourselves. We must first *be* before we can *do*, and we can *do* only to the extent to which we *are*. We cannot express powers which we do not possess; so that our doing necessarily coincides with the quality of our being. Therefore the Divine Verb reproduces the Divine Substantive by a natural sequence. It is *generated* by the Divine "I *am*," and for this reason it is called "The Son of God." So we see that The Verb, The Word, and The Son of God, are all different expressions for the same Power.

Creative vibration in the Universal Substance can, therefore, only be conceived of, as being inaugurated by the "Word" which *localizes* the activity of the Spirit in particular centres. This idea, of the localization of the Spirit through the "Word," should be fully realized as the energizing principle on the scale of the Macrocosm or "Great World," because, as we shall find later on, the same principle acts in the same way on the scale of the Microcosm or "Small World," which is the individual man. This is why these things have a personal interest for us, otherwise they would not be worth troubling about. But a mistake to be avoided at this point, is that of supposing that the "Word" is something which dictates to the Spirit when and where to operate. The "Word" is the word of the Spirit itself, and not that of some higher authority, for the Spirit being First Cause there can be nothing anterior to dictate to it; there can be nothing before that which is First. The "Word" which centralizes the activity of the Spirit, is therefore that of the Spirit itself. We have an analogy in our own case. If I go to New York the first movement in that direction is that of my Thought or Desire. It is true that in my present state of evolution I have to follow the usual methods of travel, but so far as my Thought is concerned, I have been there all the time. Indeed, such a case as the one I have mentioned, of my being seen in Edinburgh while I was physically in London, seems to point to the actual transference of some part of the personality to another locality, and similarly with my visit to Lanercost Abbey; and the reader must remember, that such phenomena are by no means uncommon—they are the natural action of some part of our personality, and must therefore follow some natural law, even though we may at present know very little of how it works.

We see, therefore, both from *a priori* reasoning, and from observed facts, that it is the Word, Thought, or Desire of the Spirit, that localizes its activity in some definite centre. The student should bear this in mind as a leading principle, for he will find that it is of general application, alike in the case of individuals, of groups of individuals, and of entire nations. It is the key to the relation between Law and Personality, the opening of the Grand Arcanum, the equilibrating of Jachin and Boaz, and it is therefore of immediate importance to ourselves.

We may take, then, as a starting-point for further enquiry, the maxim that Volition creates Centres of Spiritual Activity. But perhaps you will say: "If this be true, what word or words am I to employ?" This is a question which has puzzled a good many people before you. This "Word" which so many have been in search of, has been variously called "the Lost Word," "the Word of Power," "the Schemhammaphorasch or Secret Name of God," and so on. A quaint Jewish legend of the Middle Ages says that the "Hidden Name" was secretly inscribed in the innermost recesses of the Temple; but that, even if discovered, which was most unlikely, it could not be retained because, guarding it, were sculptured lions, which gave such a supernatural roar as the intruder was quitting the spot, that all memory of the "Hidden Name" was driven from his mind. Jesus, however, says the legend, knew this and dodged the lions. He transcribed the Name, and cutting open his thigh, hid the writing in the incision, which, by magical art, he at once closed up; then, after leaving the Temple, he took the writing out and so retained the knowledge of the Name. In this way the legend accounts for his power to work miracles.

Jesus, indeed, possessed the Word of Power, though not in the way told in the legend, and he repeatedly proclaimed it in his teaching:—"According to your Faith be it unto you"—"Verily, I say unto you, whosoever shall say to this mountain, 'Be thou taken up and cast into the sea'; and shall not doubt in his heart, but shall believe that what he saith shall come to pass, he shall have whatsoever he saith" (Mark xi, 23). And similarly in the Old Testament we are told that the Word is nigh to us, even in our hearts and in our mouth (Deut. xxx, 14). What keeps the Word of Power hidden, is our belief that nothing so simple could possibly be it.

At the same time, simple though it be, it has Law and Reason at the back of it, like everything else. The ancient Egyptians seem to have had clearer ideas on this subject than we have. "The name was to the Egyptians the *idea* of the thing, without which it could not exist, and the knowledge of which therefore gave power over that which answered to it." "The *idea* of the thing represented its *soul*."[2] This is the same conception as the "archetypal ideas" of Plato, only carried further, so as to apply, not only to classes, but to each individual of the class, and, as we shall see later, there is a good deal of truth in it. Put broadly, the conception is this—every external fact must have a spiritual origin, an internal energizing principle, which causes it to exist in the particular form in which it does. The outward fact is called the Phenomenon, and the corresponding inward principle is called the Noumenon. The dictionary definition of these two words is as follows: "Phenomenon—the appearance which anything makes to our consciousness as distinguished from what it is in itself." "Noumenon—an unknown and unknowable substance or thing as it is in itself—the opposite to the Phenomenon or form through which it becomes known to the senses or the understanding" (Chambers' Twentieth Century Dictionary). Whether the dictionary be right in saying that the "noumena" of things are entirely unknowable, the reader must decide for himself; but the present book is an attempt to learn something about the "noumena" of things in general, and of ourselves in particular, and what I want to convey is, that the "noumenon" of anything is its essence, *in terms of the Universal Energy and the Universal Substance, in their relation to the particular Form in question.* Probably the Latin word "Nomen," a Name, is derived from this Greek word, and in this sense everything has its "hidden name"; and the region in which Thought-Power works, is this region of spiritual beginnings. It deals with "hidden names"—that inward essence which determines the outward form of things, persons, and circumstances alike; and it is in order to make this clearer, that I have commenced by sketching briefly the general principles of Substance and Energy as now recognized by modern science.

If I have made my meaning clear, you will see that what is wanted is not the knowledge of particular words, but an understanding of general principles. At the same time I would not assert that the reciting of certain forms of words, such as the Indian "mantras" or the word *aum*, to which

Oriental teachers attach a mystic significance, is entirely without power. But the power is not in the words *but in our belief in their power.* I will give an amusing instance of this. On several occasions I have been consulted by persons who supposed themselves to be under the influence of "malicious magnetism," emanating in some cases from known, and in others from unknown, sources; and the remedy I have prescribed has been this. Look the adverse power, mentally, full in the face, and then assuming an attitude of confidence say "Cock-a-doodle-doo." The enquirers have sometimes smiled at first, but in every case the result has been successful. Perhaps this is why Æsculapius is represented as accompanied by a cock. Possibly the ancient physicians were in the habit of employing the "Cock-a-doodle-doo" treatment; and I might recommend it to the faculty to-day as very effective in certain cases. Now I do not think the reader will attribute any particularly occult significance to "Cock-a-doodle-doo." The power is in the mental attitude. To "cock-a-doodle-doo" at any suggestion is to treat it with scorn and derision, and to assume the very opposite of that receptive attitude which enables a suggestion to affect us. That is the secret of this method of treatment, and the principle is the same in all cases.

It matters, then, very little what particular words we use. What does matter is the intention and faith with which we use them. But perhaps some reader will here take the rôle of cross-examining counsel, and say: "You have just said it is a case of synchronous vibration—then surely it is the actual sound of the particular syllables that counts—how do you square this with your present statement?" The answer is that the Law is always the same, but the mode of response to the Law is always according to the nature of the medium in which it is operating. On the plane of physical matter the vibrations are in tune with physical sounds, as in the experiments with the eidophone; and similarly, on the plane of ideas or "noumena," the response is in terms of that plane. The word which creates "noumena," or spiritual centres of action, must itself belong to the world of "noumena," so that it is not illogical to say that it is the intention and faith that counts, and not the external sound. In this is the secret of the Power of Thought. It is the reproduction, on the miniature scale of the individual, of the same mode of Power that makes the worlds. It is that Power of Personality, which, combined with the action of the Law, brings out results which the Law alone could never do—as the old maxim has it, "Nature unaided fails."

This brings us to another important question—is not the creative power of the Word limited by the immutability of the Law? If the Law cannot be altered in the least particular, how can the Word be free to do what it likes? The answer to this is contained in another maxim: "Every creation carries its own mathematics along with it." You cannot create anything without at the same time creating its relation to everything else, just as in painting a landscape, the contour you give to the trees will determine that of the sky. Therefore, whenever you create anything, you thereby start a train of causation, which will work out in strict accordance with the sort of thought that started it. The stream always has the quality of its source. Thought which is in line with the Unity of the Great Whole, will produce correspondingly harmonious results, and Thought which is disruptive of the great Principle of

Unity, will produce correspondingly disputive results—hence all the trouble and confusion in the world. Our Thought is perfectly free, and we can use it either constructively or destructively as we choose; but the immutable Law of Sequence will not permit us to plant a thought of one kind, and make it bear fruit of another.

Then the question very naturally suggests itself: Why did not God create us so that we could not think negative or destructive thoughts? And the answer is: Because He could not. There are some things which even God cannot do. He cannot do anything that involves a contradiction in terms. Even God could not make twice two either more or less than four. Now I want the student to see clearly why making us incapable of wrong-thinking would involve a contradiction in terms, and would therefore be an impossibility. To see this we must realize what is our place in the Order of the Universe. The name "Man" itself indicates this. It comes from the Sanscrit root MN, which, in all its derivatives, conveys the idea of Measurement, as in the word Mind, through the Latin *mens*, the faculty which compares things and estimates them accordingly; Moon, the heavenly body whose phases afford the most obvious standard for the periodical measurement of time; Month, the period thus measured; "Man," the largest of the Indian weights; and so on. Man therefore means "The Measurer," and this very aptly describes our place in the order of evolution, for it indicates the relation between Personal Volition and Immutable Law.

If we grant the truth of the maxim "Nature unaided fails" the whole thing becomes clear, and the entire progress of applied science proves the truth of this maxim. To recur to an illustration I have employed in my previous books, the old ship-builders thought that ships were bound to be built of wood and not of iron, because wood floats in water and iron sinks; but now nearly all ships are made of iron. Yet the specific gravities of wood and iron have not altered, and a log of wood floats while a lump of iron sinks, just the same as they did in the days of Drake and Frobisher. The only difference is, that people thought out the *underlying principle* of the law of flotation, and reduced it to the generalized statement that anything will float, the weight of which is less than that of the mass displaced by it, whether it be an iron ship floating in water, or a balloon floating in air. So long as we restrict ourselves to the mere recollection of observed facts, we shall make no progress; but by carefully considering *why* any force acted in the way it did, under the particular conditions observed, we arrive at a generalization of principle, showing that the force in question is capable of hitherto unexpected applications if we provide the necessary conditions. This is the way in which all advances have been made on the material side, and on the principle of Continuity we may reasonably infer that the same applies to the spiritual side also.

We may generalize the whole position thus. When we first observe the working of the Law under the conditions spontaneously provided by Nature, it appears to limit us; but by seeking the *reason* of the action exhibited under these limited conditions, we discover the principle, and true nature, of the Law in question, and we then learn from the Law itself, what conditions to supply in order to give it more extended scope, and direct its energy to the accomplishment of definite purposes. The maxim we have to learn is that "Every Law *contains in itself* the principle of its own Expansion," which will set us free from the limitation which that Law at first appeared to impose upon us. The limitation was never in the Law, but in the conditions under which it was working, and our power of selection and volition enables us to provide new conditions, not spontaneously provided by Nature, and thus to *specialize* the Law, and disclose immense powers which had always been latent in it, but which would for ever remain hidden unless brought to light by the co-operation of the Personal Factor. The Law itself never changes, but we can *specialize* it by realizing the principle involved and providing the conditions thus indicated. This is our place in the Order of the Universe. We give definite direction to the action of the Law, and in this way our Personal Factor is always acting upon the law, whether we know it or not; and the Law, under the influence thus impressed upon it, is all the time re-acting upon us.

Now we cannot conceive any limit to Evolution. To suppose a point where it comes to an end is a contradiction in terms. It is to suppose that the Eternal Life Principle is used up, which is to deny its Eternity; and, as we have seen, unless we assume its Eternity, it is impossible to account either for our own existence or that of anything else. Therefore, to say that a point will ever be reached where it will be used up, is as absurd as saying that a point will be reached where the sequence of numbers will be used up. Evolution, the progress from lower to higher modes of manifestation of the underlying Principle of Life, is therefore eternal, but, in regard to the human race, this progress depends entirely on the extent to which we grasp the principles of the Law of our own Being, and so learn to specialize it in the right direction. Then if this be our place in the Universal Order, it becomes clear that we could not occupy this place unless we had a perfectly free hand to choose the conditions under which the Law is to operate; and therefore, in order to pass beyond the limits of the mineral, vegetable and animal kingdoms, and reach the status of being Persons, and not things, we must have a freedom of selection and volition, which makes it equally possible for us to select either rightly or wrongly; and the purpose of sound teaching is to make us see the eternal principles involved, and thus lead us to impress our Personality upon the Law, in the way that will bring out the infinite possibilities of good which the Law, rightly employed, contains. If it were possible to do this by an automatic Law, doubtless the Creative Wisdom would have made us so. This is why St. Paul says: "If there had been a law given which could have given life, verily righteousness should have been by the law" (Gal. iii, 21). Note the words "a law *given*," that is to say, imposed by external command; but it could not be. The laws of the Universe are Cosmic. In themselves they are *impersonal*, and the infinite possibilities contained in them, can only be brought out by the co-operation of the Personal Factor. It is only as we grasp the true relation between Jachin and Boaz, that we can enter into the Temple either of our own Individuality, or of the boundless Universe in which we live. The reason, therefore, why God did not make us mechanically incapable of wrong thinking, is simply because the very idea involves a contradiction in terms, which negatives all possibility of Creation. The conception lands us in a *reductio ad absurdum*.

Therefore, we are free to use our powers of Personality as we will, only we must take the consequences. Now one error we are all very apt to fall into, is the mistaken use of the Will. Its proper function is to keep our other faculties in line with the Law, and thus enable us to specialize it; but many people seem to think that by force of will they can somehow manage to coerce the Law; in other words, that by force of will they can sow a seed of one kind and make it bear fruit of another. The Spirit of Life seeks to express itself in our individuality, through the three avenues of reason, feeling, and will; but as in the Masonic legend of the murder of Hiram Abif, the architect of Solomon's Temple, it is beaten back on the side of reasoning, by the plummet of a logic based on false premises; on the side of feeling, by the level of conventional ideas; and on the side of will, by the hammer of a short-sighted self-will, which gives the finishing blow; and it is not until the true perception of the Principle of Life is resurrected within us, that the Temple can be completed according to the true plan.

It should be remembered that the will is *not* the Creative Faculty in us. It is the faculty of Conception that is the creative agent, and the business of the Will is to keep that faculty in the right direction, which will be determined by an enlightened Reason. Conception creates ideas which are the seed, that, in due time, will produce fruit after its own kind. In a broad sense we may call it the Imaging Faculty, only we must not suppose that this necessarily implies the visualizing of mental images, which is only a subsidiary mode of using this faculty. An "immaculate conception" is therefore the only means by which the New Liberated Man can be born in each of us. The sequence is always the same. The Will holds the Conception together, and the idea thus formed gives direction to the working of the Law. But this direction may be either true or inverted; and the impersonal Law will work constructively or destructively, according to the conception which it embodies. In this way, then, will-power may be used to hold together an inverted conception—the conception that our personal force of will is sufficient to bear down all opposition. But this mental attitude ignores the fact, that the fundamental principle of creative power is the Wholeness of the Creation; and that, therefore, the idea of forcing compliance with our wishes, by the power of our individual will, is an inverted conception, which, though it may appear to succeed for a time, is bound to fail eventually, because it antagonizes the very power it is seeking to use. This inverted use of the Will is the basis of "Black Magic," a term some readers will perhaps smile at, but which is practised at the present day to a much greater extent than many of us have any idea of—not always, indeed, with a full consciousness of its nature, but in many ways which are the first steps on the Left-hand Path. Its mark is the determination to act by Self-will, rather than using our will to co-operate with that continuous forward movement of the Great Whole, which is the Will of God. This inverted will entirely misses the point regarding the part we are formed to play in the Creative Order, and so we miss the development of our own individuality, and retrograde instead of going forward.

But if we work *with* the Law instead of against it, we shall find that our word, that is to say our conception, will become more and more the Word of Power, because it specializes the general Law in some particular direction.

The Law will serve us exactly to the extent to which we first observe the Law. It is the same in everything. If the electrician tries to go counter to the fundamental principle, that the electric current always flows from a higher to a lower potential, he will be able to do nothing with it; but let him observe this fundamental law and there is nothing that electricity will not do for him within the field of its own nature. In this sense, then, of specializing the general Law in a particular direction, we may lay down the maxim that "The Law flows from the Word, and not *vice versa*."

When we use our Word in this way, not as expressing a self-will that seeks to crush all that does not submit to it, but as a portion, however small, of the Universal Cause, and therefore with the desire of acting in harmony with that Cause, then our word becomes a constructive, instead of a destructive power. Its influence may be very small at first, because there is still a great mass of doubt at the back of our mind, and every doubt is, in reality, a Negative Word warring against our Affirmative Word; but, by adhering to our principle, we shall gradually gain experience in these things, and the creative value of our word will grow accordingly.

THE LAW OF WHOLENESS

It may seem a truism to say that the whole is made up of its parts, but all the same we often lose sight of this in our outlook on life.

The reason we do so is because we are apt to take too narrow a view of the whole; and also because we do not sufficiently consider that it is not the mere arithmetical sum of the parts that makes the whole, but also the harmonious agreement of each part with all the other parts. The extent of the whole and the harmony of the parts is what we have to look out for, and also its objective; this is a universal rule, whatever the whole in question may be.

Take, for instance, the case of the artist. He must start by having a definite objective, what in studio phrase is called a "motif"; something that has given him a certain impression which he wants to convey to others, but which cannot be stated as an isolated fact without any surroundings. Then the surroundings must be painted so as to have a natural relation to the main motif; they must lead up to it, but at the same time they must not compete with it. There must be only one definite interest in the picture, and minor details must not be allowed to interfere with it. They are there only because of the main motif, to help to express it. Yet they are not to be treated in a slovenly manner. As much as is seen of them must be drawn with an accuracy that correctly suggests their individual character; but they must not be accentuated in such a way as to emphasize details to the detriment of the breadth of the picture. This is the artistic principle of unity, and the same principle applies to everything else.

What, then, is the "Motif" of Life? Surely it must be, to express its own Livingness. Then in the True Order all modes of life and energy must converge towards this end, and it is only our short-sightedness that prevents us from seeing this,—from seeing that the greater the harmony of the whole Life, the greater will be the inflow of that Life in each of the parts that are giving it expression. This is what we want to learn with regard to ourselves, whether as individuals, classes or nations. We have seen the cosmic workings of the Law of Wholeness in the discovery of the planet Neptune. Another planet was absolutely necessary to complete the unity of our solar system, and it was found that there is such a planet, and similarly in other branches of natural science. The Law of Unity is the basic law of Life, and it is our ignorant or wilful infraction of this Law that is the root of all our troubles.

If we take this Law of Unity as the basis of our Thought we shall be surprised to find how far it will carry us. Each part is a complete whole in itself. Each inconceivably minute particle revolves round the centre of the atom in its own orbit. On its own scale it is complete in itself, and by co-operation with thousands of others forms the atom. The atom again is a complete whole, but it must combine with other atoms to form a molecule, and so on. But if the atom be imperfect as an atom, how could it combine with other atoms?

Thus we see that however infinitesimal any part may be as compared with the whole, it must also be a complete whole on its own scale, if the greater whole is to be built up. On the same principle, our recognition that our personality is an infinitesimal fraction of an inconceivably greater Life, does not mean that it is at all insignificant in itself, or that our individuality becomes submerged in an indistinguishable mass; on the contrary, our own wholeness is an essential factor towards the building up of the greater whole; so that as long as we keep before us the building up of the Great Whole as the "main motif," we need never fear the expansion of our own individuality. The more we expand, the more effective units we shall become.

We must not, however, suppose that Unity means Uniformity. St. Paul puts this very clearly when he says, if the whole body be an eye, where would be the hearing, etc. (1 Cor. xii, 14). How could you paint a picture without distinction of form, colour, or tone? Diversity in Unity is the necessity for any sort of expression, and if it be the case in our own bodies, as St. Paul points out, how much more so in the expressing of the Eternal Life through endless ages and limitless space! Once we grasp this idea of the unity and progressiveness of Life going on *ad infinitum*, what boundless vistas of possibility open before us. It would be enough to stagger the imagination were it not for our old friends, the Law and the Word. But these will always accompany us, and we may rely upon them in all worlds and under all conditions. This Law of Unity is what in natural science is known as the Law of Continuity, and the Ancient Wisdom has embodied it in the Hermetic axiom "Sicut superius, sicut inferius; sicut inferius, sicut superius"—As above, so below; as below, so above. It leads us on from stage to stage, unfolding as it goes; and to this unfolding there is no end, for it is the Eternal Life finding ever fuller expression, as it can find more and more suitable channels through which to express itself. It can no more come to an end than numbers can come to an end.

But it *must* find suitable channels. Let there be no mistake about this. Perhaps some one may say: Cannot it *make* suitable channels for any sort of expression that it needs? The answer is, that it can, and it does so up to a certain point. As we have seen, the Word, Thought, or Initial Impulse of the Ever-Living Spirit starts a centre of cosmic activity in which the mathematical element of Law at once asserts itself; thenceforward everything goes on according to certain broad principles of sequence. This is a Generic Creation, creation according to *genera* or classes, like the "archetypal ideas" of Plato. This creation is governed by a Law of Averages, and the legal maxim "De minimis non curat lex"—the Law cannot trouble about minorities—applies to it. This generic law keeps the class going, and slowly advancing, simply as a class, but it can take no notice of individuals as such. As Tennyson puts it in "In Memoriam," speaking of Nature:

"So careful of the type she seems,
So careless of the single life."

This mode of creation reaches its highest level, at any rate in our world, in Genus Homo, or the human race. We also, as a race, are under the Law of Averages. The race continues to exist, but from the moment of birth the individual life is liable to be cut short in a hundred different ways. In producing man, however, Generic Creation has produced a *type* having a mental and physical constitution capable of perceiving the underlying principle of *all* creation, that is, of seeing the relation between the Word and the Law. We cannot conceive creation by type going further than this. By the nature of this type every human being has the potential of a further evolution, which will set it free from bondage to an impersonal Law of Averages, by specializing it through the Power of the Word, that is, by bringing the Personal Factor to bear upon the Impersonal Factor, and so unfolding the possibilities which can be achieved by their united activities. We have the power of using the Word so as to specialize the action of the Law, not by altering the Law, which is impossible, but by realizing its principle, and enabling it to work under conditions which are not spontaneously provided by Nature, but are provided by our own selection. The *capacity* for this exists in all human beings, but the practical application of this capacity depends on our recognition of the principles involved; and it is for this reason that I commenced this book by citing instances of the combined working of Law and Personality in purely physical science. I wanted first to convince the reader from well ascertained facts, that the Law contains infinite possibilities, but that this can only be brought out through the operation of the mind of man.

It is here that we find the value of the maxim "Nature unaided fails." The more we consider this maxim and the principle of Unity and Continuity, the clearer it will become, that Limitation is no part of the Law itself, but results only from our own limited comprehension of it; and that St. James uses no meaningless phrase, but is stating a logical and scientific truth, when he speaks of "The perfect Law of Liberty" (Jas. i, 25). What we have to do is, to follow this up, not by petulant self-assertion, but by quietly considering the why and wherefore of the whole thing. In doing so we can fortify ourselves with another maxim, that "Principle is not limited by Precedent." When we spread the wings of thought and speculate as to future possibilities, our conventionally-minded friends may say we are talking bosh; but if you ask them why they say so, they can only reply that the past experience of the whole human race is against you. They do not speak like this in the matter of flying-machines or carriages that go without horses; they say these are scientific discoveries. But when it comes to the possibilities of our own souls, they at once set a limit to the expansion of ideas, and do not see that the scientific principle of discovery is not confined to laboratory experiments. Therefore, we must not let ourselves be discouraged by such arguments. If our friends doubt our sanity, let them doubt it. The sanity of such men as Galileo and George Stephenson was doubted by their contemporaries, so we are in good company. At the same time we must not neglect to look after our own sanity. We must know some intelligible reason for our conclusions, and realize that however unexpected, they are the logical carrying out of principles which we can recognize in the Creation around us. If we do this we need not fear to spread the wings of fancy, even though some may not be able to accompany us; only we must remember that we are using wings. Fancy, in the ordinary acceptation of the word, has really no wings; it is like a balloon that just floats wherever any passing current of air may drive it. The possession of wings implies power to direct our flight, and fancy must be converted into trained Imagination, just as the helpless balloon has been superseded by navigable air-craft. It must be "the scientific imagination"; and the "scientific imagination" carried into the world of spiritual causation becomes the Word of Power, and its Power is derived from the fact that it is always working according to Law. Then we may go on confidently, because we are following the same universal principles by which all creation has been evolved, only now we are specializing its action from the standpoint of our own individuality, according to the ancient teaching that Man, the Microcosm, repeats in himself all the laws of the Macrocosm, or great world, around him.

As we begin to see the truth of these things, we begin to transcend the simply generic stage. That first stage is necessary to provide a starting-point for the next. The first stage is that of Bondage to Law. It could not be otherwise for the simple reason that you must learn the law before you can use it. Then from the stage of Generic Creation we emerge into that of individual Creation, in which we attain liberty through Knowledge of the Law of our own Being; so that it is not a mere theological myth to talk of a New Creation, but it is the logical outcome of what we now are, if, to our recognition of the Power of the Law we add the recognition of the Power of the Word.

THE SOUL OF THE SUBJECT

We may now turn to speculate a little on some conceivable application of the general principle we have been considering. It seems to me that, as a result of the generic creation of which I have just spoken, there is in everything what, for want of a better name, I may call "The soul of the subject."

Creation being by type, everything must have a *generic* basis of being in the Cosmic Law, not peculiar to that individual thing, but peculiar to the class to which it belongs, an adaptation of the Cosmic Soul for the production of all things belonging to that particular order, in fact, what makes them what they are and not something else. Now just because this basis is generic and common to the whole genus that is built upon it, it is not specific, but it acquires *localization through Form*; the form being that of the class to which it belongs, thus producing the individual of that class, whether a cat or a cabbage. It is this underlying *generic* being of the thing, that I want the student to understand by "the soul of the subject." In fact we may call it the Noumenon or essential being of the class, as distinguished from the specific characteristics that differentiate the individual from others of the same class. It follows from this that this *generic* soul has no individuality of its own, and consequently is open to receive impressions from any source that can penetrate the sheath of outward form and specific characteristic that envelopes it. At the same time it is a manifestation of Cosmic Law, and so cannot depart from its own class-nature, and therefore any influence that may be impressed upon it from some other source will always show itself *in terms of the sort of generic soul that is thus impressed*; for instance, it would be impossible so to impress a dog as to make it write a book; and we may therefore generalize the statement, and lay down the rule, that "Every *im*press receives *ex*pression in terms of the medium through which it is expressed." This becomes almost a self-obvious truism when put into plain language like this; thus, if I paint a picture in oils, my impression is conveyed in terms of this medium, and if I paint one in water-colours my conception will be conveyed in terms of that medium, and the methods of handling will be perfectly different in the two pictures.

This applies all round; and if we keep this generalization in mind, it will render many things clear, especially in psychic matters, which would otherwise seem puzzling.

Now we ourselves are included in the general creation, and consequently we have in us a generic or *type basis* of personality, which is entirely impersonal. This is not a contradiction in terms, though it may look like one. We belong to the class Genus Homo, the distinctive quality of which is Personality, that is to say, the possession of certain faculties which constitute us persons, and not things or animals; but at the same time this merely generic personality is common to all mankind, and is not that which distinguishes one individual from another, and in this sense it is impersonal; so we may call it our Cosmic or Impersonal Personality.

Now it is upon this cosmic element, inherent in all things from mineral to man, that Thought-Power acts, because, being impersonal, it has no private purpose of its own with which to oppose the suggestion that is being impressed upon it. The only thing is, that according to the rule just laid down, the response will always be in terms of the cosmic element which we have thus set in motion. Therefore on the human plane it will always be in terms of Personality.

The whole thing comes to this, that we impart to this impersonal element the reflection of our own personality, and thereby create in it a certain personality of its own, which will express itself in terms of the inherent nature of the impersonal factor, which we have thus temporarily invested with a personal quality; we are continually doing this unconsciously, either for good or ill; but when we come to understand the law of it, we must try so to regulate the habitual current of our thoughts, that even when we are not using this power intentionally, they may only exercise a beneficial influence.

In our normal state this cosmic element in ourselves is so closely united with our more conscious powers of volition and reasoning, that they constitute a single unity; and this is how it should be, only, as we shall see later on, with a difference. But there are certain abnormal states which are worth considering, because they make clearer the existence in us of this impersonal self, which in academical language is called the subliminal consciousness. The work of the subliminal consciousness exhibits itself in various ways, such as clairvoyance, clair-audience, and conditions of trance; all of which either occur spontaneously, or are induced by experimental means, such as hypnotism; but the similarity of the phenomena in either case shows, that it is the same faculty that is in evidence.

In those hypnotic experiments in which the operator merely makes the subject do some external act, we get no further than the fact that the person's individual will has been temporarily put to sleep, and that of the hypnotist has taken its place; still even this shows a power of impressing upon the subliminal consciousness a personal quality of its own, but it does not enable it to exhibit its own powers. The object of such experiments is, to exhibit the powers of the hypnotist, not to investigate the powers of the subliminal personality, which is of more importance in the present connection. But where the hypnotist employs his power of command to tell the subliminal self of the patient to exercise its own powers, merely directing it as to the subject upon which it is to be exercised, very wonderful powers indeed are exhibited. Places unknown to the percipient are accurately described; correct accounts are given of what people are doing elsewhere; the contents of sealed letters are read; the symptoms of disease are diagnosed and suitable remedies sometimes prescribed; and so on. Distance appears to make no difference. In many cases time also does not count, and historical events of long ago, with the details of which the seer had no acquaintance, are accurately described in all their minutiæ, which have afterwards been corroborated by contemporary documents. Nor are cases wanting in which events still future have been correctly predicted, as, for example, in Cazotte's celebrated prediction of the

French Revolution, and of the fate that awaited each member of a large dinner-party when it should occur—though this was a spontaneous case, and not under hypnotism, which perhaps gives it the greater value.

The same powers are shown in spontaneous cases also, of which my own experiences related in a previous chapter may serve as a small example; but as there are many books exclusively devoted to the subject I need not go into further details here. If the reader be curious for further information, I would recommend him to read Gregory's "Letters on Animal Magnetism." It was published some fifty years ago, and, for all I know, may be out of print, but if the reader can procure it, he will find that it is a book to be relied upon, the work of a Professor of Chemistry in the University of Edinburgh, who investigated the matter calmly with a thoroughly trained scientific mind. But what I want the reader to lay hold of is the fact, that whether the action occur spontaneously or be induced by experimental means, these powers actually exist in us, and therefore in reckoning up the faculties at our disposal they must not be omitted.

In our more usual condition however, these faculties are subordinate to those which put us in touch with the every-day world, and I cannot help thinking, that at our present stage this is the best place for them. In this place they have a special function to perform, which I will speak of in another chapter, and in the meanwhile for my own part I should prefer to leave their development to the ordinary course of Nature, neither stimulating them by hypnotic influence, or auto-suggestion, nor repressing them if they manifest themselves of their own accord. However, every one must follow his or her own discretion in this matter; the only thing is, do not deny the existence of these faculties in yourself because you may not consciously exercise them, for they hold a very important place in our complex personality.

All such evidence on the subject as has come my way, appears to me to point to the fact, that it is through this impersonal or cosmic portion of our mind that Thought-Power operates upon us, whether in the form of telepathy, or of healing treatment, or in any other way; and it is through this channel also that thought currents, not specially directed towards ourselves, nevertheless affect us, just as the first wireless telephone message sent on September 29, 1915, from the office of the American Telephone Company in New York, and directed to San Francisco, was simultaneously heard at San Diego, at Darien in Panama, and even as far away as Pearl Island, Honolulu, in the Pacific Ocean.

We sometimes pick up messages which are not intended for us; so we must keep our receiver in perfect syntony of reciprocal vibration with the stations from which we require to receive messages, to the exclusion of others which would produce confusion.

But I have strayed a little from our present point, which is rather that of giving out influence than of receiving it. Through the instrumentality of this impersonal cosmic soul we can send out our Thought for the healing of disease, for the suggestion of good and happy ideas, and for many other beneficial purposes; though the extent of the result will of course be considerably influenced by the mental attitude of the recipient, which is therefore a factor to be reckoned with.

But this power of sending out a subtle influence, call it magnetism or what you will, is not confined to operations upon the human subject. Two ladies of my acquaintance experimented on two rose-trees, which, to all appearances, were both in equally good condition. They daily blessed one and cursed the other, with the result that at the end of a month the anathematized plant had withered up from the roots, while the other was in an abnormally flourishing condition. Nor are we entirely without scientific backing even in such a case as this; for Professor Bose tells us in his work on the "Response of Metals," that not only can they be poisoned by certain chemicals, so as to deprive them of their normal qualities, but that they can be mesmerized into a similar condition. Such facts as these therefore give considerable support to the theory of the existence in everything of a "soul of the subject," which responds after its own manner to the power of human thought.

In what manner, then, is this influence conveyed? It is here that our study of etheric waves comes to our assistance, by carrying the same principle further, and picturing the working of the known Law under unknown conditions. It will at least enable us to form a working hypothesis. I have stated that our actual commercial application of the etheric waves extends from the ultra-violet waves used in photography, and measuring only 1/254,000 of an inch, to those measuring many miles employed in wireless telegraphy; but this practical application by no means exhausts the conceivable possibilities of etheric vibrations; for not only do we find a gap of five octaves of as yet unknown waves between the dark heat group and the Hertzian group, but mathematically there is no limit to the greatness or smallness of the waves, and the scale may be prolonged indefinitely in either direction. Nor is this to be wondered at; for if we consider that vibration is not a progress of individual particles from one place to another, but the alternate rising and falling of the substance at the same point, and that the ether is a homogeneous and universally present substance, it is obvious that there is nothing to limit the minuteness or the greatness of the intervals at which the rising and falling will occur. Therefore we have an unlimited field for our imagination to play about in. Then, if we further reflect that all forms are built up of denser or finer aggregations of ether, and that what determines the generic form of anything is its cosmic soul, or the generating principle of the *class* to which it belongs, it follows that this soul must have a corresponding form, however inconceivably fine may be the etheric condensation which thus differentiates it from other souls, and prevents it from all being mixed up together in an indistinguishable mass. If now, we combine these two facts, that the soul of anything must have a form, however fine, and that there is no limit either to the greatness or the minuteness of etheric vibrations, we can draw certain deductions from these premises.

It is an established fact of ordinary science that, however closely particles of any substance may seem to cohere, they are in reality separated by interstices through which etheric waves can penetrate.

The principle may be illustrated by the power of the X-rays to penetrate apparently solid bodies, such as iron. Then, if we combine with this the fact, that there is no limit to the minuteness of etheric waves, we see that however fine may be the particles constituting any form, it is always possible to have etheric waves still finer and thus able to penetrate that form and set up vibrations in it. It is our familiarity with the denser modes of matter that makes it difficult for us to grasp the idea of these finer activities; but there is nothing in what we know of the denser modes to contradict the conception; on the contrary, it is just by what we have learned of these denser modes that we reach the principles on which these further conceptions are founded. Looking at this, therefore, in the light of a mathematical proposition, there is absolutely no limit to the fineness of any form, or to its susceptibilities to etheric vibrations.

Finally, to this add the power of the Word to start trains of etheric vibration, and you get the following series: The Word starts the etheric waves; these waves produce corresponding vibration in the soul of the subject; and the soul of the subject in turn communicates corresponding vibration to its body. We may thus explain the Creative Power of Thought on the basis of recognizable Law, and so we believe, because we know *why* we believe, not because somebody else has told us so. Doubt is still the creative action of Thought, only it is creating negatively; so it is helpful to feel that we have some reason for confidence in the Power of the Word. There are a great many "Thomases" among us, and as one of the number I shall be glad if I can help my "Brother Tommies" to get a grip of the why and wherefore of the things which appear at first sight so fantastic and improbable.

But the conception we are considering is not limited to concrete entities, whether persons or things. It applies to abstractions also, and it is for this reason that I have called it the "Soul of the Subject." We often speak of the "Soul of Music," or the "Soul of Poetry," and so on. Thus our ordinary talk stands on the threshold of a great mystery, which, however, is simple enough in practice. If you want to get a clearer view of any subject than you have at present, address yourself mentally to the abstract soul of that subject, and ask it to tell you about itself, and you will find that it will do so. I do not say that it will do this in any miraculous manner, but what you already know of the subject will range itself into a clearer order, and you will see connections that have not previously occurred to you. Then again, you will find that information of the class required will begin to flow towards you through quite ordinary channels, books, newspapers, or conversation, without your especially laying yourself out to hunt for it; and again, at other times, ideas will come into your mind, you do not know how, but illuminating the subject with a fresh light. I cannot explain how all this takes place. I can only say from personal experience that it happens. But of course we must not throw aside ordinary common-sense. We must sort out the information that comes to us, and compare it with our previous knowledge; in fact we must *work* at it: there is no premium for laziness. Nor must we expect to receive by a sudden afflatus a complete acquaintance with some subject of which we are entirely ignorant. I do not say that such a thing is altogether impossible, for I cannot venture to limit the possibilities of the Universe; but it is certainly not to be looked for in the ordinary course. I have sometimes been shown specimens of "inspirational painting" done by persons said to be entirely ignorant of art, and the ignorance is very apparent on the face of the work. I dare say an artist may be inspired in the production of a picture, but the technical training comes first, and the inspiration afterwards. The same I believe to be true of all other subjects, so that we come back to the maxim of the power always expressing itself in terms of the instrument through which it works. With this reservation, however, it appears to me, that every class of subject has a sort of soul of its own with which we can put ourselves *en rapport* by, so to say, mentally unifying our own personality with its abstract principle.

We are told by some teachers, that we can in the same way even construct entities in the nature of our Thought, and possessing a personality of their own with which we have endowed them. Whether this be the case I cannot say—I do not know all the secrets of the invisible. But if our thoughts do not create personal entities able to hang "on their own hook," they create forces which come to much the same thing. They start waves in the Universal etheric medium, which, like the electro-magnetic waves of telegraphy, spread all round from the point of initial impulse, and are picked up whenever a centre happens to be attuned to a similar rate of vibration, and each new centre energizes these vibrations again with a fresh impulse of its own; so in this way thought-currents become very real things.

Such, then, is the power of our Word, whether spoken or only dwelt upon in Thought, to impress itself upon the impersonal element around us, whether in persons or things. We cannot divest it of the power, though we may intensify its action by deliberate use of it, with knowledge of the principle involved, and therefore, whether consciously or unconsciously, we are sending out the influence of our personality all the time.

Now the more we know of these things the greater becomes our responsibility, and I would therefore solemnly warn the reader against any attempt to use the powers now indicated to the injury of any other person, or for the purpose of depriving any one else of that liberty of action which he would wish to enjoy himself. Such use of our mental powers is in direct opposition to the Law of Unity which I have spoken of; and since that Law is the basic principle of the whole Universe, any opposition to it places us in antagonism with a force immeasurably greater than ourselves.

Our Thought always continues to be creative; but in destructive use it becomes creative for destructive forces, and, since it has its origin in our own personality, we are certain sooner or later to feel its effects, on the principle that every action always produces a corresponding reaction. As we have seen, the Law knows nothing of persons, but acts automatically in strict accord with the nature of the power which has set it in motion. Under negative conditions the great Law of the Universe becomes your adversary, and must continue to be so, until by your altered mode of Thought you put yourself in line with it.

But on the other hand, if our intention be to co-operate with the Great Law, we shall find that in it also exists a mysterious "Soul of the Subject," which will respond to us, however imperfectly we may understand its *modus operandi*. It is the intention that counts, not the theoretical knowledge. The knowledge will grow by experience and meditation, and its value is measured entirely by the intention that is at the back of it.

THE PROMISES

We have now, I hope, laid a sufficiently broad foundation of the relation between the Law and the Word. The Law cannot be changed, and the Word can. We have two factors, one variable, and the other invariable; so that from this combination any variety of resultants may be expected. The Law cannot be altered, but it can be specialized, just as iron can be made to float by the same law by which it sinks. Now let us try to figure out in our imagination an ideal of the sort of results we should want to bring out from these two factors.

In the first place I think we should like to be free from all worry and anxiety; for a life of continual worry is not worth living. And in the second we should like always to have something to look forward to and feel an interest in; for a life entirely devoid of all interest is also not worth living. But, granted that these two conditions be fulfilled, I think we should all be well pleased to go on living *ad infinitum*. Now can we conceive any combination of the Law and the Word which would produce such results? that is the question before us. The first step is to generalize our principle as widely as possible, for the wider the generalization, the larger becomes the scope for specialization. The invariable factor we already know. It is the Law, always creating in accordance with the Word that sets it in motion, whether constructive or destructive; so what we really have to consider is the sort of Word (i.e. Thought or Desire) which will set the Law working in the right direction. It must be a Word of confidence in its own power; otherwise by the hypothesis of the case it would be giving contradictory directions to the Law, or to borrow a simile from what we have learnt about waves in ether, it would be sending out vibrations that would cancel one another and so produce no effect. Then it must be a Word that does not compromise itself by antagonizing the Law of unity, and so producing disruptive forces instead of constructive ones. And finally, we must be quite sure that it really is the right Word, and that we have been making no mistake about it. If these conditions be fulfilled the logical result will be entire freedom from anxiety. Similarly with regard to maintaining a continued interest in life. We must have a continued succession of ideals, whether great or small, that will carry us on with something always just ahead of us; and we must work the ideals out, and not let them evaporate in dreams. If these conditions be fulfilled we have before us a life of never-ending interest and activity, and therefore a life worth living. Where then are we to find the Word which will produce these conditions: perfect freedom from anxiety and continual, happy interest? I do not think it is to be found in any way but by identifying our own Word with the Word which brings all creation into existence, and keeps it always moving onward in that continuous forward movement which we call Evolution. We must come back to the old teaching, that the Macrocosm is reproduced in the Microcosm, with the further perception that this identity of principle can only be produced by identity of cause. Law cannot be other than eternal and self-demonstrating, just as 2 × 2 must eternally = 4; but it remains only an abstract conception until the Creative Word affords it a field of operation, just as twice two is four remains only a mathematical abstraction until there is something for you to count; and accordingly, as we have already seen, all our reasoning concerning the origin of Creation, whether based on metaphysical or scientific grounds, brings us to the conception of a Universal and Eternal Living Spirit localizing itself in particular areas of cosmic activity by the power of the Word. Then, if a similar Creative Power is to be reproduced in ourselves, it must be by the same method: the localizing of the same Spirit in ourselves by the power of the same "Word." Then our Word, or Thought, will no longer be that of separate personality, but that of the Eternal Spirit finding a fresh centre from which to specialize the working of the Law, and so produce still further results than that of the First or simply Cosmic and Generic Creation, according to the two maxims that "Nature unaided fails," and that "Principle is not limited by Precedent."

I want to make this sequence clear to the student before proceeding further:

1. Localization of the Spirit in specific areas of Creative Activity.

2. Cosmic or Generic Creation, including ourselves as a race resulting from this, and providing both the material and the instruments for carrying the work further by *specializing the Original Creative Power* through individual Thought, just as in all cases of scientific discovery.

3. Then, since what is to be specialized through our individual Thought is the Word of the Originating Power itself, in order to do this we must think in terms of the Originating Word, on the general principle, that any power must always exhibit itself in terms of the instrument through which it works.

This, it appears to me, is a clear logical sequence, just as a tree cannot make itself into a box, unless there be first the idea of a box which does not exist in the tree itself, and also the tools with which to fashion the wood into a box; while on the other hand there could never be any box unless there be first a tree. Now it is just such a sequence as this that is set before us in the Bible, and I do not find it adequately set forth in any other teaching, either philosophical or religious, with which I am acquainted. Some of these systems contain a great deal of truth, and are therefore helpful as far as they go; but they do not go the whole way, and for the most part stop short at the first or simply Cosmic Creation; or, if they attempt to pass beyond this, it is on the line of making unaided power of the individual the sole means by which to do so, and thus in fact always keeping us at the merely generic level. Such a mode of Thought as this, fails to meet the requirements of our conception of a happy life as one entirely exempt from fear and anxiety. In like manner also it fails to meet the first requirements of the whole series, viz.: the Word should be certain of itself; and if it be not certain of itself we have no assurance that it may not eventually disappoint our hopes. In short, this mode of thought leaves us to bear the whole burden from which we want to escape. So it is not good enough; we must look for something better.

Now this something better I find in the *Promises* contained in the Bible, and it is this that to my mind distinguishes our own Scriptures from the sacred books of all other nations, and from all systems of philosophy. I do not at all ignore the current objections to the possibility of Divine Promises, but I think that on examination they will be found to be superficial and resulting from want of careful enquiry into the true nature of the Promises themselves. How is it possible for the Laws of the Universe to make exceptions? How can God act by individual favouritism unless it be either through sheer caprice, or by the individual managing to get round Him in some way, either by supplying some need which He cannot supply for Himself, in which case God is of limited power, or else by flattering Him, in which case He is the apotheosis of absurd vanity. The two are really the same question put in different ways—the question of individual exceptions to the general Law.

The answer is that there are no individual exceptions to the general Law; but there are very various degrees of realization of the Principle of the Law, and the more a man works with the Principle the more the Law will work for him; so that the finer his perception of the Principle becomes, the more he will appear to be an exception to the Law as commonly recognized.

Edison and Marconi are not capriciously favoured by the laws of Nature, but they know more about them than most of us.

Now it is just the same with the Bible Promises. They are Promises according to Law. They are based upon the widest generalization and hence lead to the highest specialization through the combined action of the Law and the Word—Jachin and Boaz, the Two Pillars of the Universe.

These Promises comprise all sorts of desirable things: health of body, peace of mind, earthly prosperity, prolongation of life, and, finally, even the conquest of death itself; but always on one condition: perfect "Confidence in the power of the All-Originating Spirit in response to our reliance on the Word." This is what the Bible calls Faith; and it is perfectly logical when we understand the principle of it, for every Thought of doubt is, in effect, the utterance of a Word which produces negative results by the very same law by which the Word of Faith produces positive ones. This is the only condition which the Bible imposes for the fulfilment of its Promises, and this is because it is inherent in the nature of the Law by which their fulfilment is to be brought about.

A few texts will suffice as examples of the Bible Promises, and no doubt most of my readers are familiar with many others; but it would be worth while to read the Bible through, marking all such texts, and classifying them according to the sort of promises they contain.

Read, for instance, Job xxii, 21, etc. This is a most remarkable passage containing among other things the promise of earthly wealth; or again Job v, 19, etc., where we find promises of protection in time of danger, power over material nature, and prolonged life. While in Job xxxiii, 23, etc., there is promise of return to youth, a promise which is repeated in Psalm ciii, 5. Again in Isaiah lxi, 20, etc., there is the promise of immensely extended physical life, death at the age of one hundred being counted so premature as to resemble that of an infant, and the normal standard of age being compared to a tree which lives for centuries; and the same passage also promises immediate answer to prayers. The Psalms are full of such promises, and they are scattered throughout the Bible.

Now there is an unfortunate tendency among people who read their Bible with reverence, to what they call "spiritualize" such passages as these, which means that they do not believe them. They say such things are impossible; and therefore they must have some other meaning, and accordingly they interpret the words metaphorically, as referring to something to be experienced in another life, but quite impossible in this one.

Of course there are spiritual equivalents to these things, and the teaching of the Bible is, that they are the outward correspondences of inward spiritual states; but to "spiritualize" them in the way I am speaking of, is nothing but unbelief in the power of God to work on the plane of Nature. How such readers square their opinion with the fact that God has created Nature, I do not know. Even in the animal world we find wonderful instances of longevity. If an elephant be not overworked before he is twenty, he is in full working power up to eighty, and will then be capable of light work for another twenty years, after which he may yet enjoy another twenty years of quiet old age as the reward of his labours, while crocodiles and tortoises have been known to live for centuries. If then such things be possible in the ordinary course of Nature in the animal world, why need we doubt the specializing power of the Word to produce far greater results in the case of man? It is because we will not accept the maxim, that "Principle is not limited by Precedent" in regard to ourselves, though we see it demonstrated by every new scientific discovery. We rely more on the past experience of the race, than on the Creative Power of God. We call Him Almighty, and then say that in His Book He promises things which He is not able to perform. But the fault is with ourselves. We limit "the Holy *One* of Israel," and as a consequence get only so much as by our mental attitude we are able to receive—again the old maxim that "Power can only work in terms of the instrument it works through." I do not say that it is at all easy for us to completely rid ourselves of negative race-thought ingrained into us from childhood, and subtly playing upon that generic impersonal self in us of which I have spoken, and which readily responds to those thought-currents to which we are habitually attuned. It is a matter of individual growth. But the promises themselves contain no inherent impossibility, and are logical deductions from the principles of the Creative Law.

If the power of the Spirit over things of the material plane be an impossibility, then by what power did Jesus perform his miracles? Either you must deny his miracles, or you must admit the power of the Spirit to work on the material plane—there is no way out of the dilemma. Perhaps you may say: "Oh, but He was God in person!" Well, all the promises affirm that it is God who does these things; so what it is possible for God to do at one time, it is equally possible for Him to do at all times. Or perhaps you hold other theological views, and will say that Jesus was an exception to the rest of the race; but, on the contrary, the whole Bible sets Him forth as the Example—an exception certainly to men as we now know them, but the Example of what we all have it in us to become—otherwise what use is He to us? But apart from all argument on the subject we have his own words, telling us that those who believe in Him, i.e., believe what He said about Himself—shall be able to do works as great as His own, and even greater (John xiv, 12). For these reasons it appears to me that on the authority of the Bible itself, and also on metaphysical and scientific grounds we are justified in taking such promises as those I have quoted in a perfectly literal sense.

Then there are promises of the power that will attend our utterance of the Word. "Thou shalt also decree a thing and it shall be established unto thee" (Job xxii, 28). "All things are possible unto you" (Mark ix, 23). "Whosoever ... shall believe that what he sayeth cometh to pass, he shall have whatsover he sayeth" (Mark xi, 23), and so on.

Other passages again promise peace of mind. "Thou wilt keep him in perfect peace whose mind is staid on Thee, because he trusteth in Thee" (Isaiah xxvi, 3). "Let him take hold of my strength that he may make peace with me" (Isaiah xxvii, 5). St. Paul speaks of "The God of Peace" in many passages, e.g., Rom. xv, 33; 2 Cor. xiii, 11; 1 Thess. v, 23, and Hebr. xiii, 20; and Jesus, in his final discourse recorded in the fourteenth, fifteenth and sixteenth chapters of St. John's Gospel, lays peculiar stress on the gift of Peace.

And lastly there are many passages which promise the overcoming of death itself; as for instance Job xix, 25-27; John viii, 51, and x, 28, and xi, 25 and 26; Hebr. ii, 14 and 15; 1 Cor. xv, 50-57; 2 Tim. i, 10; Rom. vi, 23 ("The gift of God is eternal life in Jesus Christ, our Lord").

"God commanded the blessing, even Life for evermore" (Ps. cxxxiii, 3).

Now I hope the reader will take the trouble to look up the texts to which I have referred, and not be lazy. I am sure he would do so if he were promised a ten pound note or a fifty dollar bill for his pains, and if these promises are not all bosh, there is something worth a good deal more to be got by studying them. Just run through the list: health, wealth, peace of mind, safety, creative power, and eternal life. You would be willing to pay a good premium to an Insurance Office that could guarantee you all these. Well, there is a Company that does this without paying any premium, and its name is "God and Co., Unlimited"; the only condition, is that you yourself have to take the part of "Co." and it is not a sleeping partnership, but a wide-awake one!

So I hope you will take the trouble to look up the texts; but at the same time you must remember that the reading of single texts is not sufficient. If you take any isolated phrase you choose, without reference to the rest of the Book, there is no nonsense you cannot make out of the Bible. You would not be allowed to do that sort of thing in a Court of Law. When a document is produced in evidence, the meaning of the words used in it are very carefully construed, not only in reference to the particular clause in which they occur, but also with reference to the intention of the document as a whole, and to the circumstances under which they were written. The same word may mean very different things in different connections; for instance I remember two reported cases in one of which the word "Spanish" meant a certain sort of leather, and in the other a kind of material used in brewing; and in like manner particular texts are to be interpreted in accordance with the gist of the Bible as a whole.

This is just the mistake the Jews made, of building up theories on particular texts, and which Jesus corrected when he said: "Search the Scriptures, for in them ye think ye have eternal life, and these are they which testify of me" (John v, 39), or, as the Revised Version puts it: "Ye search the

Scriptures because ye think that in them ye have eternal life; and these are they which bear witness of me," which appears to be the better rendering. The words "ye think" is the key to the whole passage. He says in effect: "You fancy that eternal life is to be found in the book. It is not to be found in the book, but in what the book tells you about, and here I am as a living example of it." It is just the same with everything else. No book can do more than tell you about a thing; it cannot produce it. You may study the cookery book from morning till night, but that will not give you your dinner.

What Jesus meant was, that we should read the Scriptures in the same way we should read any other book of practical instruction. First think what it is all about; then look at the nature of the general principles involved, and then see what instruction the book gives you for their practical application. *Then go and do it*. And remember also a further difference between reading about a thing and doing it. A book is for everybody, and can therefore, only give general instruction; but when you come to do the thing you will always find it works with some personal modifications,—not departures from the general principles you have read about, but specializations of them—and in this way you will learn much that is not to be got out of books, even the best.

I remember many years ago, when I was much younger, asking one of our leading water-colour artists,[3] how he would recommend me to study landscape painting, and he said: "Practise continually from Nature, and you will learn more than any one can teach you; that is how I have learnt, myself." On the subject, then in question, he said just what Jesus did: "Here I am as a practical example of what I tell you." And another thing is, that the more you think principles out for yourself and try to observe them in practice, the clearer the meaning of your book will become to you. I have a few excellent books on painting, but I had no idea how excellent they were when I first got them; practical experience has taught me to find much more in them than I did at first, for now I understand better what they are talking about. Well, that is the way to read the Bible, neither despising it as worthless tradition, nor treating the mere letter of it with superstitious veneration; both extremes are to be equally avoided. In fact the Bible tells us so itself: "The letter killeth, but the Spirit giveth life" (2 Cor. iii, 6); this, of course, does not mean that the letter can be tampered with, any more than a judge can alter the wording of a document put in evidence; it must be interpreted in the general sense of the document as a whole; and when the letter is thus vivified by the Spirit, it will be found fully to express it. But we require to enter into the Spirit of it first.

Now it appears to me, that taken in this way, the Bible is an exceedingly practical book, and that is why I want the reader to get at some general principles which he will find, *mutatis mutandis*, equally applicable all round, whether to electricity, or to life, and whatever may be the subject-matter, it will always be found to resolve itself into a question of the relation between Law and Personality. If now we read the Bible Promises in the light of the general principles we have considered in the earlier pages, we shall find that they are all Promises according to Law. They are statements of the results to be obtained by a truer realization of the principles of Law and Personality than we have hitherto apprehended.

We must always bear in mind that the Law is set in motion by the Word. The Word does not *make* the Law, but gives it something to work upon, so that without the Word there could be no manifestation of the Law, a truth embodied in the maxim, that "Every Creation carries its own mathematics along with it." If the reader remembers what I have said in the chapter of "The Soul of the Subject," he will see that the principle involved, is that of the susceptibility of the Impersonal to suggestions from the Personal. This follows of course from the very Conception of Impersonality; it is that which has no power of selection and volition, and which is therefore without any power of taking an initiative on its own account.

In a previous chapter I have pointed out that the only possible conception of the inauguration of a world-system, resolves itself into the recognition of one original and universal Substantive Life, out of which proceeds a corresponding Verb, or active energy, reproducing in action what the Substantive is in essence. On the other hand there must be something for this active principle to work in; and since there can be nothing anterior to the Universal Life or Energy, both these factors must be potentially contained in it. If, then, we represent this Eternal Substantive Life by a circle with a dot in the centre, we may represent these two principles as emerging from it by placing two circles at equal distance below it, one on either side, and placing the sign "+" (plus) in one, and the sign "-" (minus) in the other. This is how students of these subjects usually map out the relation of the *prima principia*, or first abstract principles. The sign "+" (plus) indicates the Active principle, and the sign "-" (minus) the Passive principle. If the reader will draw a little diagram as described, it will help to make what follows clearer.

Necessarily the initiative must be taken by the Active principle; and the taking of initiative implies selection and volition, that is to say, the essential qualities of personality; and Passivity implies the converse of all this, and therefore is Impersonality. The two principles in no way conflict with one another, but are polar opposites, like the positive and negative plates of a battery, or the two ends of a magnet. They are complementary to one another, and neither can work without the other. A little consideration will show that this is not a mere fancy, but a self-obvious generalization, the contrary to which it is impossible to conceive. It is simply the case of the box which cannot come into existence without the activity of the carpenter and the passivity of the wood.

From such considerations as this the deep thinkers of old times posited the generating of a world-system by the interaction of what they named Animus Dei, the Active principle, and Anima Mundi, or Soul of the Universe, the Passive principle—the one Personal, and the other Impersonal; and by the hypothesis of the case the only mode of activity possible to Anima Mundi is response to Animus Dei. But the same impersonal passivity must also make Anima Mundi receptive likewise to lesser and more individualized modes of Personality, and it becomes, so to say, fecundated by the ideas thus impressed upon it. In every case "the word is the seed." We may picture this planting of an idea or "word" in the Cosmic soul as acting very much like the initial impulse that starts a train of waves in ether, and these thought-waves are reproduced in corresponding forms; or, to recur to the simile of seed, the cosmic soul acts like the soil and gives it nourishment. Looking at it in this way the old exponents of these things regarded the Active principle as Masculine, and the Passive as Feminine, the one generating and the other nutritive, corresponding to the words *rouah* and *hoshech*, the expansion and compression principles in the Hebrew text of the opening verses of Genesis.

If then we posit this impersonal Soul of the Universe as the living principle dwelling in the substance of the etheric Universal Medium it will account for a good many things. If it be asked why we should assume the presence of a living principle in the Universal Substance the answer is in the maxim "Quod ex Vivo Vivum," what proceeds from Life is living. Then as we see by our diagram, Anima Mundi equally with Animus Dei proceeds from the original Substantive of Life, and therefore, on the principle of the above maxim, that like produces like, Anima Mundi must also be a living thing whose vehicle is the Universal Substance.

We may picture then, the response of the indwelling Soul of the Universal Medium to our Thought, as starting corresponding vibrations in the Substance of the Medium, just as our own thought, acting through the vibratory system of our nerves, causes our body to make the movement we intend. But perhaps you will say: How can this be, seeing that by the hypothesis the Soul of the Universe is Impersonal, and therefore unintelligent? Well, it is just this fact of having no thought of its own, that enables us to impress our thought upon it and cause it, so to say, to "take on" an intelligence relatively to the subject of our thought, much in the same way that the impersonal soul in the human subject "takes on" or reflects the thought of the hypnotist, and not infrequently develops it to a far greater extent than the original thought of the operator expressed. Such a hypothesis—and I think some such hypothesis is needed to account for any creation at all—throws light on the *modus operandi* of the Bible Promises. We plant the Word of the Promise in the womb of Anima Mundi, and if we do not uproot it by using the same power adversely, it is bound to come to fruition in due course, by the same Law by which the world-systems are formed; and if we are to believe that the Word of the Promise is not our own word, but the Word of God, then our Thought of it is imbued with a corresponding power as we hand it over to Anima Mundi. Thus the Promises fulfil themselves automatically, in accordance with the principles of the relations between Law and Personality, and they do so, *not in our own power*, but by the Power of the Word of God.

This, then, gives us at least an intelligible working hypothesis of the rationale of the Bible Promises. The measurement of their fulfilment is exactly proportional to our belief in them, not from any unintelligible cause, and still less from any unreasoning feat of a capricious Deity, but by the working of an intelligible Law. If any of my readers happens to be an electrician, he will find an exact parallel in what is known as Ohm's Law. Such readers will be familiar with the formula $C = E/R$, but for the benefit of those to whom this formula may be unintelligible, I will give a few words of explanation. C means the current of electricity which is to be delivered for any work that is to be done. E stands for the Electro-motive force which generates the current; and R is the Resistance offered to the current by the conductor, such as the wires through which it flows. If there be no resistance, the full amount of current generated would be delivered. But without any conductor no current could be delivered, and therefore there must be *some* resistance, and so the full power of the Electro-motive force can never be delivered by the Current. The amount that will be delivered is the original power of the Electro-motive force divided by the Resistance. The Resistance therefore acts as a restricting force, limiting the extent to which the power of the original Electro-motive force shall be delivered at the point where the work is to be done, but at the same time no delivery at that point could be effected without it; so the Resistance also has a necessary part to play in the working of the circuit. Now if we want to translate the formula $C = E/R$ into terms of spiritual force we may put it thus: E stands for the limitless Potential of the Eternal Spirit; C stands for the current flowing from it; and R stands for the localizing quality of our thought. We cannot entirely dispense with this localizing quality, for our whole purpose is to transmute the *unlimited*, undifferentiated power, which subsists in the Eternal Substantive of Spirit, into a particular differentiated mode of action, which therefore implies a corresponding centralization. This is the proper function of our thought. It is this compressing power which, as I said above, the Hebrew renders by the word "*hoshech*" in the opening verses of Genesis, and which is the necessary complementary to the converse expanding power or "*rouah.*" It takes the co-operation of the two to produce any results.

Restricted, then, to its proper function our R or condensing quality is an essential factor in the work. But if it be allowed to take the form of doubt or unbelief, then it renders the flow of the current from the Spirit ineffective to the extent to which the doubt is entertained; and if doubt be allowed to degenerate into total unbelief and denial of the Power of the Spirit, we thereby cancel the originating force altogether. To put it in terms of the electrical formula, we make R greater than E, in which case no current can flow. We thus find that the words "According to your faith be it unto you" are actually the statement of a Mathematical Law, having nothing vague about them. This may be a somewhat original application of Ohm's Law, but the parallel is so exact, that I cannot help thinking it will appeal to some of my readers who may be conversant with Electrical Science. For those who are not, a simpler simile may be, that you cannot deliver a more powerful stream of water than the bore of the pipe through which it flows will admit of; or, to employ a legal truism, delivery on the part of the donor must be met by acceptance on the part of the donee before a deed of gift can become operative; or, in still simpler language, "you may take a horse to the water but you can't make him drink."

We see, then, that there is a Law of Faith, and that Faith is not a denial of the universal reign of Law, but the perception of its widest generalization, and therefore giving scope to its highest specialization. The opposition between Faith and Law, of which St. Paul so often speaks, is the opposition between this broad view of the ultimate Principle of the Creative Law and that narrower view of restriction by particular laws, which prevents us from grasping the Law of Faith; but that he does not deny the *Principle* of Law, that is the relation between C and E, is clear from his own statement in Rom.

viii, where he says: "The Law of the Spirit of Life in Christ Jesus sets me free from the law of Sin and Death;" in other words: the Law of the Good sets us free from the Law of Evil; and for the same reason St. James says, that the perfect law is the law, of Liberty (Jas. i, 25).

Of course if we suppose that faith is something contrary to the law of the Universe we at once import into our thought the negative quality which entirely vitiates our action. We rightly perceive that the laws of the Universe can never be altered, and if our notion of Faith be, that it is an attempt to work in contradiction to these laws, the best definition we can give it is that given by the little girl in the Sunday school, who said that "Faith is trying to make yourself believe what you know is not true." The reason for such a misconception is, that it entirely omits one of the factors in the calculation. It considers, only the Law, and gives no place to the Word in the scheme of things. Yet we do not carry this misconception into the sciences of chemistry and electricity. We take the immutability of the Law as the basis of these sciences, but we do not expect the immutable Law to produce a photographic apparatus, or an electric train, without the intervention of a reasoning and selective power which specializes the fundamental general Law into particular uses. We do not look to the Law for those powers of reasoning and selection, through which we make it work in all the highly complex ways of our ordinary commercial applications of it—we know better than that. We look to Personality for this. In our every-day pursuits we always act on the maxim that "Nature unaided fails," and that the infinite possibilities stored up in the Law, can only be brought to light by a power of reasoning and selection working through the Law. This co-operation of the Personal with the Impersonal is the Law *of* the Law; and since the Law is unchangeable, this Law *of* the Law must also be unchangeable, and must therefore apply on all planes, and through all time—the Law, that without co-operation of the Law and the Word nothing can be brought into existence, from a solar system to a pin; while on the other hand there is no limit to what can be got out of the Law by the operation of the Word.

If the student will look at the Bible Promises in the light of the general principles, he will find that they are perfectly logical, whether from the metaphysical or from the scientific standpoint, and that their working is only from the same Law through which all scientific developments are made. If this be apprehended it will be clear that the Word of Faith is not "trying to make ourselves believe what we know is not true," but, as St. Paul puts it, it is "giving substance to things not yet seen" (Heb. xi, 1, R.V.).

DEATH AND IMMORTALITY

I think most of my readers will agree with me, that the greatest of all the promises is that of the overcoming of death, for, as the greater includes the less, the power which can do *that* can do anything else. We think that there are only two things that are certain in this world—death and taxes, and no doubt, under the ordinary past conditions, this is quite true; but the question is: are they really inherent in the essential nature of things; or are they not the outcome of our past limited, and often inverted modes of Thought? The teaching of the Bible is that they are the latter. On the subject of taxes the Master says: "Render unto Cæsar the things that are Cæsar's" (Matth. xxii, 21), but on another occasion he said that the children of the King were not liable to taxation (Matth. xvii, 26). However we may leave the "taxes" alone for the present, with the remark that their resemblance to death consists in both being, under present conditions, regarded as compulsory. Under other conditions, however, we can well imagine "taxes" disappearing in a unity of thought which would merge them in co-operation and voluntary contribution; and it appears to me quite possible for death to disappear in like manner.

In whatever way we may interpret the story of Eden, whether literally, or if, like some of the Fathers of the church such as Origen, we take it as an allegory, the result is the same—that Death is not in the essence of man's creation, but supervened as the consequence of an inverted mode of thinking. The Creative Spirit thought one way, and Eve thought another; and since the Thought of the Creating Spirit is the origin of Life, this difference of opinion naturally resulted in death. Then, from this starting-point, all the rest of the Bible is devoted to getting rid of this difference of opinion between us and the Spirit of Life, and showing us that the Spirit's opinion is truer than ours, and so leading us to adopt it as our own. The whole thing turns on the obvious proposition, that if you invert the cause you also invert the effect. It is the principle that division is the inversion of multiplication, so that if $2 \times 2 = 4$ then you cannot escape from the consequence that $4/2 = 2$. The question then is, which of the two opinions is the more reasonable—that death is essentially inherent in the nature of things, or that it is not?

Probably ninety-nine out of a hundred readers will say, the whole experience of mankind from the earliest ages proves that Death is the unchangeable Law of the Universe, and there have been no exceptions. I am not quite sure that I should altogether agree with them on this last point; but putting that aside, let us consider whether it really is the essential Law of the Universe. To say that this is proved by the past experience of the race, is what logicians call a *petitio principii*—it is assuming the whole point at issue. It is the same argument which our grandfathers would have used against aerial navigation—no one had ever travelled in the air, and that proved that no one ever could. My father, who was a junior officer in India when the first railway was run in England, used to tell a story of one of his senior officers, who, on being asked what he thought of the rapidity of the new mode of travelling, said he thought it was "all a damned lie," which opinion appeared to him to settle the whole question. But I hope that none of my readers will hold the same opinion regarding the overcoming of death, even though they might express it in more polite language. At any rate it may be worth while to examine the theoretical possibility of the idea.

To begin with, it involves a self-contradiction to say that the energy of any force can stop the working of that force. If a force stops working, it is for one of two reasons, either that the supply of it is exhausted, or that it is overcome by an opposite and neutralizing force. But we have seen that the Originating Cause of all things can only be an inexhaustible Power of Life, and therefore the hypothesis of it becoming exhausted is eliminated; and similarly, since all the forces of the Universe proceed from this Source, it is impossible for any of them to have a nature diametrically opposite to that of the source from which they flow. So the alternative must be eliminated also. Accordingly, the outflow, undifferentiated, of Life and Energy from the Eternal Substantive of Spirit, is never stopped *by its own current* in any of its differentiated streams; it is impossible for a current to be stopped by its own flow, whether it be a current of electricity, steam, water, or anything else. What then does stop the flow of any sort of current? It is the Resistance or *inertia* of the channel through which it flows; so that we come back to the formula of Ohm's Law, C = E/R as a general proposition applicable to any conceivable sort of energy.

The neutralizing power then, is not that of the flowing of any sort of energy, but the rigidity, or inertia of the medium through which the energy has to make its way; thus bringing us back to *rouah* and *hoshech*, the expansive and compressive principles of the opening verses of Genesis. It is the broad scientific generalization of the opposition between Ertia, or Energy, and Inertia, or Absence of Energy; and since, for the reasons just given, Ertia cannot go against itself, the only thing that can stop it is Inertia.

Now the components of the human body are simply various chemical elements—so much carbon, so much hydrogen, etc., as any textbook on the subject will tell you; and although, of course, every sort of substance is the abode of ceaseless *atomic* energy, we all recognize that merely atomic energy is not that of the powers of thought, will, and perception, which make us organized mentalities instead of a mere aggregation of the various substances exposed to view in a biological museum, as constituting the human body—you might take all these substances in their proper proportions, and shake them up together, but you would not make an intelligent man of them. We are therefore safe in saying that the physiological body represents the principle of inertia in us, while the something that thinks in us represents the principle of Ertia.

The balance of power between the Life Principle in us and the Death Principle, is then, necessarily, a question of the balance between these two, the spirit and the flesh, or ertia and inertia.

Why then does the balance preponderate to the life-side for a certain length of time, and then go over to the opposite side?

Now this brings us to the distinction which the old writers drew, between the "Vital Soul" of any living thing and the Spirit. Their conception of the

"Vital Soul" was very much the same as I have set forth in the chapter on "The Soul of the Subject." It is the individual's particular share of the Cosmic Soul or Anima Mundi, whether it be an individual tree, or an individual person; and the ordinary maximum length of time, during which the Vital Soul will be able to overcome the inertia of its physical vehicle, depends upon the particular class to which the individual belongs. What the ordinary maximum is in regard to any species is a matter of experience, and it is in this way that we have fixed the usual limit of human life at three-score years and ten.

Now it is here that we shall begin to profit by some knowledge about the invisible part of ourselves. The actual molecules of our body, as I have just said, are only so much dead matter. This inert material is pulled about in various directions by strings which we call muscles, according to the movements we wish our bodies to make, and these muscles are set in motion by the vibrations of the nerves.[4] But what is it that occasions these vibrations of the nerves? Here we begin to pass beyond the limits of official Science, though not beyond the limits of recognizable Law. We have to recognize the existence of an etheric body acting as an intermediary between intention, desire, or (in the case of human beings) thought of the soul and the physical vibrations of the nerves. This is why, in an earlier chapter, I have drawn attention to our power of sending out etheric vibrations beyond the limits of the physical body, as in the case of De Rocha's experiments. Such experiments show that there is in us something not composed of dense matter, which is able to convey vibrations to dense matter; and it is this something which we speak of as the etheric body.

But if we wish to trace the links by which our thought operates upon the physical body, we find ourselves compelled to postulate yet another intermediary, what I have spoken of as the "Vital Soul"—a vehicle which does not *consciously think*, but in which what we may call race-consciousness becomes centred in the individual. This race-consciousness is none other than the ever-present "will-to-live" which is the basis of physical evolution—that automatically acting principle—which causes plants to turn towards the sun, animals to seek their proper food, and both animals and men to try instantly to escape from immediate danger. It is what we call instinct which does not reason. I may give a laughable experience of my own to illustrate the fact that conscious reason is not the method of this faculty. Once when on leave from India I was walking along a street in London in the heat of a summer's day and suddenly noticed just at my feet a long dark thing apparently wriggling across the white glare of the pavement. "Snake!" I exclaimed, and jumped aside for all I was worth, and the next moment was laughing at myself for not recollecting that cobras were not common objects in the London streets. But it looked just like one, and of course turned out to be nothing but a piece of rag. Well, instinct did its duty even if it did make a fool of me; but there is certainly no conscious reasoning in the matter, only the automatic action of inherent Law—"Self-preservation is the first law of Nature."

This Vital Soul, then, is the seat of all those instincts which go towards the preservation of the individual's physical body, and towards the propagation of the race; and it is on this account that our theosophical friends call it the "Desire Body" or, to use the Indian term "Kama rupa." It acts with conscious intention, but not with conscious *reasoning*. It is thus distinguished on the one hand from the etheric body, which is a mere vehicle for finer vibrations than can take place in the denser matter of the physical body, but which has *no intention*; and on the other from the *mind* which acts by conscious reasoning, and it thus forms an intermediary between the two.

The importance of recognizing the place of this higher intermediary in the ascending scale of living principle is, that for all practical purposes the animal world does not rise higher than this in the scale. It is true that in particular instances we find the first dawning of the mental faculty in an animal, but it is only very faint; so this does not affect the broad general principle. The point to be noted is that up to this stage human beings are built on the same lines as animals, and what distinguishes us, is the addition in ourselves of a higher factor,—that of the reasoning mind exercising the power of conscious thought.

Now it is the direction of this thought that influences the three lower factors. The sequence, going upwards, is as follows:—movement is communicated to the physical body by the etheric body; and movement is communicated to the etheric body by the Vital Soul; then, in proportion as the purely instinctive action of the Vital Soul is controlled by the conscious thought, so its action upon the two lowest principles is modified.

Here, then, is the crucial point. In what direction is the conscious thought going to modify the action of the three principles that are below it? If it takes the soul of mere racial desire and the physical body as its standard of thought, then it naturally follows that it cannot raise it any higher. It has descended to *their* level and so cannot pour any stream of life into it, on the simple principle that no current can ever flow from a lower to a higher level, whether the difference in level be that of actual elevation, as in the case of water, or different in potential, as in the case of electricity. On the other hand if the conscious mind recognizes that itself proceeds from some higher source, it looks to receive life from that source, and its thought is modified accordingly, and in turn re-acts correspondingly upon the lower principles.

If this is clear to the student, he will now see how it is that by limiting our conception of life to the current ideas entertained by the race, we impress these ideas on our three lower principles. It is true that these three principles are not capable of reasoning themselves, but the highest of them, the Vital Soul, has its action modified by the reasoning principle above it, and so communicates to the two lowest principles corresponding waves of vibration. And in this connection we must remember the distinction between the two systems of nerves; the voluntary system connected with the brain and forming the medium of all voluntary action, and the involuntary, or sympathetic system connected with the solar plexus and controlling all the automatic actions of the body, and thus being the agent of that continual renewal of the physical organism which is always going on, and keeps in existence for a life time a body which begins to disintegrate immediately the soul has left it.[5] Now it is through this inner Builder of the Body that our Thought re-acts upon our physical organism. The response is purely automatic, for the simple reason that there is no original thinking power in the three lower principles; the action is that of the Law as directed by Thought or Word.

In this way then, it appears to me, the Personal in us acts upon the Impersonal in us; and if we assume, as I think we may, that this action takes place by means of etheric waves, we have, on general scientific principles, a clue to what we read in the Bible about the transmutation of the body. The theory of the constitution of the atom shows us that its nature is determined by the number of its particles and their rate of revolution, and that a change in the rate of revolution results in the throwing off of some of the particles. Then the number of particles being altered, there results a change in the distribution of the positive and negative charges within the sphere of the atom, since they must always exactly balance one another; and this change in the distribution of the positive and negative charges must instantly result in a corresponding change in the geometrical configuration of particles constituting the atom.

That the particles automatically arrange themselves into groups of different geometrical form within the sphere of the atom, has been demonstrated both mathematically and experimentally by Professor J.J. Thompson,[6] these geometrical forms resulting of course from the balance of attraction and repulsion between the positive and negative charges of the particles.

That the transmutation of one substance into another is not a mere dream of the mediæval alchemists is now already shown by Modern Science. Under suitable conditions an atom of Radium breaks down into atoms of another sort known as Radium Emanations, and these again break down into yet another sort of atoms to which the name of Radium Emanations X has been given, while Radium Emanation also gives rise to the atom of Helium (N.K. 124). Thorium also behaves in the same manner, transmuting into atoms called Thorium X, which again change into atoms of another sort to which the name of Thorium Emanations has been given and these in turn transmute into atoms of yet another kind, known as Thorium Emanations X. The same is the case also with Uranium which, however, so far as is yet known, undergoes only one transmutation into what is known as Uranium X.

The transmutation of one sort of atom into another is therefore not a mere visionary fancy, but an established fact; and although our laboratory experiments in this direction may not as yet have gone very far, they have gone far enough to show that a Law of Transmutation does exist in Nature. Then, since the difference between one sort of atom and another results from the difference and arrangement of their particles, and the difference in the number and arrangement of the particles results from the difference in the speed of their rotation, and this again results from the difference in the energy or rate of vibration of the particles, we come back to different rates of etheric vibrations as the commencement of the whole series of changes; and as is proved by the facts of wireless telephoning, different rates of etheric vibrations can be set in motion by the varying sounds of the human voice, even on the physical plane. May it not be then, that by the same law, vibrations of other wave-lengths, yet unknown to science, will be set in motion by the unspoken word of our thought?

The substance known as Polonium, even by its near approach to an electric bell, causes it to ring, and if etheric waves can thus be started by an inanimate substance, why should we suppose that our thought has less power, especially when metaphysically we cannot avoid the conclusion that the whole creation must have its origin in the Divine Thought?

From such considerations as these, I think we may reasonably infer that if the mind be illuminated by a range of thought coming from a higher mind, there is no limit to the power which may thus be exercised over the material world, and that therefore St. Paul's statement regarding the transmutation of the present physical body, is one which should be included in the circle of our ideas, as being within the scope of the Laws of the Universe when their action is specialized by the power of the Word (1 Cor. xv); and similarly with regard to other statements to the same effect contained in the Bible. What is wanted is the realization of a greater Word than that which we form from the current experience of the race. The race has formed its Word on the basis of the lower principles of our being, and if we are to advance beyond this, the Law of the subject clearly indicates that it can only be by adopting a more fundamental Word, or Idea, than that which we have hitherto thought to include the entire range of possibilities. The Law of our further Evolution demands a Word not formed from past experiences, but based upon the eternal principle of the All-Originating Life itself. And this is in strict accord with scientific method. If we had always allowed ourselves to be ruled by past experiences we should still be primitive savages; and it is only by the gradual perception of underlying principles, that we have attained the degree of civilization we have reached to-day; so what the Bible puts before us is simply the application to the life in ourselves of the maxim that "Principle is not limited by Precedent."

Now the Bible Promises serve to put us on the track of this Principle: they suggest lines of enquiry. And the enquiry leads to the conclusion that the two ultimate factors are the Law and the Word. What we have missed hitherto is the conception of the limitless possibilities of the Law, and the limitless power of the Word. On one occasion the Master said to the Jews "Ye know not the Scriptures neither the power of God" (Matth. xxii, 29) and the same is the case with ourselves. The true "Scripture" is the "scriptura rerum" or the Law indelibly written in the nature of things, and the written Scriptures are true only because they contain the statement of the Principle of the Law. Therefore until we see the Principle of the Law we "know not the Scriptures." On the other hand, until we see the Principle of the operation of the Word through the Law, we do not know "the Power of God"; and it is only as we come to perceive the interaction of the Law and the Word that we see the beginning of the way that leads to Life and Liberty.

But although it is evident from the text just quoted, as well as from other intimations in his Epistles, that St. Paul fully grasped the principle of the transmutation of the body, he himself tells us that he has not yet realized it in practice. He says he has not yet "attained to the resurrection from the dead," but is still pressing on towards its attainment (Ph. iii, 12). And it is to be remarked that he is not here speaking of a general "resurrection *of* the dead," but, as the word *exanastasis* in the original Greek indicates, of a special resurrection from among the dead; this indicates an *individual* achievement, not merely something common to the whole race. From this and other

passages it is evident that by "the dead" it means those whose conception of
Life is limited to the four lower principles, thus
unifying
the mind with the three principles which are below it; and the same idea is
expressed in a variety of ways all through the Bible. This therefore shows that
he is quite aware that knowledge of a principle does not enable us then and
there to attain the completeness of the application, and if this be the case with
St. Paul, we cannot be surprised to find it the same with ourselves. But on the
other hand knowledge of the principle is the first step towards getting it to
work.

Well, St. Paul is dead and buried, and so I suppose will most of us be in a
few years; so the question confronts us, what becomes of us then?

As Milton puts it in "Il Penseroso" we want:

"to unsphere
The spirit of Plato and unfold
What worlds or what vast regions hold
The immortal mind that hath forsook
Her mansion in the fleshly nook."

Yes, this is a question of deep personal interest to us; but as I cannot
speak from experience, I will restrict myself to seeing whether we can form
any sort of general hypothesis on the basis of the principles we have
recognized. What then is likely to survive? The physical body is of course
disintegrated by the chemistry of Nature. The etheric body probably
continues to retain its form longer, because it is a condensation of etheric
particles wrought together by the etheric waves sent out by the Vital Soul,
and is therefore not subject to the laws of chemical affinity. The Vital Soul,
being the race-principle of life in the individual,—that principle which
automatically seeks to preserve the individual from disintegration, —probably
survives longer still, until, ceasing to receive any reflex vibrations from the
body, it grows gradually weaker in its sense of individual guardianship, and
so is eventually absorbed into the group-soul or generic essence of the class to
which it belongs. This is probably what happens in the case of animals for
want of any higher vivifying principle, and would be the same with us were
it not for the fact of having such a higher principle. In our case I should
imagine that the influx of etheric waves, received from the thought action of
the mind, would have the effect of continuing to impress the Vital Soul with
a sense of individuality, in terms of its own plane, which would prevent it from
being absorbed into the group-soul so long as the vital current from the mind
continued to reach it. But eventually that current would cease to reach it, and
in some cases, because the individual mind that governed it would gradually
realize that its connection with the physical plane had ceased, and in others,
because through a higher illumination the mind had, of its own volition,
turned its thought in another direction. In either case, on the ceasing of the
influx of that vitalizing current, the Vital Soul of the human being would
likewise be absorbed into the Cosmic Soul, or Anima Mundi.

How long the processes of the disintegration of the etheric body, and absorption of the vital soul may take, is a question on which I can offer no opinion beyond saying that certain psychic phenomena suggest that in some cases they may take a long period of time. But for the reasons I have now given, it appears to me that the permanently surviving factor is the thinking mind which is our real self, and is positively our centre of consciousness after the physical body has been put off.

By the facts of the case its consciousness is no longer affected by vibrations received from the physical body; and therefore, to the extent to which our idea of life has been centred in that body, we shall feel its loss. If our motto has been "Let us eat and drink, for to-morrow we die" we shall feel very dead indeed—a living death, a consciousness of being cut off from all that constituted our enjoyment of life—a thirst for the satisfaction of our customary ideas, which we have no power to quench; and, in proportion as our habitual mode of thought is raised above that lowest level, so will our sense of loss be less. Then, by the same Law, if our habitual mode of thought is turned towards pure, beautiful, and helpful ideals, we shall feel no loss at all, for we shall carry our own ideals with us, and, I hope, see them more clearly by reason of their disentanglement from mundane considerations. In what precise way we may then be able to work out our ideals I will not now stop to discuss. What we want first is a reasonable theory, based upon the principle of that universal Law which is only varied in its actions by the conditions under which it works; so, instead of speculating as to precise details, we may generalize the question of how we can work out the good ideals which we carry over with us, and put it this way:—Our ideas are embodied in thoughts; thoughts start trains of etheric waves, which waves induce reciprocal action whenever they meet with a receiver capable of vibrating synchronously with them, and so eventually the thought becomes a fact, and our helpful and beautiful ideal becomes a work of power, whether in this world or in any other.

Now it is to the forming of such ideals that the Bible, from first to last is trying to lead us. From first to last it is working upon one uniform principle, that the Thought is the Word, that the Word sets in motion the Law, and that when the Law is set in motion it acts with mathematical precision. The Bible is a handbook of instruction for the use of our Creative Power of Thought, and this is the sequence which it follows—one definite method, so fundamental in its nature, that it applies equally to the making of a packing-case or the making of a solar system.

Now we have formed a generalized conception, based on this universal method, of the sort of consciousness we are likely to have when we pass out of the physical body. Then our thought naturally passes on to the question what will happen after this?

It is here that some theory of the reconstitution of the physical body appears to me to hold a most important place in the order of our evolution. Let us try to trace it out on the general lines of the Creative Power of Thought indicated above, the keynote to which is that the Law is specialized by the Word, and cannot of itself bring out the infinite possibilities contained in it without such specializing, just as in all scientific development of ordinary life.

The clue to the whole question is, that our place in the Universal Order is to develop the infinite resources of the Original Life and Substance into actual facts. "Nature unaided fails." The Personal Factor must co-operate with the Impersonal, alike for setting up an electric bell, or for the furtherance of cosmic evolution; and the reason it is so is, because it could not possibly be otherwise.

If now we start by recognizing this as our necessary place in the Progressive Order of the Universe, I think it will help us to form a reasonable theory as to the reconstruction of the body. First of all, why have we any physical body at all? As a matter of fact we have one, and no amount of transcendental philosophizing will alter the fact, and so we may conclude that there is some reason for it. We have seen the truth of the maxim "Omne vivum ex vivo," and therefore that all particular forms of life are differentiations of the one Basic Life. This means a localizing of the Life-Principle in individual centres. The formation of a centre implies condensation; for where there is no condensation the Energy, whether electricity or Life, is simply *dispersed* and *achieving no purpose*. Therefore distinctness from the undifferentiated Original Life is a necessity of the case. Consequently the higher the degree of Consciousness of Individuality, the greater must be the Consciousness of *Distinctness of Personality*.

We say of a "wobbly" sort of person: "That fellow is no use, you can't depend on him." We say of a person whose ideas, intentions, and methods are subject to continual variations under all sorts of outside influences, whether of opinions or circumstances, that he has "no backbone," meaning that he is in want of individuality. He has no real thought of his own, and so has no Word of Power by which to co-operate with the Law; therefore, to the extent to which this is the case with any of us, we are of no use in furthering the unfoldment of Evolution, whether in ourselves or anywhere else.

Now we talk a lot about Evolution or the *un*folding, but we seem often not to realize that there must be something to unfold; and that therefore *In*volution, or the concentration of the Life-principle, must be a condition precedent to its *E*volution. This process of Involution must therefore be a process of gradually increasing concentration of the Life-principle, by association with denser and denser modes of the Universal Substance. Then, on the principle of Vibration, the less dense the substance in which the Life is immersed, the more it must be subject to being stirred by vibratory currents other than those produced by the conscious action of the Ego, or inherent Life, of the individuality that is being formed.

But "*the Sum of the Vibrations in anything determines the mode, power, and direction of its action*"; therefore, the less the Ego be concentrated through association with a dense vehicle, the more "wobbly" it must be, and consequently the less able to take any effective part in the further work of Creation. But in proportion as the Ego builds up an *Individual Will*, the more it gets out of the "wobbly" state—or, to refer once more to the idea of etheric waves—it becomes able to select what vibrations it will receive, and what vibrations it will send out.

The involution of the Ego into the physical body, such as we at present know it, is therefore a necessity of the case, if any effective Individuality is to be brought into existence, and the work of Creation carried on instead of being cut short, not for want of material, but for want of workmen capable of using the tools of the builders' craft—the Law as "Strength" and the Word as "Beauty."

The Descending Arc of the Circle of Being is therefore that of the Involution of Spirit into denser and denser modes of Substance,—a process called in technical language by the Greek name "Eleusin," and the process continues until a point is reached where Spirit and Substance are in equal balance, which is where we are now. Then comes the tug of war. Which of the two is to predominate? They are the Expansive and Constrictive primal elements, the "rouah" and "hoshech" of the Hebrew Genesis.

If the Constrictive element be allowed to go further than giving necessary form to the Expansive element, it imprisons the latter. The condensation becomes too dense for the Ego to receive or send forth vibrations according to its free will, and so the Individuality becomes lost. If the condensation process be not carried far enough, no Individuality can be built up, and if it be carried too far, no Individuality can emerge; so in both cases we get the same result that there is no one to speak the Word of Power without which "Nature unaided fails."

Thus we are now exactly at the bottom of the Circle of Being. We have completed the Descending Arc and reached the point where the realization of the Distinctness of Conscious Individuality enables us to choose our own line, whether that of progressing through the stages of the Ascending Arc of Being, or of falling out from the living Circle of Progression, at least for a period, into what is sometimes mystically spoken of as "the Moon," or (in descending order) the "Eighth Sphere," and which is called in Scripture "The Outer Darkness,"—the rigidity which stops the action of Life.

Therefore it is with regard to this stage of our career that the Bible lays so much stress on the conflict between the Spirit and the Flesh—it is a fact in the course of our evolution, and the purpose of the Bible is to teach us how to move forward along the Ascending Arc of the Circle of Being, so as to build up individualities which will be able to use the tools of Intelligence and Will in the great work of Evolution, both Personal and Cosmic.

Now what is shown diagrammatically as the Ascending Arc of the Circle of Life is the Return from its lowest point, or the *Full Consciousness of Personal Distinctness*, gained through *the Material Body*, back to its highest point or the Originating Life itself. This is the truth embodied in the parable of the Prodigal Son. It is a Cosmic truth, and this return journey is technically called by the Green name "Anaktorion." It is the Rising-again, that is from matter to Spirit, and is the Resurrection Principle.

But what is accomplished by the journey of the Ego round the Circle of Life?

A New Centre of Intelligence and volition is established; from this the Creative Word of Power can be spoken—a *Complete Man* has been brought into existence, who can take a *free and intelligent* part in the further work of Creation, by his understanding of the interaction between the Law and the Word. The "Volume of the Sacred Law" lies open before us, and the Vibratory Power of the Word to give effect to it is the "Blazing Star" that illuminates its contents, and so we become fellow-workers with the Great Architect of the Universe.

For these reasons it appears to me that our self-recognition in a physical body is a necessary step in our growth. But why should the reconstruction of a physical body be either necessary or desirable? The answer is as follows:

Obviously self-recognition is the necessary basis for all use of those powers of selection and volition by which the Impersonal Law is to be specialized so as to bring to light its limitless potentialities; and self-recognition means the recognition of our personal Distinctness from our environment. Therefore it must always mean the possessing of a body as a vehicle, by means of which to act upon that environment, and to receive the corresponding reaction from it. In other words it must always be a body constituted in terms of the plane upon which we are functioning. But it does not follow that we should always be tied down to one plane.

On the contrary, the very conception of the power of the Word to specialize the action of the Law, implies the power of functioning on any plane we choose; but always subject to the Law, that if we want to act on any particular plane in *propria persona*, and not merely by influencing some other agent, we can only do so by assuming a body in terms of the nature of that plane. Therefore, if we want to act on the physical plane, we must put on a physical body. But when we have fully grasped the Power of the Word we cannot be tied to a body. We shall no longer regard it as composed of so many chemical elements, but we shall see beyond them into the real primary etheric substance of which they are composed, and so by our volition shall be able to put the physical body on or off at pleasure,—that at least is a quite logical deduction from what we have learnt in the preceding pages.

Seen in this light the "Resurrection Body" is not the old body resuscitated, but a new body, just as real and tangible as the old one, only not subject to any of its disabilities,—no longer a limitation, but the ever ready instrument for any work we may desire to do upon the physical plane.

But perhaps you will say, "Why should we want to have anything more to do with the physical plane? surely we have had enough of it already!" Yes; in its old sense of limitation; but not in the new sense of a world of glorious possibilities, a new field for our creative activities; not the least of which is the helping of those who are still in those lower stages which we have already passed through.

I think if we realize the position of the Fully Risen Man, we shall see that he is not likely to turn his back upon the Earth as a rotten, old thing. Therefore a new physical body is a necessary part of his equipment.

If, then, we take it as a general principle, that for self-recognition upon any plane a body in terms of that plane is a necessity, this will throw some light on the Bible narrative of our Lord's appearances after his Resurrection. It is noteworthy that he himself lays stress on the body as an integral part of the individuality. When the disciples thought they had seen an apparition he said: "Handle me and see that it is I *myself*, and *not* a spirit, for a spirit hath not flesh and bones as ye see I have" (Luke xxiv, 39). This very clearly states that the spirit without a corresponding body is not the complete "I myself"; yet from the same narrative we gather that the solid body in which he appeared eNTA

is able to pass through closed doors, and to be disintegrated and re-integrated at will. Now on the electronic theory of the constitution of matter which I have spoken of in the earlier part of this book, there is nothing impossible in this; on the contrary it is only the known Law of synchronous vibration carried into those further ranges of wave-lengths which, though not yet produced by laboratory experiment, are unavoidably recognized by the mathematicians.

In this way then the Resurrection of the Body appears to me to be the legitimate termination of our present stage of existence. What further developments may follow, who shall say? for we must remember that the end of one series is always the commencement of another—that is the doctrine of the Octave. But this is far enough to look forward in all conscience. As to *when* the completion of our present stage of evolution will be attained, it is impossible even to hazard a guess; but that the *individual* attainment of such a Resurrection is not dependent on any particular date in the world's history, is clearly the teaching of Scripture. When Martha said to Jesus that she knew her brother would rise again "at the last day," he ignored the question of "the last day," and said "I am the Resurrection and the Life" (St. John xi, 25); and similarly St. Paul puts it forward as a thing to be attained (Ph. iii, 15). It is not a resurrection *of* the dead but *from among* the dead that St. Paul is aiming at—not an "anastasis ton nekron," but an "anastasis *ek* ton nekron."

Doubtless there are other passages of Scripture which speak of a general resurrection, which to some will be a resurrection to condemnation (St. John v, 29), a resurrection to shame and everlasting contempt (Dan. xii, 2). This is a subject upon which I will not attempt to enter—I have a great many things to learn, and this is one of them; but if the Bible statements regarding resurrection are to be taken as a whole, these passages cannot be passed over without notice. On the other hand the Bible statements regarding *individual* resurrection are there also, and the general principle on which they are based becomes clear when we see the fundamental relation between the Law and the Word. Only we must remember that the Word that can thus set in motion the Law of Life, and make it triumph over the Law of Death, cannot be spoken by the limited personality which only knows itself as John Smith or Mary Jones. We must attain a larger personality than that, before we can speak the Word. And this larger personality is not just John Smith or Mary Jones magnified; that is the mistake we are all so apt to fall into. Mere magnification will not do it. A square will continue to be a square however large you make it; it will never become a circle. But on the other hand, there is such a thing as stating the area of a circle in the form of a square; and when we learn to regard our square as not existing on its own account, but as an expression of the circle in another form, our attention will be directed to the circle first, as the generating figure, and *then* to the square as a particular mode of expressing the same area. If we look at it in this way we shall never mistake the square for the circle, but we shall see that as the circle grows, the corresponding square will grow with it. It is this dependence of the square on the circle that makes all the difference, and makes it a living, growing square. For the true circle represents Infinitude. It is not bounded by a limiting circumference as in the merely symbolic geometrical figure, but is rather represented by the impulse which generates an ever widening circle of electro-magnetic waves; and when we realize this, our square becomes a living thing. The "Word" that we speak with this recognition is no longer ours, but His who sent us—the expression, on the plane of individuality, of the Thought that sent us into existence and so it is the "Word of Life." This is the true Resurrection of the Individual.

TRANSFERRING THE BURDEN

The more we grow into a clear perception of what is really meant by "Squaring the Circle," the freer we shall find ourselves from the burden of anxiety. We shall rise to a larger generalization of the Law of Cause and Effect. We shall learn in all things to reach out to First Cause as operating through the channels of secondary causation,—"causa causas" as producing, and therefore controlling "causa causata"—and so we cease to worry about secondary causes. On the plane of the lower personality we see certain facts, and argue that they are bound to produce certain results, which would be quite true if we really saw *all* the facts; or, again, allowing that in any particular case we actually did see all the facts as they now exist, we can either deny the operation of First Cause, or recognize its infinite capacity for creating new facts. Therefore, whatever may be the nature of our anxiety, we should endeavour to dispel it by the consideration that there may be already existing other facts we do not know of, which will produce a different result from the one we fear, and that in any case there is a power which can produce new facts in answer to our appeal to it.

But I can imagine some one saying to us, "You bumptious little midget, do you think First Cause is going to trouble Itself about you and your petty concerns? Do you not know that First Cause works by universal Law, and makes no exceptions?" Well, I would not have written this book if I did not suppose that First Cause works by universal Law, and it is just because It does so that I believe It *will* work for me and my concerns. The Law makes no exceptions, but it can be specialized through the power of the Word. Then our sceptic says, "What, do you think *your* word can do that?" To which I reply, "It is not my word because I am not using it in my lower personality, as John Smith or Mary Jones, but in that higher personality which recognizes only one all-embracing Personality and itself as included in that."

Which comes first, the Law or the Word?

The distribution of the solar systems in space, the localization of the Spirit in specific areas of cosmic activity, proclaims the starting of all manifestation through the "Word." Then the operation of Law follows with mathematical precision, just as when we write 2 × 2 we cannot avoid getting 4 as the result—only there is no reason why we should not write 2 × 3 and so get 6 instead of 4. Let it be borne in mind that the Law flows from the Word, and not *vice versa*, and you have got the clue to the enigma of Life.

How far we shall be able to make practical use of this clue depends, of course, on our acceptance of its principle.

The Directing Power of the Word is *inherent* in the Word, and we cannot alter it. It is the *Law Of the Law*, and so, like any other law, it cannot be broken, but its action can be inverted. We cannot deprive the Word of its efficacy, but our denial of it as the Word of Expansion is equivalent to an affirmation of it as the Word of Contraction, and so the Law acts towards us as a Limitation. But the fault is not in the Law, but in the way we use the Word. Now if the reader grasps this, he will see that the less we trouble ourselves about what appear to us to be the visible and calculable causes of things, the freer we must become from the burden of anxiety; and as we advance step by step to a clearer recognition of the true order of Cause and Effect, so all intermediate causes will fade from our view. Only the two extremes of the sequence of Cause and Effect will remain in sight. First Cause, moving as the Word, starting a sequence, and the desired result terminating it, as the Word taking Form in Fact. The intermediate links in the chain will be there, but they will be seen as effects, not causes. The wider the generalization we thus make, the less we shall need to trouble about particulars, knowing that they will form themselves by the natural action of the Law; and the widest generalization is therefore, to state not what we want to *have*, but what we want to *be*. The only reason we ever want to *have* anything, is because we think it will help us to be something—something more than we are now; so that the "having" is only a link in the chain of secondary causes, and may therefore be left out of consideration, for it will come of itself through the natural workings of the Law, set in operation by the Word as First Cause. This principle is set forth in the statement of the Divine Name given to Moses (Ex. iii, 13-14). The Name is simply "I *am*"—it is Being, not having—the having follows as a natural consequence of the Being; and if it be true that we are made in the likeness and image of God, that is to say on the same Principle, then what is the Law of the Divine nature must be the Law of ours also—and as we awake to this we become "partakers of the Divine Nature" (2 Pet. i, 4).

What we really want, therefore, is to *be* something—something more than we are now; and this is quite right. It is our consciousness of the continually generative impulse of the Eternal Living Spirit, which is the *fons et origo* (fountain and source) of all differentiated life working within us for ever more and more perfect individual expression of all that is in Itself. If the reader remembers what I said at the beginning of this book about the Verb Substantive of Being, he will see that each of us is in truth a "Word (verbum) of God." Let not the orthodox reader be shocked at this—I am only saying what the Bible does. Look up the following passages: "I will write upon him the name of my God and my own new name" (Rev. xiii, 12). "I saw, and behold a lamb standing on the Mount Zion (note, the word Zion means the principle of Life), and with him a hundred and forty and four thousand, having his name and the name of his Father written on their foreheads" (Rev. xiv, 1). "His name shall be on their foreheads" (Rev. xxii, 4). Read particularly the whole passage Rev. xix, 11-16, where we are expressly told that the name in question is "the Word of God"; and that this name is the one put upon those who follow their Leader, is shown by the same description being given of the followers as of the Leader. They all ride upon "white horses," and the "horse" is the symbol of the intellect. Also in the case of the Leader, the peculiarity of his Name is that "no one knows it but himself," and in Rev. ii, 17, exactly the same thing is said of the "New Name" to be given "to him that overcometh." Again, in Isaiah lxii, 2, "Thou shalt be called by a new name, which the mouth of the Lord shall name"; and again in Num. vi, 27, "They shall put my name upon the children of Israel."

Then as the meaning of that Name "the Word of God." In Ps. cxix, 160: "Thy word is true from the beginning," and Jesus said: "Thy Word is Truth" (John xvii, 17).

This also corresponds with the description in Rev. xix, 11-16 where another name for "the Word of God" is "Faithful and True"; and the same metaphor of the Truth *"riding into action"* is contained in Ps. xlv, 3, 4. "Gird thy sword upon thy thigh, O most mighty, with thy glory and thy majesty; and in thy majesty ride prosperously because of Truth." The same symbol of "riding" also occurs in Ps. lxviii: "Extol him that rideth upon the heavens," "Sing praises to him that rideth upon the heaven of heavens which were of old (i.e., *ab initio*); lo, he doth send out his Voice and that a mighty Voice"—and the word "Voice" is the Hebrew Word [Hebrew: "K[=o]l"], meaning "Sound" or "Word"—so that here again we have the idea of "The Word" riding into action. Once more—"Thou hast magnified thy Word above all thy Name" (Ps. cxxxviii, 2), thus repeating the idea of the Word as the Name.

In other passages we have the idea of the Word as a Weapon. "The Sword of the Spirit which is the Word of God" (Eph. vi, 17), which answers to the description in Revelations of the Sword proceeding out of the mouth of the Word; and we have the same metaphor of the Word riding into action in Habakkuk iii, 8 and 9. "Thou didst ride upon thine horses and thy chariots of salvation. Thy bow was made quite naked ... even thy Word"; and similarly those that oppose the Word are "killed with the sword of him that sat upon the horse, which sword proceeded out of his mouth."

In other passages we have the Word put before us as a Defence. "His Truth shall be thy shield and buckler" (Ps. xci, 4); and again "The Name of the Lord is a strong tower; the righteous runneth into it and is safe" (Prov. xviii, 10); and we have already seen that this Name is "The Word of God"; and similarly in Ps. cxxiv, 8: "Our help is in the name of the Lord, who made heaven and earth."

Lastly, we get "the Word" as the final deliverance from all ill; "Into thy hand I commit my spirit: thou hast redeemed me, O Lord God of Truth" (Ps. xxxi, 5).

And the reason of all this is because "His Truth endureth to all generations" (Ps. c, 5); it is everlasting, Changeless Principle. "By the Word of the Lord were the heavens made; and all the host of them by the breath of his mouth" (Ps. xxxiii, 6), as is also said of the Word in the opening of St. John's Gospel and First Epistle.

Now a careful comparison of these and similar passages will make it clear that the sequence presented to us is as follows: The "Word" is the passing of the Verb Substantive of Being into Action. It is always the same in Principle, on whatever scale, and therefore applies to ourselves also, so that each one of us is a "Word of God." We are this by the very essence of our being, and that is why the first thing we are told about Man is, that he is made in the image and likeness of God. But how far any of us will become a really effective "Word," depends upon our acceptance of the New Name which is ready to be bestowed upon each one. "To as many as *receive* him, to them gives he power to become Sons of God, even to them that believe on his Name" (John 1-12). We get the New Name by realizing the Truth, which Truth is that we ourselves are included in *the name*, and that name is called "The Word of God."

The meaning of which becomes clear if we remember that the spiritual name of anything is its "Noumenon" or essential being, which is manifested through its "Phenomenon" or outward reproduction in Form; so that the true order is first our "Name" or essential Being, then our "Word" or active manifestation of this essential Being, then the "Truth" or the unchangeable Law of Being passing into Manifestation—and these three are *One*. Then when we see that this is true of ourselves, not because of some arbitrary favouritism making us exceptions to the human race, but because it is the working on the plane of Human Individuality of the same Power and the same Law by which the world has come into existence, we can see that we have here a Principle which we can trust to work as infallibly as the principle of Mathematics; and that therefore the desire to become something more than we now are is nothing else than the Eternal Spirit of Life seeking ever fuller expression.

The correction which our mode of thinking needs therefore is to start with Being, not with Having, and we may then trust the Having to come along in its right order; and if we can get into this new manner of thinking, what a world of worry it will save us! If we realize that the Law flows from the Word, and not vice versa, then the Law of attraction must work in this manner, and will bring to us all those conditions through which we shall be able to express the more expanded Being towards which we are directing our Word; and as a consequence, we shall have no need to trouble about forcing particular conditions into existence—they will grow spontaneously out of the seed we have planted. All we have to do now, or at any time, is to take the conditions that are ready to hand and use them on the lines of the sort of "being" towards which we are directing our Thought—use them just as far as they go at the time, without trying to press them further—and we shall find by experience that out of the present conditions thus used to-day, more favourable conditions will grow in a perfectly natural manner to-morrow, and so on, day by day, until, when later on we look back, we shall be surprised to find ourselves expressing all, and more than all, the sort of "*being*" we had thought of. Then, from this new standpoint of our being, we shall continue to go on in the same way, and so on *ad infinitum*, so that our life will become one endless progress, ever widening as we go on. And this will be found a very quiet and peaceful way, free from worry and anxiety, and wonderfully effective. It may lead you to some position of authority or celebrity; but as such things belong to the category of "Having" and not of "Being" they were not what you aimed at, and are only by-products of what you have become in yourself. They are conditions, and like all other conditions should be made use of for the development of still more expanded "being"; that is to say, you will go on working on the more extended scale which such a position makes possible to you. But the one thing you would not try to do with it would be to "boss the show." The moment you do this you are no longer using the Word of the larger Personality, and have descended to your old level of the smaller personality, just John Smith or Mary Jones, ignorant of yourselves as being anything greater. It is true your Word still directs the operation of the Law towards yourself—it always does this—but your word has become inverted, and so calls into operation the Law of Contraction instead of the Law of Expansion. A higher position means a wider field for usefulness—that is all; and to the extent to which you fit yourself for it, it will come to you. So, if you content yourself with always speaking in your Thought the Creative Word of "Being" from day to day, you will find it the Way of Peace and the Secret of a Happy Life—by no means monotonous, for all sorts of unexpected interests will be continually opening out to you, giving you scope for all the activities of which your present degree of "being" renders you capable. You will always find plenty to do, and find pleasure in doing it, so you need never be afraid of feeling dull.

But perhaps you will say:

"How am I to know that I am not speaking my own Word instead of that of the Creative Spirit?"

Well, the word of the smaller personality is always based on the idea of possessing, and the Word of the Spirit is always based on the idea of Becoming—that is the criterion. And also, if we base our speaking of the Word on the Promises of Spirit, we may be sure that we are on the right track.

We may be sure of it, because when we come to analyze these promises we shall find that they are all statements of the Creative Law of Being, and the nature of this Law is obvious from the facts of the Visible Creation.

These things are not true because they are written in the Bible, but the Bible is true because these things are written in it. The more we examine the Bible Promises, the more they will impress themselves upon us as being Promises according to Law; and since the Law can never be broken, we can feel quite secure of it, subject to the one condition that we do not stop the Law from working to the fulfilment of the Promise, by our own inverted use of the Word. But if we take the *Word of the Promise* and make it our own Word, then we know that we are speaking the right Word, which will so specialize the action of the Law, as to produce the fulfilment of the Promise. Apart from the Word there is no Foundation. In all other systems we have either Law without Will, or Will without Law.

Then we know that we are not speaking of ourselves, but are speaking the Word of the Power that sent us into the World. The Law alone cannot fulfil the Promises. It is in itself Cosmic and Impersonal, and, as every scientific discovery amply demonstrates, it needs the co-operation of the Personal Factor to bring out its latent possibilities; so that the Word is as necessary as the Law for the fulfilment of the Promises; but if the Word which we speak is that of the Creating Spirit, we may reckon it as being just as certain in its operation as the Law, and the two together form an infallible Power.

But there is one thing we must not forget, and this is the Law of Growth. If the Law which we plant is the seed, then we must allow time for it to grow; we must leave it alone and go about our business as usual, and the seed we have sown will spring and grow up of itself, we know not how, a truth which we have been told by the Master himself (Mark iv, 26, 29).

We must not be like children who plant a seed one day, and dig it up the next to see whether it is growing. Our part is to plant the seed, not to make it grow,—the Creative Law of Life will do that. It is for this reason that the Bible gives us such injunctions as "Study to be quiet" (1 Thess. iv, 11). "He that believeth shall not make haste" (Is. xxviii, 16). "In quietness and in confidence shall be your strength" (Is. xxx, 15). To make ourselves anxious as to whether the Word we have planted will fructify is just to dig it up again, and then of course it will not grow.

The fundamental maxim, then, which we must always keep in mind is that "Every creation carries its own Mathematics along with it," and that therefore "The Law flows from the Word, and not *vice versa*;" and consequently *"The Word is the Foundation of every creative series,"* whether that series be great or small, cosmic or individual, constructive or destructive. Every series commences with Intention; and remember the exact meaning of the Word. It is from the two Latin words "in," towards, and "tendere," to stretch, and it therefore means a "reaching out in a certain direction." This "reaching out in a certain direction" is the Conception of ourself as arrived at the destination towards which our Thought tends, and is therefore *the conceiving of an idea*, and our formulated idea is stated, if only mentally, in Words—and the termination of the series is the realization of the idea in actual fact. Therefore it is equally true of every series, whether it be the creation of a lady's blouse or the creation of a world, that "in the Beginning is the Word"—the Word is *the Point of Origination*.

Then, since the Word is the Point of Origination, what is our conception of the best thing we can originate with it? There is a great variety of opinion as to what is desirable; and it is only natural and right that it should be so, for otherwise we should be without any individuality, which means that we should have no real life in us—in fact such a world is unthinkable; it would be a world that had ceased to move, it would be a dead world. So it is the varied conception of "the Good" that makes the world go on. Uniformity means reducing things to one dead level. But on the other hand there must be Unity—unity of action resulting from unity of purpose, otherwise the world logically terminates in internecine strife. If then the world is to go on, it can only be by means of Unity expressing itself in Variety, and therefore the question is: What is the *unifying Desire* which underlies all the varieties of expression? It is a very simple one—it is just to *enjoy living*. Our ideas of an enjoyable life may be very various, but that is what we all really want; so what we want to get at is: What is the basis of an enjoyable life?

I have no hesitation in saying that the secret of enjoying life is *to take an interest in it*. The opposite of Livingness is Deadness, that is, inertia and stagnation. Dying of "ennui" is a very real thing indeed, and if we would not die of this malady we must have an interest in life that will always keep going on.

Now for anything to interest us we must enter into the spirit of it. If we do not enter into the spirit of a game it does not interest us; if we do not enter into the spirit of a book, it does not interest us, we are bored to death with it; and so on with everything. So from our own experience we may lay down the maxim that "To enjoy anything we must enter into the spirit of it," and if this be so, then, to enjoy the "Living Quality of Life" we must enter into the Spirit of Life itself. I say the "Living Quality of Life" so as to dissociate it from all ideas of particular conditions; because what we are trying to get at is the fundamental principle of Life which creates conditions, and not the reflex of sensations, whether physical or mental, which any particular set of conditions may induce in us for the time being. In this way we come back to the initial proposition with which we started—that the origin of everything is only to be found in a Universal Ever-Living Spirit, and that our own life proceeds from this Spirit in accordance with the maxim "Omne vivum ex vivo." Thus we are logically brought to the conclusion that the ultimate Desire of all Humanity is to consciously enter into the Spirit of Life as it is *in itself*, antecedently to all conditions. This is the widest of all generalizations, and so opens the door to the highest of all specializations; for it is a scientific fact that the more widely we can generalize the principle of any Law, the more highly we can specialize its working. It is only as our conception of it is limited that any Law limits us.

A principle *per se* is always undifferentiated, and capable of any sort of differentiation into particular modes of expression that are not in opposition to the principle itself; and it is true of the Principle of Life as of all others. There is therefore no limit to its expression except that which inverts it,—that is to say, anything which tends towards Death; and, accordingly, what we have to avoid is the negative mode of Thought, which starts an inverted action of the Law, logically resulting in destructiveness instead of constructiveness. But the mistake we make from not seeing the basic principle of the whole thing, is that of looking to the conditions to form the Life, instead of looking to the Life to form the conditions; and therefore what we require is a *Standard of Measurement* for our Thought, by which we shall be able to form *The Perfect Word* which will set in motion the Law of Cause and Effect in such a manner as to fulfil that *Basic Desire of Life* which is common to all Humanity. The Perfect Word must therefore fulfil two Conditions—it must have the essential Quality of the Undifferentiated Eternal Life, and it must have the essential Quality of "Genus Homo." It must say with Horace "Homo sum; nihil humani mihi alienum puto" (I am Man; I regard nothing human as alien to myself). When we think it out carefully, there is no escaping the conclusion that this must be the essential Quality of the Perfect Word we are in search of. It is the final logical inference from all that we have learnt regarding the interaction between Law and Personality, that the Perfect Word must combine in itself the Quality of each—it must be at once both Human and Divine.

Of course all my readers know where the description of such a Word is to be found; but what I want them to realize is the way in which we have now reached a similar description of the Perfect Word. We have not accepted it unquestioningly as the teaching of a scholastic theology, but have arrived at it by a course of careful reasoning from the facts of physical Nature and from our experience of our own mental powers. This way of getting at it makes it really our own. We know what we mean by it, and it is no longer a mere traditional form of words. It is the same with everything else; nothing becomes our own by being just told about it.

For instance, if I show an artist a picture, and he tells me that a boat in it is half a mile away from the spectators, I may accept this on his authority, because I suppose he knows all about it. But if next day a friend shows me a picture of a bit of coast with a fishing-boat in the distance, and asks me how far off that boat is, I am utterly stumped because I do not know how the artist was able to judge the distance. But if I understand the principle, I give my friend a very fair approximation of the distance of the boat. I work it out like this. I say:—the immediate foreground of the picture shows an amount of detail which could not be seen more than twenty yards away, and the average size of such details in nature shows that the bottom edge of the picture must measure about ten yards across. Then from experience I know that the average length of craft of the particular rigging in the picture is, say, about eighty feet, and I then measure that this length goes sixteen and a half times across the picture on the level where the boat is situated, and so I know that a line across the picture at this level measures 80 x 16-1/2 = 1320 ft. = 440 yards. Then I make the calculation: 10 yds.: 440 yds.:: 20 yds.: the distance required to be ascertained 440 x 20 / 10 = 880 yds. 1760 yds. = 1 mile and 1760 / 2 = 880 yds. Therefore I know that the boat in the picture is represented as being about half a mile from the spectator. I really know the distance and do not merely guess it, and I know *how* I know it. I know it simply from the geometrical principle that with a given angle at the apex of a triangle the length of a perpendicular dropped from the apex to the base of the triangle will always bear the same ratio to the length of the base, whatever the size of the triangle may be. In this way I know the distance of the boat in the picture by combining mathematics and my own observation of facts—once again to co-operation of Law and Personality. Now a familiar instance like this shows the difference between being told a thing and really knowing it, and it is by an analogous method that we have now arrived at the conclusion that the Perfect Word is a combination of the Human and the Divine. We have definite reasons for seeing this as the ultimate fact of human development—the power to give expression to the Perfect Word—, and that this follows naturally from the fact of our own existence and that of some originating source from which we derive it.

But perhaps the reader will say: How can a Word take form as a Person? Well, words which do not eventually take form as facts only evaporate into thin air, and we cannot conceive the Divine Ideals of Man doing this. Therefore the expression of the Perfect Word on the plane of Humanity must take substance in the Form of Humanity. It is not the manifestation of any limited personality with all his or her idiosyncrasies, but the manifestation of the basic principle of Humanity itself common to us all.

To quote Dryden's words—but in a very different sense to that intended in "Absolom and Achitophel,"—such a one must be "Not one, but all Mankind's epitome." The manifestation must be the Perfect Expression of that fundamental Life which is the Root Desire in us all, and which is therefore called "The Desire of all nations."

Here then we have reached (Haggai ii, 7) the foundation fact of Human Personality. It is the Eternal "Will-to-live," as Schopenhauer calls it, which works subconsciously in all creation; therefore it is the root from which all creation springs. In the atom it becomes atomic energy, in the plant it becomes vegetable life, in the animal it becomes animal life, and in man it becomes personal life, and therefore, if a Perfect Standard of the Eternal Life is to be set before us, it must be in terms of Human Personality.

But some one will say: Why should we need such a Standard? The answer is that since the working of the Law towards each of us is determined by our mode of Thought, we require to be guarded against an inverted use of the Word. "Ignorantia Legis nemini excusat" (ignorance of the Law does not excuse you from its operation), is a scientific, as well as a forensic maxim, for the Law of Cause and Effect can never be altered. Our ignorance of the laws of electricity will not prevent us from being electrocuted if we get into the circuit of some powerful voltage.

Therefore, because the Law is *Impersonal* and knows no exceptions, and will bring us either Life or Death according to the direction which we give it by our Word, it is of the first importance for us to have a Standard by which to measure the Word expressed through our own Personality. This is why St. Paul speaks of our growing to "the measure of the stature of the fulness of Christ," (Eph. iv, 13) and why we find the symbol of "Measurement" so frequently employed in the Bible.

Therefore, if a great scale of measurement for our Word is to be exhibited, it can only be by its presentation in human form.

Then if the purpose be to establish such a standard of measurement, the scale must be expressed in units of the same denomination as that of our own nature—you cannot divide miles by ampères—and it is because the scale of our potential being is laid out in the same denomination as that of the Spirit of Life itself that we can avail ourselves of the standard of "the Word made Flesh."

When this is clearly seen it removes those intellectual difficulties which so many feel with regard to the doctrine of the Atonement. If we want to avail ourselves of the Bible Promises on the basis of the Bible teaching, we cannot throw the teaching overboard. As I have said before, if a doctrine is to be rightly interpreted, it must be interpreted as a whole, and in one form or another the doctrine of the Atonement is the pivot point of the whole Bible. To omit it is like trying to play "Hamlet" with Hamlet left out, and you may put your Bible out on the rubbish-heap. How, then, does the Atonement come in?

Here are the usual intellectual difficulties. To whom is the sacrifice offered? To God or to the Devil? If it be to the Devil, then the Devil is a greater power than God. If it be to God, then how can a God who demands a sacrifice of blood be Love? And in either case how can guilt be transferred from one person to the other?

Now as a matter of fact none of these questions arise. They are beside the real point at issue, which is: How can we so combine the Personal action of the Word with the Impersonal action of the Law, as to make the Law become to us the Law of Life instead of the Law of Death (Rom. viii, 2)?

Let us recur to the principles which we have worked out. The Law flows from the Word and not *vice versa* —it acts for good or ill according to the Quality of the Word which calls it into action. Therefore to get the Law of Life we must speak the Word of Life. Then, on the principle of "Omne vivum ex vivo," the Word of Fundamental Basic Life, which is not subject to conditions because it is antecedent to all conditions, can only be spoken through consciousness of participating in the Eternal Life which is the "fons et origo" of all particular being. Therefore, to be able to speak this Word we must have a foundation of assurance that we are in no way separated from the Eternal Life, and since this foundation is required for all men, it must be broad enough to accommodate all grades of perceptions.

Theologically the separation from the Eternal Life is said to be caused by "Sin." But what do we mean by "Sin"?

We can only judge of what a thing *is* by what it *does*; and so, if "Sin" is that which prevents the inflowing of the Eternal Life, which we know is the root of our individual being, then it must be the transgression of the inherent Law of our own Being. The truth is that we live simultaneously in two worlds, the visible and the invisible, just as trees draw their life from the earth beneath and from the air and light above, and the transgression consists in limiting ourselves only to the lower world, and thereby cutting ourselves off from the essential part of our own life, that which *really lives* .

We do not realize the true function of the three lower principles of our nature, viz.: Vital Spirit, etheric body, and outward form; the function of which is to give concentration to the current of spiritual life flowing from the Eternal Spirit, and thus enable the undifferentiated Life to differentiate itself into Individual Consciousness, which will be able to specialize the action of the Law into higher manifestations than it can produce without the co-operation of Personality.

On the analogy of Ohm's Law our error is making our "R" so rigid that it ceases to be a conductor, and so no current is delivered and no work done. This is the true nature of sin, and it is this opposition of our R to E.M.F. or Eternal Motive Force that has to be removed. We have to realize the true function of our R, as the channel through which the E.M.F. is enabled to carry on its work. When we awake to the fact that our true place in the Order of the Universe is to be fellow-workers with God in carrying on the work of Creation, then we see that hitherto we have entirely missed the purpose of our calling, and have misused the Divine image in which we were created; and therefore we want an assurance that our past errors will not stand in the way of our future advance into continually fuller participation in the Divine Creative Work, which, in virtue of our true nature should be our rightful inheritance.

That our future destiny is to actually take an individual part, however small, in guiding the great work of Evolution, may not be evident to us in the earlier stages of our awakening; but what is clear as a matter of feeling, but not yet intellectually, is, that in some way or other we have been cutting ourselves off from the Great Source of Light, and that what we therefore want, is to be re-united to it. What is wanted, then, is something which will give us a firm ground of assurance that we *are* re-united to it, and that that something must be of such a nature as never to lose anything of its efficiency at any stage of our progress—it must cover the whole ground.

Now, if we think deeply upon this question, we shall gradually come to see that this expansive quality is to be found in the doctrine of the Atonement. It meets all the needs of our spiritual nature in a way that no other theory does, and responds to every stage of our progress. There is only one thing that will prevent it working, and that is, saying that we have no need of it. That is why St. John said, that if we say we have no sin, we deceive ourselves, and the truth is not in us (1 John i, 8). But the more we come into the light of Truth, and realize that sin is everything that is not in accordance with the Law of our own essential being as related to the Eternal Life, the more we shall see, not only that we have transgressed the Law in the past, but also that even now we are very far from completely fulfiling it; and the more light we get the more clearly we shall see this to be the case. Therefore, whatever may be the stage of our mental development, the assurance which we all need for the basis of our new life is that of the removal of sin—the sins of the past, and the daily errors of the present. We may form various theories, each to our own satisfaction, as to *how* this takes place. For instance we may argue that, since "the Word" is the undifferentiated potential of Humanity, every human soul is included in the Self-offering of Christ, and that in Him we ourselves suffered on the Cross. Or we may say that our confession that such an offering is needed amounts to our participation in it. Or we may say with St. Paul that, as in Adam all are sinners, so in Christ all are made free from sin (1 Cor. xv, 22). That is, taking Adam and Christ as the representatives of two orders of men. Or we may fall back on the statement "Sacrifice and burnt offerings Thou wouldst not" (Ps. xl, 6), and on Jesus' own explanation of his death, that He offered himself in testimony to the Truth—that is, that the Eternal Life will no more exercise a retrospective vengeance upon us for our past misunderstanding of It, than would electricity or any other force. We may explain the *modus operandi* of the great offering in any of these ways, for the Scripture presents it in all of them—but the great thing is to accept it; for by the nature of our mental constitution, such an acceptance, whether with or without an intellectual explanation, affords the assurance which we stand in need of; and building upon the Foundation we can safely rear the edifice of our future development.

Also it affords us a continual safeguard in all the further stages of our evolution. As our psychic consciousness increases, we become more and more responsive to psychic stimulus whether that stimulus proceed from a good or evil influence; and therefore the recognition of our Redemption in Christ surrounds us with a protecting barrier, through which no evil spirit or malign influence can pass; so that, resting upon this Truth, we need never be in fear of any such invasion, but shall at all times be clothed with the whole armour of God (Eph. vi, 11).

From whatever point of view we regard it, we therefore find in the One Offering once made for the sin of the whole world, a standpoint such as is provided by no other teaching, whether religious or philosophical; and we shall see on examination that it is not an arbitrary decree for which we can give no account, but that it is based on the psychological constitution of man—a provision so perfectly adapted to our requirements at every stage of our evolution, that we can only attribute it to the Divine Wisdom acting through One, who by Perfect Love, thus willingly offered himself, in order to provide the Foundation of complete assurance for all who recognize their need of it.

On this basis, then, of reunion with the Eternal Source of Life, all the Promises of the Bible are found to be according to Law—that is, according to the inherent Law of our Being; so that, in the laying of this Foundation, we find the supreme manifestation of the interaction between the Law and the Word, which, when its significance is apprehended, opens out vistas of limitless possibilities to the individual and to the race.

But the race, as a whole, is yet very far from apprehending this, and for the most part has no perception of spiritual causation. Where some dim perception of spiritual causation is beginning to emerge, it is very frequently inverted, because people only apprehend it as giving them an additional power of exercising compulsion over their fellow-men, and thus depriving them of that individuality which it is the one purpose of Evolution to develop. This is because people do not look beyond the three lower principles of life, those principles which animals have in common with man; and consequently the higher principle of mind, which distinguishes man, is brought down to the lower level, so that the man is distinguished from the beast only by the possession of intellectual faculties, which by their perversion make him not merely a beast, but a devil of a beast. Therefore the recognition of psychic powers, when not safeguarded by the higher principles of Truth, plunges man even deeper into darkness than does a simple materialism; and so the two go hand in hand on the downward path. There is abundant evidence that this is increasingly the case at the present day; and therefore it is that the Bible Promises culminate in the Promise of the return of Him who offered himself in order to lay the foundation of Peace. As I have said before, we must either take the Bible as a whole, or reject it entirely. We cannot pick and choose what pleases us, and refuse what does not. No legal document could be treated in this way; and in like manner the Bible is one great whole, or else it is just—"skittles."

Therefore, if that Divine "Word" was manifested to save the world from destruction, by opening the way for the *individual* through recognition of his true relation to God, then it is only a reasonable carrying out of the same thought that, when the bulk of mankind fail to realize the beneficent use of these powers, and persist in using them invertedly, the same Being should again appear to save the race from utter self-destruction, but not by the same method, for that would be impossible.

The individual method is that of individual self-recognition in the light of Truth; but that cannot be *forced* upon any one. The headlong downward career of the race as a whole cannot therefore be stopped *vi et armis* , and this can only be done by first letting it have a bitter experience of what intellect, depraved to the service of the Beast in Man, leads to, and then forcibly restraining those who persist in this madness. Therefore a Second Coming of the Divine Man is a logical sequence to the first, and equally logical, this Second Coming must be as One who will rule the nations with irresistible power; so that men, reflecting upon the evils of the past, and enquiring into their cause, may be led to see that cause in the inverted action of the Law of their own being, and may therefore learn so to renew their thoughts in accordance with the Divine Thought as to bring them into the glorious liberty of the Sons of God.

This, then, is the Promise we have to look forward to at the present day, and though it might not be wise to speculate as to the precise time and manner of its fulfilment, there can be no doubt as to the nature of the general principles involved; and I trust the reader has at least learned from this book that principles unfold themselves with unfailing accuracy, though it depends on our Word, or mental attitude, in what way their unfoldment will affect us personally.

For such reasons as these, it appears to me, that the current objections to the doctrine of Atonement are entirely beside the mark. They miss the whole point of the thing. Punishment for Sin? Of course there is punishment for sin so long as it is persisted in. It is the natural working of the Law of Cause and Effect. Forgiveness of sin? Of course there is forgiveness of sin as soon as, through knowledge, we make a right use of the Law of our own Being. It could not be otherwise. It is the natural working of the Law of Cause and Effect.

"This is the covenant that I will make with them after those days, saith the Lord, I will put my laws into their hearts, and in their minds will I write them; and their sins and iniquities will I remember no more" (Heb. x, 16); and similarly in Jer. xxxi, 32, from which the writer of the Epistles to the Hebrews quotes this. "Now the Lord is the Spirit" (2 Cor. iii, 17, R.V.), i.e., the Originating Spirit of life, and therefore "my laws" means the inherent Law of the Originating Principle of Being, so that here we have a plain statement that the realization of the True Law of our Being *ipso facto* results in the cancelling of all our past errors. When once we see the principle of it the whole sequence becomes perfectly plain.

There is nothing arbitrary in all this. It results naturally from a New mode of Thought producing a New order of Consciousness; and it is written that "if any man be in Christ he is a new creature" or, as it says in the margin, "a new creation" (2 Cor. v, 17), and on the principle that "every Creation carries its own mathematics with it," every such man has passed from the Law of Death into the Law of Life. The full fruition may not yet be visible—we must allow for the Law of Growth—but the Principle is in him and has become the central, generating point of his consciousness, and is therefore bound, sooner or later, to develop into perfect manifestation by the Law of its own nature. If the Principle be accepted it will work all the same, whether we accept it by simple trust in the written Word, or whether we analyze the grounds of our trust; just as an electric bell will ring when you press the button, whether you are an electrical engineer or not. But there will be this difference, that if you *are* an electrical engineer you will see the principle implied in the ringing of the bell, and you will find in it the promise of infinite possibilities which it is open to you to develope; and in like manner, the more clearly you see the relation which necessarily exists between yourself and the All-Originating Living Spirit, the more clear it will become to you, that this relation opens up an endless vista of boundless potentialities which can never be exhausted. This is the true nature of the Bible Promises; they were not made by some external Deity about whose ideas we can never have any certainty, but by the Indwelling God, who is at once the Life, the Law, and the Substance of all things, and therefore they are Promises according to Law, containing in themselves the principle of their own fulfilment.

But, as I trust the reader is now convinced, the Law can fulfil the Promise which is latent in it only by the co-operation of the Word; that is, the Personal Factor which provides the necessary conditions for the Law to work under; and therefore, if the Promise is to be fulfilled, we must meet the All-originating Life, the "Premium mobile," not only on the Plane of Law, but on the Plane of Personality also. This becomes evident if we consider that this Originating Life must be *entirely undifferentiated* in Itself; for otherwise it could not be the origin of all differentiated modes of Life and Energy. As long as we find differentiation, on however wide a scale, we have not arrived at First Cause. There will still be something further back, out of which the differentiations have proceeded; and it is this "Something" which is at the back of "Everything" that we are in search of. Therefore the Originating Spirit must be *absolutely undifferentiated* , and consequently the Personal Factor in ourselves must be the differentiation into individuality of a Quality eternally subsisting in the All-Originating Undifferentiated Spirit.

Then, since our individual differentiation of this Quality must depend on the mode of our recognition of it, it follows that a Standard of Measurement is needed, and the Standard is presented to us in the form of the Personality around whom the whole Bible centres, and who, as the Standard of the Divine Infinitude differentiating Himself into units of individual personality, can only be described as at once The Son of God and The Son of Man. If we see that the Eternal Life, by reason of its non-differentiation in itself, must needs become to each of us *exactly what we take it to be* , then it follows that in order to realize it on our own plane of Personality we must see it *through the medium of Personality* , and it is therefore not a theological figment, but the Supreme Psychological Truth that no man can come to "the Father"—that is, to the Parent Spirit—except through the Son (John xiv, 6).

When we see the reason at the back of it, the Bible becomes a New Book to us, and we learn that the interpretation of it is not to be found in learned commentaries, but in ourselves. Then we find that it is indeed The Book of Promises, not vague and uncertain, but logical and scientific, teaching us how to combine the instrumentality of the Law with the freedom of the Word; so that through the Perfect Word, manifested as the Perfect Man, we reach the Perfect Law, and find that *The perfect law is the law of liberty.*

FOOTNOTES:

[1] For various reasons I am not giving the actual names of places and persons in this story.

[2] "Out of Egypt" by Miss Crouse. Gorham Press, Boston, U.S.A.

[3] R.W. Allen.

[4] See Chapters on "Body, Soul, and Spirit" in my "Edinburgh Lectures on Mental Science."

[5] See "Edinburgh Lectures."

[6] "New Knowledge."

The Creative Process in the Individual

FOREWORD

In the present volume I have endeavored to set before the reader the conception of a sequence of creative action commencing with the formation of the globe and culminating in a vista of infinite possibilities attainable by every one who follows up the right line for their unfoldment.

I have endeavored to show that, starting with certain incontrovertible scientific facts, all these things logically follow, and that therefore, however far these speculations may carry us beyond our past experience, they nowhere break the thread of an intelligible connection of cause and effect.

I do not, however, offer the suggestions here put forward in any other light than that of purely speculative reasoning; nevertheless, no advance in any direction can be made except by speculative reasoning going back to the first principles of things which we do know and thence deducing the conditions under which the same principles might be carried further and made to produce results hitherto unknown. It is to this method of thought that we owe all the advantages of civilization from matches and post-offices to motor-cars and aeroplanes, and we may therefore be encouraged to hope such speculations as the present may not be without their ultimate value. Relying on the maxim that Principle is not bound by Precedent we should not limit our expectations of the future; and if our speculations lead us to the conclusion that we have reached a point where we are not only able, but also *required* , by the law of our own being, to take a more active part in our personal evolution than heretofore, this discovery will afford us a new outlook upon life and widen our horizon with fresh interests and brightening hopes.

If the thoughts here suggested should help any reader to clear some mental obstacles from his path the writer will feel that he has not written to no purpose. Only each reader must think out these suggestions for himself. No writer or lecturer can convey an idea *into* the minds of his audience. He can only put it before them, and what they will make of it depends entirely upon themselves—assimilation is a process which no one can carry out for us.

To the kindness of my readers on both sides of the Atlantic, and in Australia and New Zealand, I commend this little volume, not, indeed, without a deep sense of its many shortcomings, but at the same time encouraged by the generous indulgence extended to my previous books.

T.T.

June, 1910.

TABLE OF CONTENTS

I say no man has ever yet been half devout enough,
None has ever yet adored or worship'd half enough,
None has begun to think how divine he himself is, and
how certain the future is.
I say that the real and permanent grandeur of these States
must be their religion,
Otherwise there is no real and permanent grandeur. —Walt Whitman.

THE STARTING-POINT

It is an old saying that "Order is Heaven's First Law," and like many other old sayings it contains a much deeper philosophy than appears immediately on the surface. Getting things into a better order is the great secret of progress, and we are now able to fly through the air, not because the laws of Nature have altered, but because we have learnt to arrange things in the right order to produce this result—the things themselves had existed from the beginning of the world, but what was wanting was the introduction of a Personal Factor which, by an intelligent perception of the possibilities contained in the laws of Nature, should be able to bring into working reality ideas which previous generations would have laughed at as the absurd fancies of an unbalanced mind. The lesson to be learnt from the practical aviation of the present day is that of the triumph of principle over precedent, of the working out of an *idea* to its logical conclusions in spite of the accumulated testimony of all past experience to the contrary; and with such a notable example before us can we say that it is futile to enquire whether by the same method we may not unlock still more important secrets and gain some knowledge of the unseen causes which are at the back of external and visible conditions, and then by bringing these unseen causes into a better order make practical working realities of possibilities which at present seem but fantastic dreams? It is at least worth while taking a preliminary canter over the course, and this is all that this little volume professes to attempt; yet this may be sufficient to show the lay of the ground.

Now the first thing in any investigation is to have some idea of what you are looking for—to have at least some notion of the general direction in which to go—just as you would not go up a tree to find fish though you would for birds' eggs. Well, the general direction in which we all want to go is that of getting more out of Life than we have ever got out of it—we want to be more alive in ourselves and to get all sorts of improved conditions in our environment. However happily any of us may be circumstanced we can all conceive something still better, or at any rate we should like to make our present good permanent; and since we shall find as our studies advance that the prospect of increasing possibilities keeps opening out more and more widely before us, we may say that what we are in search of is the secret of getting more out of Life in a continually progressive degree. This means that what we are looking for is something personal, and that it is to be obtained by producing conditions which do not yet exist; in other words it is nothing less than the exercise of a certain creative power in the sphere of our own particular world. So, then, what we want is to introduce our own Personal Factor into the realm of unseen causes. This is a big thing, and if it is possible at all it must be by some sequence of cause and effect, and this sequence it is our object to discover. The law of Cause and Effect is one we can never get away from, but by carefully following it up we may find that it will lead us further than we had anticipated.

Now, the first thing to observe is that if *we* can succeed in finding out such a sequence of cause and effect as the one we are in search of, somebody else may find out the same creative secret also; and then, by the hypothesis of the case, we should both be armed with an infallible power, and if we wanted to employ this power against each other we should be landed in the "impasse" of a conflict between two powers each of which was irresistible. Consequently it follows that the first principle of this power must be Harmony. It cannot be antagonizing itself from different centers—in other words its operation in a simultaneous order at every point is the first necessity of its being. What we are in search of, then, is a sequence of cause and effect so universal in its nature as to include harmoniously all possible variations of individual expression. This primary necessity of the Law for which we are seeking should be carefully borne in mind, for it is obvious that any sequence which transgresses this primary essential must be contrary to the very nature of the Law itself, and consequently cannot be conducting us to the exercise of true creative power.

What we are seeking, therefore, is to discover how to arrange things in such an order as to set in motion a train of causation that will harmonize our own conditions without antagonizing the exercise of a like power by others. This therefore means that all individual exercise of this power is the particular application of a universal power which itself operates creatively on its own account independently of these individual applications; and the harmony between the various individual applications is brought about by all the individuals bringing their own particular action into line with this independent creative action of the original power. It is in fact another application of Euclid's axiom that things which are equal to the same thing are equal to one another; so that though I may not know for what purpose some one may be using this creative power in Pekin, I do know that if he and I both realize its true nature, we cannot by any possibility be working in opposition to one another. For these reasons, having now some general idea of what it is we are in search of, we may commence our investigation by considering this common factor which must be at the back of all individual exercise of creative power, that is to say, the Generic working of the Universal Creative Principle.

That such a Universal Creative Principle is at work we at once realize from the existence of the world around us with all its inhabitants, and the inter-relation of all parts of the cosmic system shows its underlying Unity—thus the animal kingdom depends on the vegetable, the vegetable kingdom on the mineral, the mineral or globe of the earth on its relation to the rest of the solar system, and possibly our solar system is related by a similar law to the distribution of other suns with their attendant planets throughout space. Our first glance therefore shows us that the All-originating Power must be in essence Unity and in manifestation Multiplicity, and that it manifests as Life and Beauty through the unerring adaptation of means to ends—that is so far as its cosmic manifestation of ends goes: what we want to do is to carry this manifestation still further by operation from an individual standpoint. To do this is precisely our place in the Order of Creation, but we must defer the question why we hold this place till later on.

One of the earliest discoveries we all make is the existence of Matter. The bruised shins of our childhood convince us of its solidity, so now comes the question, Why does Matter exist? The answer is that if the form were not expressed in solid substance, things would be perpetually flowing into each other so that no identity could be maintained for a single moment. To this it might be replied that a condition of matter is conceivable in which, though in itself a plastic substance, in a fluent state, it might yet by the operation of will be held in any particular forms desired. The idea of such a condition of matter is no doubt conceivable, and when the fluent matter was thus held in particular forms you would have concrete matter just as we know it now, only with this difference, that it would return to its fluent state as soon as the supporting will was withdrawn. Now, as we shall see later on, this is precisely what matter really is, only the will which holds it together in concrete form is not individual but cosmic.

In itself the Essence of Matter is precisely the fluent substance we have imagined, and as we shall see later on the knowledge of this fact, when realized in its proper order, is the basis of the legitimate control of mind over matter. But a world in which every individual possessed the power of concreting or fluxing matter at his own sweet will irrespective of any universal coordinating principle is altogether inconceivable—the conflict of wills would prevent such a world remaining in existence. On the other hand, if we conceive of a number of individuals each possessing this power and all employing it on the lines of a common cosmic unity, then the result would be precisely the same stable condition of matter with which we are familiar—this would be a necessity of fact for the masses who did not possess this power, and a necessity of principle for the few who did. So under these circumstances the same stable conditions of Nature would prevail as at present, varied only when the initiated ones perceived that the order of evolution would be furthered, and not hindered, by calling into action the higher laws. Such occasions would be of rare occurrence, and then the departure from the ordinary law would be regarded by the multitude as a miracle. Also we may be quite sure that no one who had attained this knowledge in the legitimate order would ever perform a "miracle" for his own personal aggrandizement or for the purpose of merely astonishing the beholders—to do so would be contrary to the first principle of the higher teaching which is that of profound reverence for the Unity of the All-originating Principle. The conception, therefore, of such a power over matter being possessed by certain individuals is in no way opposed to our ordinary recognition of concrete matter, and so we need not at present trouble ourselves to consider these exceptions.

Another theory is that matter has no existence at all but is merely an illusion projected by our own minds. If so, then how is it that we all project identically similar images? On the supposition that each mind is independently projecting its own conception of matter a lady who goes to be fitted might be seen by her dressmaker as a cow. Generations of people have seen the Great Pyramid on the same spot; but on the supposition that each individual is projecting his own material world in entire independence of all other individuals there is no reason why any two persons should ever see the same thing in the same place. On the supposition of such an independent action by each separate mind, without any common factor binding them all to one particular mode of recognition, no intercourse between individuals would be possible—then, without the consciousness of relation to other individuals the consciousness of our own individuality would be lost, and so we should cease to have any conscious existence at all. If on the other hand we grant that there is, above the individual minds, a great Cosmic Mind which imposes upon them the necessity of all seeing the same image of Matter, then that image is not a projection of the individual minds but of the Cosmic Mind; and since the individual minds are themselves similar projections of the Cosmic Mind, matter is for them just as much a reality as their own existence. I doubt not that material substance is thus projected by the all-embracing Divine Mind; but so also are our own minds projected by it, and therefore the relation between them and matter is a real relation and not a merely fictitious one.

I particularly wish the student to be clear on this point, that where two factors are projected from a common source their relation to each other becomes an absolute fact in respect of the factors themselves, notwithstanding that the power of changing that relation by substituting a different projection must necessarily always continue to reside in the originating source. To take a simple arithmetical example—by my power of mental projection working through my eyes and fingers I write 4 X 2. Here I have established a certain numerical relation which can only produce eight as its result. Again, I have power to change the factors and write 4 X 3, in which case 12 is the only possible result, and so on. Working in this way calculation becomes possible. But if every time I wrote 4 that figure possessed an independent power of setting down a different number by which to multiply itself, what would be the result? The first 4 I wrote might set down 3 as its multiplier, and the next might set down 7, and so on. Or if I want to make a box of a certain size and cut lengths of plank accordingly, if each length could capriciously change its width at a moment's notice, how could I ever make the box? I myself may change the shape and size of my box by establishing new relations between the bits of wood, but for the pieces of wood themselves the proportions determined by my mind must remain fixed quantities, otherwise no construction could take place.

This is a very rough analogy, but it may be sufficient to show that for a cosmos to exist at all it is absolutely necessary that there should be a Cosmic Mind binding all individual minds to certain *generic* unities of action, and so producing all things as realities and nothing as illusion. The importance of this conclusion will become more apparent as we advance in our studies.

We have now got at some reason why concrete material form is a necessity of the Creative Process. Without it the perfect Self-recognition of Spirit from the Individual standpoint, which we shall presently find is the means by which the Creative Process is to be carried forward, would be impossible; and therefore, so far from matter being an illusion, it is the necessary channel for the self-differentiation of Spirit and its Expression in multitudinous life and beauty. Matter is thus the necessary Polar Opposite to Spirit, and when we thus recognize it in its right order we shall find that there is no antagonism between the two, but that together they constitute one harmonious whole.

THE SELF-CONTEMPLATION OF SPIRIT

If we ask how the cosmos came into existence we shall find that ultimately we can only attribute it to the Self-Contemplation of Spirit. Let us start with the facts now known to modern physical science. All material things, including our own bodies, are composed of combinations of different chemical elements such as carbon, oxygen, nitrogen, &c. Chemistry recognizes in all about seventy of these elements each with its peculiar affinities; but the more advanced physical science of the present day finds that they are all composed of one and the same ultimate substance to which the name of Ether has been given, and that the difference between an atom of iron and an atom of oxygen results only from the difference in the number of etheric particles of which each is composed and the rate of their motion within the sphere of the atom, thus curiously coming back to the dictum of Pythagoras that the universe has its origin in Number and Motion. We may therefore say that our entire solar system together with every sort of material substance which it contains is made up of nothing but this one primary substance in various degrees of condensation.

Now the next step is to realize that this ether is everywhere. This is shown by the undulatory theory of light. Light is not a substance but is the effect produced on the eye by the impinging of the ripples of the ether upon the retina. These waves are excessively minute, ranging in length from 1-39,000th of an inch at the red end of the spectrum to 1-57,000th at the violet end. Next remember that these waves are not composed of advancing particles of the medium but pass onwards by the push which each particle in the line of motion gives to the particle next to it, and then you will see that if there were a break of one fifty-thousandth part of an inch in the connecting ether between our eye and any source of light we could not receive light from that source, for there would be nothing to continue the wave-motion across the gap. Consequently as soon as we see light from any source however distant, we know that there must be a continuous body of ether between us and it. Now astronomy shows us that we receive light from heavenly bodies so distant that, though it travels with the incredible speed of 186,000 miles per second, it takes more than two thousand years to reach us from some of them; and as such stars are in all quarters of the heavens we can only come to the conclusion that the primary substance or ether must be universally present.

This means that the raw material for the formation of solar systems is universally distributed throughout space; yet though we find that millions of suns stud the heavens, we also find vast interstellar spaces which show no sign of cosmic activity. Then something has been at work to start cosmic activity in certain areas while passing over others in which the raw material is equally available. What is this something? At first we might be inclined to attribute the development of cosmic energy to the etheric particles themselves, but a little consideration will show us that this is mathematically impossible in a medium which is equally distributed throughout space, for all its particles are in equilibrium and so no one particle possesses *per se* a greater power of originating motion than any other. Consequently the initial movement must be started by something which, though it works on and through the particles of the primary substance, is not those particles themselves. It is this "Something" which we mean when we speak of "Spirit."

Then since Spirit starts the condensation of the primary substance into concrete aggregation, and also does this in certain areas to the exclusion of others, we cannot avoid attributing to Spirit the power of Selection and of taking an Initiative on its own account.

Here, then, we find the *initial* Polarity of Universal Spirit and Universal Substance, each being the complementary of the other, and out of this relation all subsequent evolution proceeds. Being complementary means that each supplies what is wanting in the other, and that the two together thus make complete wholeness. Now this is just the case here. Spirit supplies Selection and Motion. Substance supplies something from which selection can be made and to which Motion can be imparted; so that it is a *sine qua non* for the Expression of Spirit.

Then comes the question, How did the Universal Substance get there? It cannot have made itself, for its only quality is inertia, therefore it must have come from some source having power to project it by some mode of action not of a material nature. Now the only mode of action not of a material nature is Thought, and therefore to Thought we must look for the origin of Substance. This places us at a point antecedent to the existence even of primary substance, and consequently the initial action must be that of the Originating Mind upon Itself, in other words, Self-contemplation.

At this primordial stage neither Time nor Space can be recognized, for both imply measurement of successive intervals, and in the primary movement of Mind upon itself the only consciousness must be that of Present Absolute Being, because no external points exist from which to measure extension either in time or space. Hence we must eliminate the ideas of time and space from our conception of Spirit's *initial* Self-contemplation.

This being so, Spirit's primary contemplation of itself as simply Being necessarily makes its presence universal and eternal, and consequently, paradoxical as it may seem, its independence of Time and Space makes it present throughout all Time and Space. It is the old esoteric maxim that the point expands to infinitude and that infinitude is concentrated in the point. We start, then, with Spirit contemplating itself simply as Being. But to realize your being you must have consciousness, and consciousness can only come by the recognition of your relation to something else. The something else may be an external fact or a mental image; but even in the latter case to conceive the image at all you must mentally stand back from it and look at it—something like the man who was run in by the police at Gravesend for walking behind himself to see how his new coat fitted. It stands thus: if you are not conscious of something you are conscious of nothing, and if you are conscious of nothing, then you are unconscious, so that to be conscious at all you must have something to be conscious of.

This may seem like an extract from "Paddy's Philosophy," but it makes it clear that consciousness can only be attained by the recognition of something which is not the recognizing *ego* itself—in other words consciousness is the realization of some particular sort of *relation* between the cognizing subject and the cognized object; but I want to get away from academical terms into the speech of human beings, so let us take the illustration of a broom and its handle—the two together make a broom; that is one sort of relation; but take the same stick and put a rake-iron at the end of it and you have an altogether different implement. The stick remains the same, but the difference of what is put at the end of it makes the whole thing a broom or a rake. Now the thinking and feeling power is the stick, and the conception which it forms is the thing at the end of the stick, so that the quality of its consciousness will be determined by the ideas which it projects; but to be conscious at all it must project ideas of some sort.

Now of one thing we may be quite sure, that the Spirit of Life must *feel alive* . Then to feel alive it must be conscious, and to be conscious it must have something to be conscious of; therefore the contemplation of itself as standing related to something which is not its own originating self *in propria persona* is a necessity of the case; and consequently the Self-contemplation of Spirit can only proceed by its viewing itself as related to something standing out from itself, just as we must stand at a proper distance to see a picture—in fact the very word "existence" means "standing out." Thus things are called into existence or "outstandingness" by a power which itself does not stand out, and whose presence is therefore indicated by the word "subsistence."

The next thing is that since in the beginning there is nothing except Spirit, its primary feeling of aliveness must be that of being alive *all over* ; and to establish such a consciousness of its own universal livingness there must be the recognition of a corresponding *relation* equally extensive in character; and the only possible correspondence to fulfil this condition is therefore that of a universally distributed and plastic medium whose particles are all in perfect equilibrium, which is exactly the description of the Primary Substance or ether. We are thus philosophically led to the conclusion that Universal Substance must be projected by Universal Spirit as a necessary consequence of Spirit's own inherent feeling of Aliveness; and in this way we find that the great Primary Polarity of Being becomes established.

From this point onward we shall find the principle of Polarity in universal activity. It is that relation between opposites without which no external Motion would be possible, because there would be nowhere to move from, and nowhere to move to; and without which external Form would be impossible because there would be nothing to limit the diffusion of substance and bring it into shape. Polarity, or the interaction of Active and Passive, is therefore the basis of all *Evolution* .

This is a great fundamental truth when we get it in its right order; but all through the ages it has been a prolific source of error by getting it in its wrong order. And the wrong order consists in making Polarity the originating point of the Creative Process. What this misconception leads to we shall see later on; but since it is very widely accepted under various guises even at the present day it is well to be on our guard against it. Therefore I wish the student to see clearly that there is something which comes before that Polarity which gives rise to Evolution, and that this something is the original movement of Spirit *within itself*, of which we can best get an idea by calling it Self-contemplation.

Now this may seem an extremely abstract conception and one with which we have no practical concern. I fancy I can hear the reader saying "The Lord only knows how the world started, and it is His business and not mine," which would be perfectly true if this originating faculty were confined to the Cosmic Mind. But it is not, and the same action takes place in our own minds also, only with the difference that it is ultimately subject to that principle of Cosmic Unity of which I have already spoken. But, subject to that unifying principle, this same power of origination is in ourselves also, and our personal advance in evolution depends on our right use of it; and our use of it depends on our recognition that we ourselves give rise to the particular polarities which express themselves in our whole world of consciousness, whether within or without. For these reasons it is very important to realize that Evolution is not the same as Creation. It is the unfolding of potentialities involved in things already created, but not the calling into existence of what does not yet exist—*that* is Creation.

The order, therefore, which I wish the student to observe is, first the Self-contemplation of Spirit producing Polarity, and next Polarity producing Manifestation in Form—and also to realize that it is in this order his own mind operates as a subordinate center of creative energy. When the true place of Polarity is thus recognized, we shall find in it the explanation of all those relations of things which give rise to the whole world of phenomena; from which we may draw the practical inference that if we want to change the manifestation we must change the polarity, and to change the polarity we must get back to the Self-contemplation of Spirit. But in its proper place as the root-principle of all *secondary* causation, Polarity is one of those fundamental facts of which we must never lose sight. The term "Polarity" is adopted from electrical science. In the electric battery it is the connecting together of the opposite poles of zinc and copper that causes a current to flow from one to the other and so provides the energy that rings the bell. If the connection is broken there is no action. When you press the button you make the connection. The same process is repeated in respect of every sort of polarity throughout the universe. Circulation depends on polarity, and circulation is the *manifestation* of Life, which we may therefore say depends on the principle of polarity. In relation to ourselves we are concerned with two great polarities, the polarity of Soul and Body and the polarity of Soul and Spirit; and it is in order that he may more clearly realize their working that I want the student to have some preliminary idea of Polarity as a general principle.

The conception of the Creative Order may therefore be generalized as follows. The Spirit wants to enjoy the reality of its own Life—not merely to vegetate, but to enjoy giving—and therefore by Self-contemplation it projects a polar opposite, or complementary, calculated to give rise to the particular sort of *relation* out of which the enjoyment of a certain mode of self-consciousness will necessarily spring. Let this sentence be well pondered over until the full extent of its significance is grasped, for it is the key to the whole matter Very well, then: Spirit wants to Enjoy Life, and so, by thinking of itself as *having* the enjoyment which it wishes, it produces the conditions which, by their re-action upon itself, give rise to the reality of the sort of enjoyment contemplated. In more scientific language an opposite polarity is induced, giving rise to a current which stimulates a particular mode of sensation, which sensation in turn becomes a fresh starting-point for still further action; and in this way each successive stage becomes the stepping-stone to a still higher degree of sensation—that is, to a Fuller Enjoyment of Life.

Such a conception as this presents us with a Progressive Series to which it is impossible to assign any limit. That the progression must be limitless is clear from the fact that there is never any change in the method. At each successive stage the Creating Power is the Self-consciousness of the Spirit, as realized at that stage, still reaching forward for yet further Enjoyment of Life, and so always keeping on repeating the *one* Creative Process at an ever-rising level; and since these are the sole working conditions, the progress is one which logically admits of no finality. And this is where the importance of realizing the Singleness of the Originating Power comes in, for with a Duality each member would limit the other; in fact, Duality as the Originating Power is inconceivable, for, once more to quote "Paddy's Philosophy," "finality would be reached before anything was begun."

This Creative Process, therefore, can only be conceived of as limitless, while at the same time strictly progressive, that is, proceeding stage by stage, each stage being necessary as a preparation for the one that is to follow. Let us then briefly sketch the stages by which things in our world have got as far as they have. The interest of the enquiry lies in the fact that if we can once get at the principle which is producing these results, we may discover some way of giving it personal application.

On the hypothesis of the Self-contemplation of Spirit being the originating power, we have found that a primary ether, or universal substance, is the necessary correspondence to Spirit's simple awareness of its own being. But though awareness of being is the necessary foundation for any further possibilities it is, so to say, not much to talk about. The foundation fact, of course, is to know that I Am; but immediately on this consciousness there follows the desire for Activity—I want to enjoy my I Am-ness by doing something with it. Translating these words into a state of consciousness in the Cosmic Mind they become a Law of Tendency leading to *localised* activity, and, looking only at our own world, this would mean the condensation of the universal etheric substance into the primary nebula which later on becomes our solar system, this being the correspondence to the Self-contemplation of Spirit as passing into specific activity instead of remaining absorbed in simple awareness of Being. Then this self-recognition would lead to the conception of still more specific activity having its appropriate polar opposite, or material correspondence, in the condensation of the nebula into a solar system.

Now at this stage Spirit's conception of itself is that of Activity, and consequently the material correspondence is Motion, as distinguished from the simple diffused ether which is the correspondence of mere awareness of

Being, But what sort of motion? Is the material movement evolved at this stage bound to take any particular form? A little consideration will show us that it is. At this initial stage, the first awakening, so to say, of Spirit into activity, its consciousness can only be that of activity *absolute* ; that is, not as related to any other mode of activity because as yet there is none, but only as related to an all-embracing Being; so that the only possible conception of Activity at this stage is that of *Self-sustained* activity, not depending on any preceding mode of activity because there is none. The law of reciprocity therefore demands a similar self-sustained motion in the material correspondence, and mathematical considerations show that the only sort of motion which can sustain a self-supporting body moving *in vacuo* is a rotary motion bringing the body itself into a spherical form. Now this is exactly what we find at both extremes of the material world. At the big end the spheres of the planets rotating on their axes and revolving round the sun; and at the little end the spheres of the atoms consisting of particles which, modern science tells us, in like manner rotate round a common center at distances which are astronomical as compared with their own mass. Thus the two ultimate units of physical manifestation, the atom and the planet, both follow the same law of self-sustained motion which we have found that, on *a priori* grounds, they ought in order to express the primary activity of Spirit. And we may note in passing that this rotary, or *absolute* , motion is the combination of the only two possible *relative* modes of motion, namely, motion from a point and motion to it, that is to say centrifugal and centripetal motion; so that in rotary, or absolute, motion we find that both the polarities of motion are included, thus repeating on the purely mechanical side the primordial principle of the Unity including the Duality in itself.

But the Spirit wants something more than mechanical motion, something more alive than the preliminary Rota, and so the first step toward individualized consciousness meets us in plant life. Then on the principle that each successive stage affords the platform for a further outlook, plant life is followed by animal life, and this by the Human order in which the liberty of selecting its own conditions is immensely extended. In this way the Spirit's expression of itself has now reached the point where its polar complementary, or Reciprocal, manifests as Intellectual Man—thus constituting the Fourth great stage of Spirit's Self-recognition. But the Creative Process cannot stop here, for, as we have seen, its root in the Self-contemplation of Spirit renders it of necessity an Infinite Progression. So it is no use asking what is its ultimate, for it has no ultimate—its word is "Excelsior"—ever Life and "Life more Abundant." Therefore the question is not as to finality where there is none, but as to the next step in the progression. Four kingdoms we know: what is to be the Fifth? All along the line the progress has been in one direction, namely, toward the development of more perfect Individuality, and therefore on the principle of continuity we may reasonably infer that the next stage will take us still further in the same direction. We want something more perfect than we have yet reached, but our ideas as to what it should be are very various, not to say discordant, for one person's idea of better is another person's idea of worse. Therefore what we want to get at is some broad generalization of principle which will be in advance of our past experiences.

This means that we must look for this principle in something that we have not yet experienced, and the only place where we can possibly find principles which have not yet manifested themselves is *in gremio Dei* —that is, in the innermost of the Originating Spirit, or as St. John calls it, "in the bosom of the Father." So we are logically brought to personal participation in the Divine Ideal as the only principle by which the advance into the next stage can possibly be made. Therefore we arrive at the question, What is the Divine Ideal like?

THE DIVINE IDEAL

What is the Divine Ideal? At first it might appear hopeless to attempt to answer such a question, but by adhering to a definite principle we shall find that it will open out, and lead us on, and show us things which we could not otherwise have seen—this is the nature of principle, and is what distinguishes it from mere rules which are only the application of principle under some particular set of conditions. We found two principles as essential in our conception of the Originating Spirit, namely its power of Selection and its power of Initiative; and we found a third principle as its only possible Motive, namely the Desire of the *living* for ever increasing Enjoyment of Life. Now with these three principles as the very essence of the All-originating Spirit to guide us, we shall, I think, be able to form some conception of that Divine Ideal which gives rise to the Fifth Stage of Manifestation of Spirit, upon which we should now be preparing to enter.

We have seen that the Spirit's Enjoyment of Life is necessarily a *reciprocal* —it must have a corresponding fact in manifestation to answer to it; otherwise by the inherent law of mind no consciousness, and consequently no enjoyment, could accrue; and therefore by the law of continuous progression the required Reciprocal should manifest as a being awakening to the consciousness of the principle by which he himself comes into existence.

Such an awakening cannot proceed from a comparison of one set of existing conditions with another, but only from the recognition of a Power which is independent of all conditions, that is to say, the absolute Self-dependence of the Spirit. A being thus awakened would be the proper correspondence of the Spirit's Enjoyment of Life at a stage not only above mechanical motion or physical vitality, but even above intellectual perception of existing phenomena, that is to say at the stage where the Spirit's Enjoyment consists in recognizing itself as the Source of all things. The position in the Absolute would be, so to speak, the awakening of Spirit to the recognition of its own Artistic Ability. I use the word "Artistic" as more nearly expressing an almost unstatable idea than any other I can think of, for the work of the artist approaches more closely to creation *ex nihilo* than any other form of human activity. The work of the artist is the expression of the self that the artist is, while that of the scientist is the comparison of facts which exist independently of his own personality. It is true that the realm of Art is not without its methods of analysis, but the analysis is that of the artist's own feeling and of the causes which give rise to it. These are found to contain in themselves certain principles which are fundamental to all Art, but these principles are the laws of the creative action of mind rather than those of the limitations of matter. Now if we may transfer this familiar analogy to our conception of the working of the All-Originating Mind we may picture it as the Great Artist giving visible expression to His feeling by a process which, though subject to no restriction from antecedent conditions, yet works by a

Law which is inseparable from the Feeling itself—in fact the Law *is* the Feeling, and the Feeling *is* the Law, the Law of Perfect Creativeness.

Some such Self-contemplation as this is the only way in which we can conceive the next, or Fifth, stage of Spirit's Self-recognition as taking place. Having got as far as it has in the four previous stages, that is to the production of intellectual man as its correspondence, the next step in advance must be on the lines I have indicated—unless, indeed, there were a sudden and arbitrary breaking of the Law of Continuity, a supposition which the whole Creative Process up to now forbids us to entertain. Therefore we may picture the Fifth stage of the Self-contemplation of Spirit as its awakening to the recognition of its own Artistic Ability, its own absolute freedom of action and creative power—just as in studio parlance we say that an artist becomes "free of his palette." But by the always present Law of Reciprocity, through which alone self-consciousness can be attained, this Self-recognition of Spirit in the Absolute implies a corresponding objective fact in the world of the Relative; that is to say, the coming into manifestation of a being capable of realizing the Free Creative Artistry of the Spirit, and of recognizing the same principle in himself, while at the same time realizing also the *relation* between the Universal Manifesting Principle and its Individual Manifestation.

Such, it appears to me, must be the conception of the Divine Ideal embodied in the Fifth Stage of the progress of manifestation. But I would draw particular attention to the concluding words of the last paragraph, for if we miss the *relation* between the Universal Manifesting Principle and its Individual Manifestation, we have failed to realize the Principle altogether, whether in the Universal or in the Individual—it is just their interaction that makes each become what it does become—and in this further becoming consists the progression. This relation proceeds from the principle I pointed out in the opening chapter which makes it necessary for the Universal Spirit to be always harmonious with itself; and if this Unity is not recognized by the individual he cannot hold that position of Reciprocity to the Originating Spirit which will enable it to recognize itself as in the Enjoyment of Life at the higher level we are now contemplating—rather the feeling conveyed would be that of something antagonistic, producing the reverse of enjoyment, thus philosophically bringing out the point of the Scriptural injunction, "Grieve not the Spirit." Also the re-action upon the individual must necessarily give rise to a corresponding state of inharmony, though he may not be able to define his feeling of unrest or to account for it. But on the other hand if the grand harmony of the Originating Spirit within itself is duly regarded, then the individual mind affords a fresh center from which the Spirit contemplates itself in what I have ventured to call its Artistic Originality—a boundless potential of Creativeness, yet always regulated by its own inherent Law of Unity.

And this Law of the Spirit's Original Unity is a very simple one. It is the Spirit's necessary and basic conception of itself. A lie is a statement that something is, which is not. Then, since the Spirit's statement or conception of anything necessarily makes that thing exist, it is logically impossible for it to conceive a lie. Therefore the Spirit is Truth. Similarly disease and death are the negative of Life, and therefore the Spirit, as the Principle of Life, cannot embody disease or death in its Self-contemplation. In like manner also, since it is free to produce what it will, the Spirit cannot desire the presence of repugnant forms, and so one of its inherent Laws must be Beauty. In this threefold Law of Truth, Life, and Beauty, we find the whole underlying nature of the Spirit, and no action on the part of the individual can be at variance with the Originating Unity which does not contravert these fundamental principles.

This it will be seen leaves the individual absolutely unfettered except in the direction of breaking up the fundamental harmony on which he himself, as included in the general creation, is dependent. This certainly cannot be called limitation, and we are all free to follow the lines of our own individuality in every other direction; so that, although the recognition of our relation to the Originating Spirit safeguards us from injuring ourselves or others, it in no way restricts our liberty of action or narrows our field of development. Am I, then, trying to base my action upon a fundamental desire for the opening out of Truth, for the increasing of Livingness, and for the creating of Beauty? Have I got this as an ever present Law of Tendency at the back of my thought? If so, then this law will occupy precisely the same place in My Microcosm, or personal world, that it does in the Macrocosm, or great world, as a power which is in itself formless, but which by reason of its presence necessarily impresses its character upon all that the creative energy forms. On this basis the creative energy of the Universal Mind may be safely trusted to work through the specializing influence of our own thought[1] and we may adopt the maxim "trust your desires" because we know that they are the movement of the Universal in ourselves, and that being based upon our fundamental recognition of the Life, Love, and Beauty which the Spirit is, their unfoldments must carry these initial qualities with them all down the line, and thus, in however small a degree, becomes a portion of the working of the Spirit in its inherent creativeness.

This perpetual Creativeness of the Spirit is what we must never lose sight of, and that is why I want the student to grasp clearly the idea of the Spirit's Self-contemplation as the only possible root of the Creative Process. Not only at the first creation of the world, but at all times the plane of the innermost is that of Pure Spirit,[2] and therefore at this, the originating point, there is nothing else for Spirit to contemplate excepting itself; then this Self-contemplation produces corresponding manifestation, and since Self-contemplation or recognition of its own existence must necessarily go on continually, the corresponding creativeness must always be at work. If this fundamental idea be clearly grasped we shall see that incessant and progressive creativeness is the very essence and being of Spirit. This is what is meant by the Affirmativeness of the Spirit. It cannot *per se* act negatively, that is to say uncreatively, for by the very nature of its Self-recognition such a negative action would be impossible. Of course if *we* act negatively then, since the Spirit is always acting affirmatively, we are moving in the opposite direction to it; and consequently so long as we regard our own negative action as being affirmative, the Spirit's action must appear to us negative, and thus it is that all the negative conditions of the world have their root in negative or inverted thought: but the more we bring our thought into harmony with the

Life, Love, and Beauty which the Spirit is, the less these inverted conditions will obtain, until at last they will be eliminated altogether. To accomplish this is our great object; for though the progress may be slow it will be steady if we proceed on a definite principle; and to lay hold of the true principle is the purpose of our studies. And the principle to lay hold of is the Ceaseless Creativeness of Spirit. This is what we mean when we speak of it as The Spirit of the Affirmative, and I would ask my readers to impress this term upon their minds. Once grant that the All-originating Spirit is thus the Spirit of the Pure Affirmative, and we shall find that this will lead us logically to results of the highest value.

If, then, we keep this Perpetual and Progressive Creativeness of the Spirit continually in mind we may rely upon its working as surely in ourselves as in that great cosmic forward movement which we speak of as Evolution. It is the same power of Evolution working within ourselves, only with this difference, that in proportion as we come to realize its nature we find ourselves able to facilitate its progress by offering more and more favorable conditions for its working. We do not add to the force of the Power, for we are products of it and so cannot generate what generates *us* ; but by providing suitable conditions we can more and more highly specialize it. This is the method of all the advance that has ever been made. We never create any force (*e.g.* electricity) but we provide special conditions under which the force manifests *itself* in a variety of useful and beautiful ways, unsuspected possibilities which lay hidden in the power until brought to light by the cooperation of the Personal Factor.

Now it is precisely the introduction[3] of this Personal Factor that concerns us, because to all eternity we can only recognize things from our own center of consciousness, whether in this world or in any other; therefore the practical question is how to specialize in our own case the *generic* Originating Life which, when we give it a name, we call "the Spirit." The method of doing this is perfectly logical when we once see that the principle involved is that of the Self-recognition of Spirit. We have traced the *modus operandi* of the Creative Process sufficiently far to see that the existence of the cosmos is the result of the Spirit's seeing itself *in* the cosmos, and if this be the law of the whole it must also be the law of the part. But there is this difference, that so long as the normal average relation of particles is maintained the whole continues to subsist, no matter what position any particular particle may go into, just as a fountain continues to exist no matter whether any particular drop of water is down in the basin or at the top of the jet. This is the *generic* action which keeps the race going as a whole. But the question is, What is going to become of ourselves? Then because the law of the whole is also the law of the part we may at once say that what is wanted is for the Spirit *to see itself in us* —in other words, to find in us the Reciprocal which, as we have seen, is necessary to its Enjoyment of a certain Quality of Consciousness. Now, the fundamental consciousness of the Spirit must be that of Self-sustaining Life, and for the full enjoyment of this consciousness there must be a corresponding *individual* consciousness reciprocating it; and on the part of the individual such a consciousness can only arise from the recognition that his own life is identical with that of the Spirit—not something sent forth to wander away by itself, but something included in and forming part of the Greater Life. Then by the very conditions of the case, such a contemplation on the part of the individual is nothing else than the Spirit contemplating itself from the standpoint of the individual consciousness, and thus fulfilling the Law of the Creative Process under such specialized conditions as must logically result in the perpetuation of the individual life. It is the Law of the Cosmic Creative Process transferred to the individual.

This, it seems to me, is the Divine Ideal: that of an Individuality which recognizes its Source, and recognizes also the method by which it springs from that Source, and which is therefore able to open up in itself a channel by which that Source can flow in uninterruptedly; with the result that from the moment of this recognition the individual lives directly from the Originating Life, as being himself *a special direct creation* , and not merely as being a member of a generic race. The individual who has reached this stage of recognition thus finds a principle of enduring life *within himself* ; so then the next question is in what way this principle is likely to manifest itself.

THE MANIFESTATION OF THE LIFE PRINCIPLE

We must bear in mind that what we have now reached is a principle, or universal potential, only we have located it in the individual. But a principle, as such, is not manifestation. Manifestation is the growth proceeding *from* the principle, that is to say, some Form in which the principle becomes active. At the same time we must recollect that, though a form is necessary for manifestation, *the* form is not essential, for the same principle may manifest through various forms, just as electricity may work either through a lamp or a tram-car without in any way changing its inherent nature. In this way we are brought to the conclusion that the Life-principle must always provide itself with a body in which to function, though it does not follow that this body must always be of the same chemical constitution as the one we now possess. We might well imagine some distant planet where the chemical combinations with which we are familiar on earth did not obtain; but if the essential life-principle of any individual were transported thither, then by the Law of the Creative Process it would proceed to clothe itself with a material body drawn from the atmosphere and substance of that planet; and the personality thus produced would be quite at home there, for all his surroundings would be perfectly natural to him, however different the laws of Nature might be there from what we know here.

In such a conception as this we find the importance of the two leading principles to which I have drawn attention—first, the power of the Spirit to create *ex nihilo* , and secondly, the individual's recognition of the basic principle of Unity giving permanence and solidity to the frame of Nature. By the former the self-recognizing life-principle could produce any sort of body it chose; and by the latter it would be led to project one in harmony with the natural order of the particular planet, thus making all the facts of that order solid realities to the individual, and himself a solid and natural being to the other inhabitants of that world. But this would not do away with the individual's knowledge of how he got there; and so, supposing him to have realized his identity with the Universal Life-Principle sufficiently to consciously control the projection of his own body, he could at will disintegrate the body which accorded with the conditions of one planet and constitute one which accorded just as harmoniously with those of another, and could thus function on any number of planets as a perfectly natural being on each of them. He would in all respects resemble the other inhabitants with one all-important exception, that since he had attained to unity with his Creative Principle he would not be tied by the laws of matter as they were.

Any one who should attain to such a power could only do so by his realization of the all-embracing Unity of the Spirit as being the Foundation of all things; and this being the basis of his own extended powers he would be the last to controvert his own basic principle by employing his powers in such a way as to disturb the natural course of evolution in the world where he was.

He might use them to help forward the evolution of others in that world, but certainly never to disturb it, for he would always act on the maxim that "Order is Heaven's First Law."

Our object, however, is not to transfer ourselves to other planets but to get the best out of this one; but we shall not get the best out of this one until we realize that the power which will enable us to do so is so absolutely universal and fundamental that its application in this world is precisely the same as in any other, and that is why I have stated it as a general proposition applicable to all worlds.

The principle being thus universal there is no reason why we should postpone its application till we find ourselves in another world, and the best place and time to begin are Here and Now. The starting point is not in time or locality, but in the mode of Thought; and if we realize that this Point of Origination is Spirit's power to produce something out of nothing, and that it does this in accordance with the natural order of substance of the particular world in which it is working, then the spiritual ego in ourselves, as proceeding direct from the Universal Spirit, should be able first, to so harmoniously combine the working of spiritual and physical laws in its own body as to keep it in perfect health, secondly to carry this process further and renew the body, thus eradicating the effects of old age, and thirdly to carry the process still further and perpetuate this renewed body as long as the individual might desire.

If the student shows this to one of his average acquaintances who has never given any thought to these things, his friend will undoubtedly exclaim "Tommy rot!" even if he does not use a stronger expletive. He will at once appeal to the past experience of all mankind, his argument being that what has not been in the past cannot be in the future; yet he does not apply the same argument to aeronautics and is quite oblivious of the fact that the Sacred Volume which he reverences contains promises of these very things. The really earnest student must never forget the maxim that "Principle is not bound by Precedent"—if it were we should still be primitive savages.

To use the Creative Process we must Affirm the Creative Power, that is to say, we must go back to the Beginning of the series and start with Pure Spirit, only remembering that this starting-point is now to be found *in ourselves*, for this is what distinguishes the individual Creative Process from the cosmic one. This is where the importance of realizing only *one* Originating Power instead of two interacting powers comes in, for it means that we do not derive our power from any existing polarity, but that we are going to establish polarities which will start secondary causation on the lines which we thus determine. This also is where the importance comes in of recognizing that the only possible originating movement of spirit must be Self-contemplation, for this shows us that we do not have to contemplate existing conditions but the Divine Ideal, and that this contemplation of the Divine Ideal of Man is the Self-contemplation of the Spirit from the standpoint of Human Individuality.

Then the question arises, if these principles are true, why are we not demonstrating them? Well, when our fundamental principle is obviously correct and yet we do not get the proper results, the only inference is that somewhere or other we have introduced something antagonistic to the fundamental principle, something not inherent in the principle itself and which therefore owes its presence to some action of our own. Now the error consists in the belief that the Creative Power is limited by the material in which it works. If this be assumed, then you have to calculate the resistances offered by the material; and since by the terms of the Creative Process these resistances do not really exist, you have no basis of calculation at all—in fact you have no means of knowing where you are, and everything is in confusion. This is why it is so important to remember that the Creative Process is the action of a Single Power, and that the interaction of two opposite polarities comes in at a later stage, and is not creative, but only distributive—that is to say, it localizes the Energy already proceeding from the Single Power. This is a fundamental truth which should never be lost sight of. So long, however, as we fail to see this truth we necessarily limit the Creative Power by the material it works in, and in practise we do this by referring to past experience as the only standard of judgment. We are measuring the Fifth Kingdom by the standard of the Fourth, as though we should say that an intellectual man, a being of the Fourth Kingdom, was to be limited by the conditions which obtain in the First or Mineral Kingdom—to use Scriptural language we are seeking the Living among the dead.

And moreover at the present time a new order of experience is beginning to open out to us, for well authenticated instances of the cure of disease by the invisible power of the Spirit are steadily increasing in number. The facts are now too patent to be denied—what we want is a better knowledge of the power which accounts for them. And if this beginning is now with us, by what reason can we limit it? The difference between the healing of disease and the renewal of the entire organism and the perpetuation of life is only a difference of degree and not of kind; so that the actual experience of increasing numbers shows the working of a principle to which we can logically set no limits.

If we get the steps of the Creative Process clearly into our minds we shall see why we have hitherto had such small results.

Spirit creates by Self-contemplation;
Therefore, What it contemplates itself
as being, that it becomes.
You are individualized Spirit;
Therefore, What you contemplate as
the Law of your being becomes the
Law of your being.

Hence, contemplate a Law of Death arising out of the Forces of the Material reacting against the Power of the Spirit and overcoming it, and you impress this mode of self-recognition upon Spirit in yourself. Of course you cannot alter its inherent nature, but you cause it to work under negative conditions and thus make it produce negative results so far as you yourself are concerned.

But reverse the process, and contemplate a Law of Life as inherent in the very Being of the Spirit, and therefore as inherent in spirit in yourself; and contemplate the forces of the Material as practically non-existent in the Creative Process, because they are products of it and not causes—look at things in this way and you will impress a corresponding conception upon the Spirit which, by the Law of Reciprocity, thus enters into Self-contemplation on *these* lines from the standpoint of your own individuality; and then by the nature of the Creative Process a corresponding externalization is bound to take place. Thus our initial question, How did anything come into existence at all, brings us to the recognition of a Law of Life which we may each specialize for ourselves; and in the degree to which we specialize it we shall find the Creative Principle at work within us building up a healthier and happier personality in mind, body, and circumstances.

Only we must learn to distinguish the vehicles of Spirit from Spirit itself, for the distinction has very important bearings. What distinguishes the vehicles from the Spirit is the Law of Growth. The Spirit is the Formless principle of Life, and the vehicle is a Form in which this principle functions. Now the vehicle is a projection by the Spirit of substance coordinate with the natural order of the plane on which the vehicle functions, and therefore requires to be built up comformably to that order. This building up is what we speak of as Growth; and since the principle which causes the growth is the individualized Spirit, the rate at which the growth will go on will depend on the amount of vitalizing energy the Spirit puts into it, and the amount of vitalizing energy will depend on the degree in which the individualized Spirit appreciates its own livingness, and finally the degree of this appreciation will depend on the quality of the individual's perception of the Great All-originating Spirit as reflecting itself in him and thus making his contemplation of It nothing else than the Creative Self-contemplation of the Spirit proceeding from an individual and personal center. We must therefore not omit the Law of Growth in the vehicle from our conception of the working of the Spirit. As a matter of fact the vehicle has nothing to say in the matter for it is simply a projection from the Spirit; but for this very reason its formation will be slow or rapid in exact proportion to the individual spirit's vitalizing conception. We could imagine a degree of vitalizing conception that would produce the corresponding form instantaneously, but at present we must allow for the weakness of our spiritual power—not as thinking it by any means incapable of accomplishing its object, but as being far slower in operation now than we hope to see it in the future—and so we must not allow ourselves to be discouraged, but must hold our thought knowing that it is doing its creative work, and that the corresponding growth is slowly but surely taking place—thus following the Divine precept that men ought always to pray and not to faint. Gradually as we gain experience on these new lines our confidence in the power of the Spirit will increase, and we shall be less inclined to argue from the negative side of things, and thus the hindrances to the inflow of the Originating Spirit will be more and more removed, and greater and greater results will be obtained.

If we would have our minds clear on this subject of Manifestation we should remember its threefold nature:—First the General Life-Principle, secondly the Localization of this principle in the Individual, and thirdly the Growth of the Vehicle as it is projected by the individualized spirit with more or less energy. It is a sequence of progressive condensation from the Undifferentiated Universal Spirit to the ultimate and outermost vehicle—a truth enshrined in the esoteric maxim that "Matter is Spirit at its lowest level."

The forms thus produced are in true accord with the general order of Nature on the particular plane where they occur, and are therefore perfectly different from forms temporarily consolidated out of material drawn from other living organisms. These latter phantasmal bodies are held together only by an act of concentrated volition, and can therefore only be maintained for a short time and with effort; while the body which the individualized spirit, or ego, builds for itself is produced by a perfectly natural process and does not require any effort to sustain it, since it is kept in touch with the whole system of the planet by the continuous and effortless action of the individual's sub-conscious mind.

This is where the action of sub-conscious mind as the builder of the body comes in. Sub-conscious mind acts in accordance with the aggregate of suggestion impressed upon it by the conscious mind, and if this suggestion is that of perfect harmony with the physical laws of the planet then a corresponding building by the sub-conscious mind will take place, a process which, so far from implying any effort, consists rather in a restful sense of unity with Nature.[4]

And if to this sense of union with the Soul of Nature, that Universal Sub-conscious Mind which holds in the cosmos the same place that the sub-conscious mind does in ourselves—if to this there be superadded a sense of union with the All-creating Spirit from which the Soul of Nature flows, then through the medium of the individual's sub-conscious mind such specialized effects can be produced in his body as to transcend our past experiences without in any way violating the order of the universe. The Old Law was the manifestation of the Principle of Life working under constricted conditions: the New Law is the manifestation of the same Principle working under expanding conditions. Thus it is that though God never changes we are said to "increase with the increase of God."

THE PERSONAL FACTOR

I have already pointed out that the presence of a single all-embracing Cosmic Mind is an absolute necessity for the existence of any creation whatever, for the reason that if each individual mind were an entirely separate center of perception, not linked to all other minds by a common ground of underlying mentality independent of all individual action, then no two persons would see the same thing at the same time, in fact no two individuals would be conscious of living in the same world. If this were the case there would be no common standard to which to refer our sensations; and, indeed, coming into existence with no consciousness of environment except such as we could form by our own unaided thought, and having by the hypothesis no standard by which to form our thoughts, we could not form the conception of any environment at all, and consequently could have no recognition of our own existence. The confusion of thought involved even in the attempt to state such a condition shows it to be perfectly inconceivable, for the simple reason that it is self-contradictory and self-destructive. On this account it is clear that our own existence and that of the world around us necessarily implies the presence of a Universal Mind acting on certain *fixed lines of its own* which establish the basis for the working of all individual minds. This paramount action of the Universal Mind thus sets an unchangeable standard by which all individual mental action must eventually be measured, and therefore our first concern is to ascertain what this standard is and to make it the basis of our own action.

But if the independent existence of a common standard of reference is necessary for our self-recognition simply as inhabitants of the world we live in, then *a fortiori* a common standard of reference is necessary for our recognition of the unique place we hold in the Creative Order, which is that of introducing the Personal Factor without which the possibilities contained in the great Cosmic Laws would remain undeveloped, and the Self-contemplation of Spirit could never reach those infinite unfoldments of which it is logically capable.

The evolution of the Personal Factor is therefore the point with which we are most concerned. As a matter of fact, whatever theories we may hold to the contrary, we do all realize the same cosmic environment in the same way; that is to say, our minds all act according to certain generic laws which underlie all our individual diversities of thought and feeling. This is so because we are made that way and cannot help it. But with the Personal Factor the case is different. A standard is no less necessary, but we are not so made as to conform to it automatically. The very conception of automatic conformity to a *personal* standard is self-contradictory, for it does away with the very thing that constitutes personality, namely freedom of volition, the use of the powers of Initiative and Selection. For this reason conformity to the Standard of Personality must be a matter of choice, which amounts to the same thing as saying that it rests with each individual to form his own conception of a standard of Personality; but which liberty, however, carries with it the inevitable result that we shall bring into manifestation the *conditions* corresponding to the sort of personality we accept as our normal standard.

I would draw attention to the words "Normal Standard." What we shall eventually attain is, not what we merely wish, but what we regard as normal. The reason is that since we sub-consciously know ourselves to be based upon the inherent Law of the Universal Mind we feel, whether we can reason it out or not, that we cannot force the All-producing Mind to work contrary to its own inherent qualities, and therefore we intuitively recognize that we cannot transcend the sort of personality which is normal according to the Law of Universal Mind. This thought is always at the back of our mind and we cannot get away from it for the simple reason that it is inherent in our mental constitution, because our mind is itself a product of the Creative Process; and to suppose ourselves transcending the possibilities contained in the Originating Mind would involve the absurdity of supposing that we can get the greater out of the less.

Nevertheless there are some who try to do so, and their position is as follows. They say in effect, I want to transcend the standard of humanity as I see it around me. But this is the normal standard according to the Law of the Universe, therefore I have to get above the Law of the Universe. Consequently I cannot draw the necessary power from that Law, and so there is nowhere else to get it except from myself. Thus the aspirant is thrown back upon his own individual will as the ultimate power, with the result that the onus lies on him of concentrating a force sufficient to overcome the Law of the Universe. There is thus continually present to him a suggestion of struggle against a tremendous opposing force, and as a consequence he is continually subjecting himself to a strain which grows more and more intense as he realizes the magnitude of the force against which he is contending. Then as he begins to realize the inequality of the struggle he seeks for extraneous aid, and so he falls back on various expedients, all of which have this in common that they ultimately amount to invoking the assistance of other individualities, not seeing that this involves the same fallacy which has brought him to his present straits, the fallacy, namely, of supposing that any individuality can develop a power greater than that of the source from which itself proceeds. The fallacy is a radical one; and therefore all efforts based upon it are fore-doomed to ultimate failure, whether they take the form of reliance on personal force of will, or magical rites, or austerity practised against the body, or attempts by abnormal concentration to absorb the individual in the universal, or the invocation of spirits, or any other method—the same fallacy is involved in them all, that the less is larger than the greater.

Now the point to be noted is that the idea of transcending the present conditions of humanity does not necessarily imply the idea of transcending the normal law of humanity. The mistake we have hitherto made has been in fixing the Standard of Personality too low and in taking our past experiences as measuring the ultimate possibilities of the race. Our liberty consists in our ability to form our own conception of the Normal Standard of Personality, only subject to the conditions arising out of the inherent Law of the underlying Universal Mind; and so the whole thing resolves itself into the question, What are those fundamental conditions? The Law is that we cannot transcend the Normal; therefore comes the question, What is the Normal?

I have endeavored to answer this question in the chapter on the Divine Ideal, but since this is the crucial point of the whole subject we may devote a little further attention to it. The Normal Standard of Personality must necessarily be the reproduction in Individuality of what the Universal Mind is in itself, because, by the nature of the Creative Process, this standard results from Spirit's Self-contemplation at the stage where its recognition is turned toward its own power of Initiative and Selection. At this stage Spirit's Self-recognition has passed beyond that of Self-expression through a mere Law of Averages into the recognition of what I have ventured to call its Artistic Ability; and as we have seen that Self-recognition at any stage can only be attained by the realization of a *relation* stimulating that particular sort of consciousness, it follows that for the purpose of this further advance expression through individuals of a corresponding type is a necessity. Then by the Law of Reciprocity such beings must possess powers similar to those contemplated in itself by the Originating Spirit, in other words they must be in their own sphere the image and likeness of the Spirit as it sees itself.

Now we have seen that the Creating Spirit necessarily possesses the powers of Initiative and Selection. These we may call its *active* properties—the summing up of what it *does* . But what any power does depends on what it *is* , for the simple reason that it cannot give out what it does not contain; therefore at the back of the initiative and selective power of the Spirit we must find what the Spirit *is* , namely, what are its *substantive* properties. To begin with it must be Life. Then because it is Life it must be Love, because as the undifferentiated Principle of Life it cannot do otherwise than tend to the fuller development of life in each individual, and the pure motive of giving greater enjoyment of life is Love. Then because it is Life guided by Love it must also be Light, that is to say, the primary all-inclusive perception of boundless manifestations yet to be. Then from this proceeds Power, because there is no opposing force at the level of Pure Spirit; and therefore Life urged forward by Love or the desire for recognition, and by Light or the pure perception of the Law of Infinite Possibility, must necessarily produce Power, for the simple reason that under these conditions it could not stop short of action, for that would be the denial of the Life, Love, and Light which it is. Then because the Spirit is Life, Love, Light, and Power, it is also Peace, again for a very simple reason, that being the Spirit of the Whole it cannot set one part in antagonism against another, for that would be to destroy the wholeness. Next the Spirit must be Beauty, because on the same principle of Wholeness it must duly proportion every part to every other part, and the due proportioning of all parts is beauty. And lastly the Spirit must be Joy, because, working on these lines, it cannot do otherwise than find pleasure in the Self-expression which its works afford it, and in the contemplation of the limitlessness of the Creative Process by which each realized stage of evolution, however excellent, is still the stepping-stone to something yet more excellent, and so on in everlasting progression.

For these reasons we may sum up the Substantive Being of the All-originating Spirit as Life, Love, Light, Power, Peace, Beauty, and Joy; and its Active Power as that of Initiative and Selection. These, therefore, constitute the basic laws of the underlying universal mentality which sets the Standard of Normal Personality—a standard which, when seen in this light, transcends the utmost scope of our thought, for it is nothing else than the Spirit of the Infinite Affirmative conceived in Human Personality. This standard is therefore that of the Universal Spirit itself reproduced in Human Individuality by the same Law of Reciprocity which we have found to be the fundamental law of the Creative Process—only now we are tracing the action of this Law in the Fifth Kingdom instead of in the Fourth.

This Standard, then, we may call the Universal Principle of Humanity, and having now traced the successive steps by which it is reached from the first cosmic movement of the Spirit in the formation of the primary nebula, we need not go over the old ground again, and may henceforward take this Divine Principle of Humanity as our Normal Standard and make it the starting point for our further evolution. But how are we to do this? Simply by using the one method of Creative Process, that is, the Self-contemplation of Spirit. We now know ourselves to be Reciprocals of the Divine Spirit, centers in which It finds a fresh standpoint for Self-contemplation; and so the way to rise to the heights of this Great Pattern is by contemplating it as the Normal Standard of our own Personality.

And be it noted that the Pattern thus set before us is Universal. It is the embodiment of all the great principles of the Affirmative, and so in no way interferes with our own particular individuality—*that* is something built up upon this foundation, something additional affording the differentiating medium through which this unifying Principle finds variety of expression, therefore we need be under no apprehension lest by resting upon this Pattern we should become less ourselves. On the contrary the recognition of it sets us at liberty to become more fully ourselves because we know that we are basing our development, not upon the strength of our own unaided will, nor yet upon any sort of extraneous help, but upon the Universal Law itself, manifesting through us in the proper sequence of the Creative Order; so that we are still dealing with Universal principles, only the principle by which we are now working is the Universal Principle of Personality.

I wish the student to get this idea very clearly because this is really the crux of the passage from the Fourth Kingdom into the Fifth. The great problem of the future of evolution is the introduction of the Personal Factor. The reason why this is so is very simple when we see it. To take a thought from my own "Doré Lectures" we may put it in this way. In former days no one thought of building ships of iron because iron does not float; yet now ships are seldom built of anything else, though the relative specific gravities of iron and water remain unchanged. What has changed is the Personal Factor. It has expanded to a more intelligent perception of the law of flotation, and we now see that wood floats and iron sinks, both of them by the same principle working under opposite conditions, the law, namely, that anything will float which bulk for bulk is lighter than the volume of water displaced by it, so that by including in our calculations the displacement of the vessel as well as the specific gravity of the material, we now make iron float by the very same law by which it sinks. This example shows that the function of the Personal Factor is to analyze the manifestations of Law which are spontaneously afforded by Nature and to discover the Universal Affirmative Principle which lies hidden within them, and then by the exercise of our powers of Initiative and Selection to provide such specialized conditions as will enable the Universal Principle to work in perfectly new ways transcending anything in our past experience. This is how all progress has been achieved up to the present; and is the way in which all progress must be achieved in the future, only for the purpose of evolution, or growth from within, we must transfer the method to the spiritual plane.

The function, then, of the Personal Factor in the Creative Order is to provide specialized conditions by the use of the powers of Selection and Initiative, a truth indicated by the maxim "Nature unaided fails"; but the difficulty is that if enhanced powers were attained by the whole population of the world without any common basis for their use, their promiscuous exercise could only result in chaotic confusion and the destruction of the entire race. To introduce the creative power of the Individual and at the same time avoid converting it into a devastating flood is the great problem of the transition from the Fourth Kingdom into the Fifth. For this purpose it becomes necessary to have a Standard of the Personal Factor independent of any individual conceptions, just as we found that in order for us to attain self-consciousness at all it was a necessity that there should be a Universal Mind as the *generic* basis of all individual mentality; only in regard to the generic build of mind the conformity is necessarily automatic, while in regard to the specializing process the fact that the essence of that process is Selection and Initiative renders it impossible for the conformity to the Standard of Personality to be automatic—the very nature of the thing makes it a matter of individual choice.

Now a Standard of Personality independent of individual conceptions must be the *essence* of Personality as distinguished from individual idiosyncrasies, and can therefore be nothing else than the Creative Life, Love, Beauty, etc., viewed as a Divine Individuality, by identifying ourselves with which we eliminate all possibility of conflict with other personalities based on the same fundamental recognition; and the very universality of this Standard allows free play to all our particular idiosyncrasies while at the same time preventing them from antagonizing the fundamental principles to which we have found that the Self-contemplation of the Originating Spirit must necessarily give rise. In this way we attain a Standard of Measurement for our own powers. If we recognize no such Standard our development of spiritual powers, our discovery of the immense possibilities hidden in the inner laws of Nature and of our own being, can only become a scourge to ourselves and others, and it is for this reason that these secrets are so jealously guarded by those who know them, and that over the entrance to the temple are written the words "Eskato Bebeloi"—"Hence ye Profane."

But if we recognize and accept this Standard of Measurement then we need never fear our discovery of hidden powers either in ourselves or in Nature, for on this basis it becomes impossible for us to misuse them.

Therefore it is that all systematic teaching on these subjects begins with instruction regarding the Creative Order of the Cosmos, and then proceeds to exhibit the same Order as reproduced on the plane of Personality and so affording a fresh starting point for the Creative Process by the introduction of Individual Initiative and Selection. This is the doctrine of the Macrocosm and the Microcosm; and the transition from the generic working of the Creative Spirit in the Cosmos to its specific working in the Individual is what is meant by the doctrine of the Octave.

THE STANDARD OF PERSONALITY

We have now got some general idea as to the place of the personal factor in the Creative Order, and so the next question is, How does this affect ourselves? The answer is that if we have grasped the fundamental fact that the moving power in the Creative Process is the self-contemplation of Spirit, and if we also see that, because we are miniature reproductions of the Original Spirit, our contemplation of It becomes Its contemplation of Itself from the standpoint of our own individuality—if we have grasped these fundamental conceptions, then it follows that our process for developing power is to contemplate the Originating Spirit as the source of the power we want to develop. And here we must guard against a mistake which people often make when looking to the Spirit as the source of power. We are apt to regard it as sometimes giving and sometimes withholding power, and consequently are never sure which way it will act. But by so doing we make Spirit contemplate itself as having no definite action at all, as a plus and minus which mutually cancel each other, and therefore by the Law of the Creative Process no result is to be expected. The mistake consists in regarding the power as something separate from the Spirit; whereas by the analysis of the Creative Process which we have now made we see that the Spirit itself *is* the power, because the power comes into existence only through Spirit's self-contemplation. Then the logical inference from this is that by contemplating the Spirit *as* the power, and *vice versa* by contemplating the power *as* the Spirit, a similar power is being generated in ourselves.

Again an important conclusion follows from this, which is that to generate any *particular sort* of power we should contemplate it in the abstract rather than as applied to the particular set of circumstances we have in hand. The circumstances indicate the sort of power we want but they do not help us to generate it; rather they impress us with a sense of something contrary to the power, something which has to be overcome by it, and therefore we should endeavor to dwell on the power *in itself*, and so come into touch with it in its limitless infinitude.

It is here that we begin to find the benefit of a Divine Standard of Human Individuality. That also is an Infinite Principle, and by identifying ourselves with it we bring to bear upon the abstract conception of infinite Impersonal Power a corresponding conception of Infinite Personality, so that we thus import the Personal Factor which is able *to use* the Power without imposing any strain upon ourselves. We know that by the very nature of the Creative Process we are one with the Originating Spirit and therefore one with all the principles of its Being, and consequently one with its Infinite Personality, and therefore our contemplation of it as the Power which we want gives us the power to use that Power.

This is the Self-contemplation of Spirit employed from the individual standpoint for the generating of power. Then comes the application of the power thus generated. But there is only one Creative Process, that of the Self-contemplation of Spirit, and therefore the way to use this process for the application of the power is to contemplate ourselves as surrounded by the conditions which we want to produce. This does not mean that we are to lay down a hard and fast pattern of the conditions and strenuously endeavor to compel the Power to conform its working to every detail of our mental picture—to do so would be to hinder its working and to exhaust ourselves. What we are to dwell upon is the idea of an Infinite Power producing the happiness we desire, and because this Power is also the Forming Power of the universe trusting it to give that form to the conditions which will most perfectly react upon us to produce the particular state of consciousness desired.

Thus neither on the side of in-drawing nor of out-giving is there any constraining of the Power, while in both cases there is an initiative and selective action on the part of the individual—for the generating of power he takes the initiative of invoking it by contemplation, and he makes selection of the sort of power to invoke; while on the giving-out side he makes selection of the purpose for which the Power is to be employed, and takes the initiative by his thought of directing the Power to that purpose. He thus fulfils the fundamental requirements of the Creative Process by exercising Spirit's inherent faculties of initiative and selection by means of its inherent method, namely by Self-contemplation. The whole action is identical in kind with that which produces the cosmos, and it is now repeated in miniature for the particular world of the individual; only we must remember that this miniature reproduction of the Creative Process is based upon the great fundamental principles inherent in the Universal Mind, and cannot be dissociated from them without involving a conception of the individual which will ultimately be found self-destructive because it cuts away the foundation on which his individuality rests.

It will therefore be seen that any individuality based upon the fundamental Standard of Personality thus involved in the Universal Mind has reached the basic principle of union with the Originating Spirit itself, and we are therefore correct in saying that union is attained through, or by means of, this Standard Personality. This is a great truth which in all ages has been set forth under a variety of symbolic statements; often misunderstood, and still continuing to be so, though owing to the inherent vitality of the idea itself even a partial apprehension of it produces a corresponding measure of good results. This falling short has been occasioned by the failure to recognize an Eternal Principle at the back of the particular statements—in a word the failure to see what they were talking about. All *principles* are eternal in themselves, and this is what distinguishes them from their particular manifestations as laws determined by temporary and local conditions.

If then, we would reach the root of the matter we must penetrate through all verbal statements to an Eternal Principle which is as active now as ever in the past, and which is as available to ourselves as to any who have gone before us. Therefore it is that when we discern an Eternal and Universal

Principle of Human Personality as necessarily involved in the Essential Being of the Originating Universal Spirit—*Filius in gremio Patris* —we have discovered the true Normal Standard of Personality. Then because this standard is nothing else than the principle of Personality expanded to infinitude, there is no limit to the expansion which we ourselves may attain by the operation in us of this principle; and so we are never placed in a position of antagonism to the true law of our being, but on the contrary the larger and more fundamental our conception of personal development the greater will be the fulfilment which we give to the Law. The Normal Standard of Personality is found to be itself the Law of the Creative Process working at the personal level; and it cannot be subject to limitation for the simple reason that the process being that of the Self-contemplation of Spirit, no limits can possibly be assigned to this contemplation.

We need, therefore, never be afraid of forming too high an idea of human possibilities provided always that we take this standard as the foundation on which to build up the edifice of our personality. And we see that this standard is no arbitrary one but simply the Expression in Personality of the *One* all-embracing Spirit of the Affirmative; and therefore the only limitation implied by conformity to it is that of being prevented from running on lines the opposite of those of the Creative Process, that is to say, from calling into action causes of disintegration and destruction. In the truly Constructive Order, therefore, the Divine Standard of Personality is as really the basis of the development of specific personality as the Universal Mind is the necessary basis of generic mentality; and just as without this generic ultimate of Mind we should none of us see the same world at the same time, and in fact have no consciousness of existence, so apart from this Divine Standard of Personality it is equally impossible for us to specialize the generic law of our being so as to develop all the glorious possibilities that are latent in it.

Only we must never forget the difference between these two statements of the Universal Law—the one is cosmic and generic, common to the whole race, whether they know it or not, a Standard to which we all conform automatically by the mere fact of being human beings; while the other is a personal and individual Standard, automatic conformity to which is impossible because that would imply the loss of those powers of Initiative and Selection which are the very essence of Personality; so that this Standard necessarily implies a personal selection of it in preference to other conceptions of an antagonistic nature.

RACE THOUGHT AND NEW THOUGHT

The steady following up of the successive stages of the Creative Process has led us to the recognition of an Individuality in the All-creating Spirit itself, but an Individuality which is by its very nature Universal, and so cannot be departed from without violating the essential principles on which the further expansion of our own individuality depends. At the same time it is strictly *individual*, for it is the Spirit of Individuality, and is thus to be distinguished from that merely *generic* race-personality which makes us human beings at all. Race-personality is of course the necessary *basis* for the development of this Individuality; but if we do not see that it is only the preliminary to further evolution, any other conception of our personality as members of the race will prevent our advance toward our proper position in the Creative Order, which is that of introducing the Personal Factor by the exercise of our individual power of initiative and selection.

It is on this account that Race-thought, simply as such, is opposed to the attempt of the individual to pass into a higher order of life. It limits him by strong currents of negative suggestion based on the fallacy that the perpetuation of the race requires the death of the individual;[5] and it is only when the individual sees that this is not true, and that his race- nature constitutes the ground out of which his new Individuality is to be formed, that he becomes able to oppose the negative power of race-thought. He does this by destroying it with its own weapon, that is, by finding in the race-nature itself the very material to be used by the Spirit for building-up the New Man. This is a discovery on the spiritual plane equivalent to the discovery on the physical plane that we can make iron float by the same law by which it sinks. It is the discovery that what we call the mortal part of us is capable of being brought under a higher application of the Universal Law of Life, which will transmute it into an immortal principle. When we see what we call the mortal part of us in this light we can employ the very principle on which the negative race-thought is founded as a weapon for the destruction of that thought in our own minds.

The basis of the negative race-thought is the idea that physical death is an essential part of the Normal Standard of Personality, and that the body is composed of so much neutral material with which death can do what it likes. But it is precisely this neutrality of matter that makes it just as amenable to the Law of Life as to the Law of Death—it is simply neutral and not an originating power on either side; so then when we realize that our Normal Standard of Personality is not subject to death, but is the Eternal Essence and Being of Life itself, then we see that this neutrality of matter—its inability to make selection or take initiative on its own account—is just what makes it the plastic medium for the expression of Spirit in ourselves.

In this way the generic or race-mind in the individual becomes the instrument through which the specializing power of the Spirit works toward the building up of a personality based upon the truly Normal Standard of Individuality which we have found to be inherent in the All-originating Spirit itself: and since the whole question is that of the introduction of the factor of personal individuality into the creative order of causation, this cannot be done by depriving the individual of what makes him a person instead of a thing, namely, the power of conscious initiative and selection.

For this reason the transition from the Fourth Kingdom into the Fifth cannot be forced upon the race either by a Divine fiat or by the generic action of cosmic law, for it is a *specialising* of the cosmic law which can only be effected by *personal* initiative and selection, just as iron can only be made to float under certain specialized conditions; and consequently the passage from the Fourth into the Fifth Kingdom is a strictly individual process which can only be brought about by a personal perception of what the normal standard of the New Individuality really is. This can only be done by the active laying aside of the old race-standard and the conscious adoption of the new one. The student will do well to consider this carefully, for it explains why the race cannot receive the further evolution simply as a race; and also it shows that our further evolution is not into a state of less activity but of greater, not into being less alive but more alive, not into being less ourselves but more ourselves; thus being just the opposite of those systems which present the goal of existence as re-absorption into the undifferentiated Divine essence. On the contrary our further evolution is into greater degrees of conscious activity than we have ever yet known, because it implies our development of greater powers as the consequence of our clearer perception of our true relation to the All-originating Spirit. It is the recognition that we may, and should, measure ourselves by this New Standard instead of by the old race-standard that constitutes the real New Thought. The New Thought which gives New Life to the individual will never be realized so long as we think that it is merely the name of a particular sect, or that it is to be found in the mechanical observance of a set of rules laid down for us by some particular teacher. It is a New Fact in the experience of the individual, the *reason* for which is indeed made clear to him through intellectual perception of the real nature of the Creative Process, but which can become an actual experience only by habitual personal intercourse with that Divine Spirit which is the Life, Love and Beauty that are at the back of the Creative Process and find expression through it.

From this intercourse new thoughts will continually flow in, all of them bearing that vivifying element which is inherent in their source, and the individual will then proceed to work out these new ideas with the knowledge that they have their origin in the selection and initiative power of the All-creating Spirit itself, and in this way by combined meditation and action he will find himself advancing into increasing light, liberty and usefulness. The advance may be almost imperceptible from one day to another, but it will be perceptible at longer intervals, and the one who is thus moving forward with the Spirit of God will on looking back at any time always find that he is getting more livingness out of life than he was a year previously. And this without strenuous effort, for he is not having to manufacture the power from his own resources but only to *receive* it—and as for *using* it, that is only the exercise of the power itself. So following on these lines you will find that Rest and Power are identical; and so you get the real New Thought which grows in Newness every day.

THE DÉNOUEMENT OF THE CREATIVE PROCESS

Then comes the question, What should logically be the dénouement of the progression we have been considering? Let us briefly recapitulate the steps of the series. Universal Spirit by Self-contemplation evolves Universal Substance. From this it produces cosmic creation as the expression of itself as functioning in Space and Time. Then from this initial movement it proceeds to more highly specialized modes of Self-contemplation in a continually ascending scale, for the simple reason that self-contemplation admits of no limits and therefore each stage of self-recognition cannot be other than the starting-point for a still more advanced mode of self-contemplation, and so on *ad infinitum* . Thus there is a continuous progress toward more and more highly specialized forms of life, implying greater liberty and wider scope for enjoyment as the capacity of the individual life corresponds to a higher degree of the contemplation of Spirit; and in this way evolution proceeds till it reaches a level where it becomes impossible to go any further except by the exercise of conscious selection and initiative on the part of the individual, while at the same time conforming to the universal principles of which evolution is the expression.

Now ask yourself in what way individual selection and initiative would be likely to act as expressing the Originating Spirit itself? Given the knowledge on the part of the individual that he is able by his power of initiative and selection to draw directly upon the All-originating Spirit of Life, what motive could he have for not doing so? Therefore, granted such a perfect recognition, we should find the individual holding precisely the same place in regard to his own individual world that the All-originating Spirit does to the cosmos; subject only to the same Law of Love, Beauty, &c., which we found to be necessarily inherent in the Creative Spirit—a similarity which would entirely prevent the individual from exercising his otherwise limitless powers in any sort of antagonism to the Spirit of the Great Whole.

At the same time the individual would be quite aware that he was not the Universal Spirit *in propria persona* , but that he was affording expression to it through his individuality. Now Expression is impossible except through Form, and therefore form of some sort is a necessity of individuality. It is just here, then, that we find the importance of that principle of Harmony with Environment of which I spoke earlier, the principle in accordance with which a person who had obtained complete control of matter, if he wished to transport himself to some other planet, would appear there in perfect conformity with all the laws of matter that obtained in that world; though, of course, not subject to any limitation of the Life Principle in himself. He would exhibit the laws of matter as rendered perfect by the Law of Originating Life. But if any one now living on this earth were thus perfectly to realize the Law of Life he would be in precisely the same position *here* as our imaginary visitor to another planet—in other words the dénouement of the Law of Life is not the putting off of the body, but its inclusion as part of the conscious life of the Spirit.

This does not imply any difference in the molecular structure of the body from that of other men, for by the principle of Harmony of which I have just spoken, it would be formed in strict accordance with the laws of matter on the particular planet; though it would not be subject to the limitations resulting from the average man's non-recognition of the power of the Spirit. The man who had thus fully entered into the Fifth Kingdom would recognize that, in its relation to the denser modes of matter his body was of a similar dense mode. That would be its relation to external environment as seen by others. But since the man now knew *himself* as not belonging to these denser modes of manifestation, but as an individualization of Primary Spirit, he would see that relatively to himself all matter was Primary Substance, and that from this point of view any condensations of that substance into atoms, molecules, tissues, and the like counted for nothing—for him the body would be simply Primary Substance entirely responsive to his will. Yet his reverence for the Law of Harmony would prevent any disposition to play psychic pranks with it, and he would use his power over the body only to meet actual requirements.

In this way, then, we are led to the conclusion that eternal life in an immortal physical body is the logical dénouement of our evolution; and if we reflect that, by the conditions of the case, the owners of such bodies could at will either transport themselves to other worlds or put off the physical body altogether and remain in the purely subjective life while still retaining the power to reclothe themselves in flesh whenever they chose, we shall see that this dénouement of evolution answers all possible questions as to the increase of the race, the final destruction of the planet, and the like.

This, then, is the ultimate which we should keep in view; but the fact remains that, though there may be hidden ones who have thus attained, the bulk of mankind have not, and that the common lot of humanity is to go through the change which we call death. In broad philosophical terms death may be described as the withdrawal of the life into the subjective consciousness to the total exclusion of the objective consciousness. Then by the general law of the relation between subjective and objective mind, the subjective mind severed from its corresponding objective mentality has no means of acquiring fresh impressions *on its own account* , and therefore can only ring the changes on those impressions which it has brought with it from its past life. But these may be of very various sorts, ranging from the lowest to the highest, from those most opposed to that ultimate destiny of man which we have just been considering, to those which recognize his possibilities in a very large measure, needing little more to bring about the full fruition of perfected life. But however various may be their experiences, all who have passed through death must have this in common that they have lost their physical instrument of objective perception and so have their mode of consciousness determined entirely by the dominant mode of suggestion which they have brought over with them from the objective side of life.[6] Of course if the objective mentality were also brought over this would give the individual the same power of initiative and selection that he possesses while in the body, and, as we shall see later on, there are exceptional persons with whom this is the case; but for the great majority the physical brain is a necessity for the working of the objective mentality, and so when they are deprived of this instrument their life becomes purely subjective and is a sort of dream-life, only with a vast difference between two classes of dreamers—those who dream as they must and those who dream as they will. The former are those who have enslaved themselves in various ways to their lower mentality—some by bringing with them the memory of crimes unpardoned, some by bringing with them the idea of a merely animal life, others less degraded, but still in bondage to limited thought, bringing with them only the suggestion of a frivolous worldly life—in this way, by the natural operation of the Law of Suggestion, these different classes, either through remorse, or unsatisfied desires, or sheer incapacity to grasp higher principles, all remain earth-bound, suffering in exact correspondence with the nature of the suggestion they have brought along with them. The unchangeable Law is that the suggestion becomes the life; and this is equally true of suggestions of a happier sort. Those who have brought over with them the great truth that conditions are the creations of thought, and who have accustomed themselves while in objective life to dwell on good and beautiful ideas, are still able, by reason of being imbued with this suggestion, to mold the conditions of their consciousness in the subjective world in accordance with the sort of ideas which have become a second nature to them. Within the limits of these ideas the dominant suggestion to these entities is that of a Law which confers Liberty, so by using this Law of the constructive power of thought they can determine the conditions of their own consciousness; and thus instead of being compelled to suffer the nightmare dreams of the other class, they can mold their dream according to their will. We cannot conceive of such a life as theirs in the unseen as otherwise than happy, nevertheless its range is limited by the range of the conceptions they have brought with them. These may be exceedingly beautiful and thoroughly true and logical *as far as they go* ; but they do not go the whole way, otherwise these spirits would not be in the category which we are considering but would belong to that still higher class who fully realize the ultimate possibilities which the Law of the Expression of Spirit provides.

The otherwise happy subjective life of these more enlightened souls has this radical defect that they have failed to bring over with them that power of original selection and initiative without which further progress is impossible. I wish the student to grasp this point very clearly, for it is of the utmost importance. Of course the basis of our further evolution is conformity to the harmonious nature of the Originating Spirit; but upon this foundation we each have to build up the superstructure of our own individuality, and every step of advance depends on our personal development of power to take that step. This is what is meant by taking an initiative. It is making a New Departure, not merely recombining the old things into fresh groupings still subject to the old laws, but introducing an entirely new element which will bring its own New Law along with it.

Now if this is the true meaning of "initiative" then that is just the power which these otherwise happy souls do not possess. For by the very conditions of the case they are living only in their subjective consciousness, and consequently are living by the law of subjective mind; and one of the chief characteristics of subjective mind is its incapacity to reason inductively, and therefore its inability to make the selection and take the initiative necessary to inaugurate a New Departure. The well established facts of mental law show conclusively that subjective mind argues only deductively. It argues quite correctly from any given premises, but it cannot take the initiative in selecting the premises—that is the province of inductive reasoning which is essentially the function of the objective mind. But by the law of Auto-suggestion this discarnate individual has brought over his premises with him, which premises are the sum-total of his inductions made during objective life, the conception of things which he held at the time he passed over, for this constituted his idea of Truth. Now he cannot add to these inductions, for he has parted with his instrument for inductive reasoning, and therefore his deductive reasoning in the purely subjective state which he has now entered is necessarily limited to the consequences which may be deducted from the premises which he has brought along with him.

In the case of the highly-developed individualities we are now considering the premises thus brought over are of a very far-reaching and beautiful character, and consequently the range of their subjective life is correspondingly wide and beautiful; but, nevertheless, it is subject to the radical defect that it is debarred from further progress for the simple reason that the individual has not brought over with him the mental faculty which can impress his subjective entity with the requisite forward movement for making a new departure into a New Order. And moreover, the higher the subjective development with which the individual passed over the more likely he will be to realize this defect. If during earth-life he had gained sufficient knowledge of these things he will carry with him the knowledge that his discarnate existence is purely subjective; and therefore he will realize that, however he may be able to order the pictures of his dream, yet it is still but a dream, and in common with all other dreams lacks the basis of solidity from which to take *really creative action* .

He knows also that the condition of other discarnate individualities is similar to his own, and that consequently each one must necessarily live in a world apart—a world of his own creation, because none of them possess the objective mentality by which to direct their subjective currents so as to make them penetrate into the sphere of another subjective entity, which is the *modus operandi* of telepathy. Thus he is conscious of his own inability to hold intercourse with other personalities; for though he may for his own pleasure create the semblance of them in his dream-life, yet he knows that these are creations of his own mind, and that while he appears to be conversing with a friend amid the most lovely surroundings the friend himself may be having experiences of a very different description. I am, of course, speaking now of persons who have passed over in a very high state of development and with a very considerable, though still imperfect, knowledge of the Law of their own being. Probably the majority take their dream-life for an external reality; and, in any case, all who have passed over without carrying their objective mentality along with them must be shut up in their individual subjective spheres and cease to function as centers of creative power so long as they do not emerge from that state.

But the highly advanced individuals of whom I am now speaking have passed over with a true knowledge of the Law of the relation between subjective and objective mind and have therefore brought with them a *subjective* knowledge of this truth; and therefore, however otherwise in a certain sense happy, they must still be conscious of a fundamental limitation which prevents their further advance. And this consciousness can produce only one result, an ever-growing longing for the removal of this limitation—and this represents the intense desire of the Spirit, as individualized in these souls, to attain to the conditions under which it can freely exercise its creative power. Sub-consciously this is the desire of *all* souls, for it is that continual pressing forward of the Spirit for manifestation out of which the whole Creative Process arises; and so it is that the great cry perpetually ascends to God from all as yet undelivered souls, whether in or out of the body, for the deliverance which they knowingly or unknowingly desire.

All this comes out of the well-ascertained facts of the law of relation between subjective and objective mind. Then comes the question, Is there no way of getting out of this law? The answer is that we can never get away from universal principles—*but we can specialise them*. We may take it as an axiom that any law which appears to limit us contains in itself the principle by which that limitation can be overcome, just as in the case of the flotation of iron. In this axiom, then, we shall find the clue which will bring us out of the labyrinth. The same law which places various degrees of limitation upon the souls that have passed into the invisible can be so applied as to set them free. We have seen that everything turns on the obligation of our subjective part to act within the limits of the suggestion which has been most deeply impressed upon it. Then why not impress upon it the suggestion that in passing over to the other side it has brought its objective mentality along with it?

If such a suggestion were effectively impressed upon our subjective mind, then by the fundamental law of our nature our subjective mind would act in strict accordance with this suggestion, with the result that the objective mind would no longer be separated from it, and that we should carry with us into the unseen our *whole* mentality, both subjective and objective, and so be able to exercise our inductive powers of selection and initiative as well there as here.

Why not? The answer is that we cannot accept any suggestion unless we believe it to be true, and to believe it to be true we must feel that we have a solid foundation for our belief. If, then, we can find a sufficient foundation for adequately impressing this suggestion upon ourselves, then the principles of mental law assure us that we shall carry our objective faculty of initiative and selection into the unseen. Therefore our quest is to find this Foundation. Then, since we cannot accept as true what we believe to be contrary to the ultimate law of the universe, if we are to find such a foundation at all it must be within that Law; and it is for this reason that I have laid so much stress upon the Normal Standard of Human Individuality. When we are convinced that this ideal completeness is quite normal, and is a spiritual fact, not dependent upon the body, but able to control the body, then we have got the solid basis on which to carry our objective personality along with us into the unseen, and the well-established laws of our mental constitution justify the belief that we can do so.

From these considerations it is obvious that those who thus pass over in possession of their complete mentality must be in a very different position from those who pass into a condition of merely subjective life, for they have brought their powers of selection and initiative with them, and can therefore employ their experiences in the unseen as a starting-point for still further development. So, then, the question arises, What lines will this further development be likely to follow?

We are now considering the case of persons who have reached a very high degree of development; who have succeeded in so completely uniting the subjective and objective portions of their spiritual being into a perfect whole that they can never again be severed; and who are therefore able to function with their whole consciousness on the spiritual plane. Such persons will doubtless be well aware that they have attained this degree of development by the Law of the Creative Process working in terms of their own individuality, and so they would naturally always refer to the original Cosmic Creation as the demonstration of the principle which they have to specialize for their own further evolution. Then they would find that the principle involved is that of the manifestation of Spirit in Form; and they would further see that this manifestation is not an illusion but a reality, for the simple reason that both mind and matter are equally projections from the Great Originating Spirit. Both alike are thoughts of the Divine Mind, and it is impossible to conceive any greater reality than the Divine Thought, or to get at any more substantial source of reality than that. Even if we were to picture the Divine Mind as laughing at its productions as being mere illusions *relatively to itself* (which I certainly do not), still the relation between the individual mind and material existence would be a reality for the individual, on the simple mathematical ground that like signs multiplied together invariably produce a positive result, even though the signs themselves be negative; so that, for us, at every stage of our existence substance must always be as much a reality as mind. Therefore the manifestation of Spirit in Form is the eternal principle of the Creative Process whether in the evolution of a world-system or in that of an individual.

But when we realize that by the nature of the Creative Process substance must be an eternal verity we must not suppose that this is true also of *particular forms* or of *particular modes* of matter. Substance is a necessity for the expression of Spirit, but it does not follow that Spirit is tied down to any particular mode of expression. If you fold a piece of paper into the form of a dart it will fly through the air by the law of the form which you have given it. Again, if you take the same bit of paper and fold it into the shape of a boat it will float on water by the law of the new form that you have given it. The thing formed will act in accordance with the form given it, and the same paper can be folded into different forms; but if there were no paper you could put it into any shape at all. The dart and the boat are both real so long as you retain the paper in either of those shapes; but this does not alter the fact that you can change the shapes, though your power to do so depends on the existence of the paper. This is a rough analogy of the relation between ultimate substance and particular forms, and shows us that neither substance nor shape is an illusion; both are essential to the manifestation of Spirit, only by the nature of the Creative Process the Spirit has power to determine what shape substance shall take at any particular time.

Accordingly we find the great Law that, as Spirit is the Alpha of the Creative Process, so solid material Form is its Omega; in other words the Creative Series is incomplete until solid material form is reached. Anything short of this is a condition of incompleteness, and therefore the enlightened souls who have passed over in possession of both sides of their mentality will realize that their condition, however beatific, is still one of incompleteness; and that what is wanted for completion is expression through a material body. This, then, is the direction in which such souls would use their powers of initiative and selection as being the true line of evolution—in a word they would realize that the principle of Creative Progression, when it reaches the level of fully developed mental man, necessarily implies the Resurrection of the Body, and that anything short of this would be retrogression and not progress.

At the same time persons who had passed over with this knowledge would never suppose that Resurrection meant merely the resuscitation of the old body under the old conditions; for they would see that the same inherent law which makes expression in concrete substance the ultimate of the creative series also makes this ultimate form depend on the originating movement of the spirit which produces it, and therefore that, although *some* concrete form is essential for complete manifestation, and is a substantial reality so long as it is maintained, yet the maintaining of the particular form is entirely dependent on the action of the spirit of which the form is the external clothing. This resurrection body would therefore be no mere illusory spirit-shape, yet it would not be subject to the limitations of matter as we now know it: it would be physical matter still, but entirely subject to the will of the indwelling spirit, which would not regard the denser atomic relations of the body but only its absolute and essential nature as Primary Substance. I want the student to grasp the idea that the same thing may be very different when looked at, so to say, from opposite ends of the stick. What is solid molecular matter when viewed from the outside is plastic primary substance when viewed from the inside. The relations of this new body to any stimulus proceeding from outside would be those of the external laws of Nature; but its relation to the spiritual ego working from within would be that of a plastic substance to be molded at will. The employment of such power would, however, at all times be based upon the reverent worship of the All-creating Spirit; and it would therefore never be exercised otherwise than in accordance with the harmonious progress of the Creative Process. Proceeding on these lines the spirit in the individual would stand in precisely the same relation to his body that the All-originating Spirit does to the cosmos.

This, then, is the sort of body which the instructed would contemplate as that in which he was to attain resurrection. He would regard it, not as an illusion, but as a great reality; while at the same time he would not need to trouble himself about its particular form, for he would know that it would be the perfect expression of his own conception of himself. He would know this because it is in accordance with the fundamental principle that external creation has its root in the Self-contemplation of Spirit.

Those passing over with this knowledge would obviously be in a very different position from those who passed over with only a subjective consciousness. They would bring with them powers of selection and initiative by which they could continue to impress fresh and expanding conceptions upon their subjective mind, and so cause it to carry on its work as the seed-ground of the whole individuality, instead of being shut up in itself as a mere circulus for the repetition of previously received ideas; and so in their recognition of the *principle* of physical resurrection they would have a clear and definite line of auto-suggestion. And because this suggestion is derived from the undeniable facts of the whole cosmic creation, it is one which both subjective and objective mind can accept as an established fact, and so the suggestion becomes effective. This suggestion, then, becomes the self-contemplation of the individual spirit; and because it is in strict conformity with the generic principle of the Original Creative Activity, of which the individual mind is itself a product, this becomes also the Self-contemplation of the Originating Spirit as seeing itself reflected in the individual spirit; so that, by the basic law of the Creative Process, this suggestion is bound sooner or later to work out into its corresponding fact, namely, the production of a material body free from the power of death and from all those limitations which we now associate with our physical organism.

This, then, is the hope of those who pass over in recognition of the great truth. But how about those who have passed over without that recognition? We have seen that their purely subjective condition precludes them from taking any initiative on their own account, for that requires the presence of objective mind. Their subjective mind, however, still retains its essential nature; that is, it is still susceptible to suggestion, and still possesses its inherent creativeness in working out any suggestion that is sufficiently deeply implanted in it. Here, then, opens up a vast field of activity for that other class who have passed over in possession of both sides of their mentality. By means of their powers of initiative and selection they can on the principle of telepathy cause their own subjective mind to penetrate the subjective spheres of those who do not possess those powers, and they can thus endeavor to impress upon them the great truth of the physical ultimate of the Creative Process—the truth that any series which stops short of that ultimate is incomplete, and, if insisted upon as being ultimate, must become self-destructive because in opposition to the inherent working of the Universal Creative Spirit. Then, as the perception of the true nature of the Creative Process dawned upon any subjective entity, it would by reason of accepting this suggestion begin to develop an objective mentality, and so would gradually attain to the same status as those who had passed over in full possession of all their mental powers.

But the more the objective mentality became developed in these discarnate personalities the more the need of a corresponding physical instrument would assert itself, both from their intellectual perception of the original cosmic process, and also from the inherent energy of the Spirit as centered in the ultimate ego of the individual. Not to seek material manifestation would be the contrary of all we have traced out regarding the nature of the Creative Process; and hence the law of tendency resulting from the conscious union of subjective and objective mind in the individual must necessarily be toward the production of a physical form. Only we must recollect, as I have already pointed out, that this concentration of these minds would be upon a principle and not upon a particular bodily shape. The particular form they would be content to leave to the inherent self-expressiveness of the Universal Spirit working through the particular ego, with the result that their expectation would be fixed upon a *general principle* of physical Resurrection which would provide a form suited to be the material instrument of the highest ideal of man as a spiritual and mental being. Then, since the subjective mind is the automatic builder of the body, the result of the individual's acceptance of the Resurrection principle must be that this mental conception will eventually work out as a corresponding fact. Whether on this planet or on some other, matters not, for, as we have already seen, the physical body evolved by a soul that is conscious of its unity with the Universal Spirit is bound to be in conformity with the physical laws of *any* planet, though from the standpoint of the conscious ego not limited by them.

In this way we may conceive that those who have passed over in possession of both sides of their spiritual nature would find a glorious field of usefulness in the unseen in helping to emancipate those who had passed over in possession of their subjective side only. But from our present analysis it will be seen that this can only be effected on the basis of a recognition of the principle of the Resurrection of the Body. Apart from the recognition of this principle the only possible conception which the discarnate individual could form of himself would be that of a purely subjective being; and this carries with it all the limitations of a subjective life unbalanced by an objective one; and so long as the principle of physical resurrection is denied, so long the life must continue to be merely subjective and consequently unprogressive.[7]

But it may be asked why those who have realized this great principle sufficiently to carry their objective mentality into the unseen state are liable to the change which we call death. The answer is that though they have realized *the general principle* they have not yet divested themselves of certain conceptions by which they limit it, and consequently by the law of subjective mind they carry those limitations into the working of the Resurrection principle itself.

They are limited by the race-belief that physical death is under all conditions a necessary law of Nature, or by the theological belief that death is the will of God; so then the question is whether these beliefs are well founded. Of course appeal is made to universal experience, but it does not follow that the universal experience of the past is bound to be the universal experience of the future—the universal experience of the past was that no man had ever flown across the English Channel, yet now it has been done.

What we have to do, therefore, is not to bother about past experience, but to examine the inherent nature of the Law of Life and see whether it does not contain possibilities of further development. And the first step in this direction is to see whether what we have hitherto considered limitations of the law are really integral parts of the law itself. The very statement of this question shows the correct answer; for how can a force acting in one direction be an integral part of a force acting in the opposite direction? How can the force which pulls a thing down be an integral part of the force which builds it up? To suppose, therefore, that the limitations of the law are an integral portion of the law itself is a *reductio ad absurdum*.

For these reasons the argument from the past experience of the race counts for nothing; and when we examine the theological argument we shall find that it is only the old argument from past experience in another dress. It is alleged that death is the will of God. How do we know that it is the will of God? Because the facts prove it so, is the ultimate answer of all religious systems with one exception; so here we are back again at the old race-experience as the criterion of truth. Therefore the theological argument is nothing but the materialistic argument disguised. It is in our more or less *conscious* acceptance of the materialistic argument, under any of its many disguises, that the limitation of life is to be found—not in the Law of Life itself; and if we are to bring into manifestation the infinite possibilities latent in that Law it can only be by looking steadily into the *principle* of the Law and resolutely denying everything that opposes it. The Principle of Life must of necessity be Affirmative, and affirmative throughout, without any negative anywhere—if we once realize this we shall be able to unmask the enemy and silence his guns.

Now to do this is precisely the one object of the Bible; and it does it in a thoroughly logical manner, always leading on to the ultimate result by successive links of cause and effect. People will tell you that the Bible is their authority for saying that Death is the will of God; but these are people who read it carelessly; and ultimately the only reason they can give you for their manner of interpreting the Bible is that the facts prove their interpretation to be correct; so that in the last resort you will always find you have got back to the old materialistic argument from past race-experience, which logically proves nothing. These are good well-meaning people with a limited idea which they read into the Bible, and so limit its promises by making physical death an essential preliminary to Resurrection. They grasp, of course, the great central idea that Perfected Man possesses a joyous immortal Life permeating spirit, soul and body; but they relegate it to some dim and distant future, entirely disconnected from the present law of our being, not seeing that if we are to have eternal life it must necessarily be involved in some principle which is eternal, and therefore existing, at any rate latently, at the present moment. Hence, though their fundamental principle is true, they are all the time mentally limiting it, with the result that they themselves create the conditions they impose upon it, and consequently the principle will work (as principles always do) in accordance with the conditions provided for its action.

Unless, therefore, this limiting belief is entirely eradicated, the individual, though realizing the fundamental principle of Life, is bound to pass out of physical existence; but on the other hand, since he does take the recognition of this fundamental principle with him, it is bound to bear fruit sooner or later in a joyous Resurrection, while the intermediate state can only be a peaceful anticipation of that supreme event. This is the answer to the question why those who have realized the great principle sufficiently to carry their objective mentality into the unseen world are still liable to physical death; and in the last analysis it will be found to resolve itself into the remains of race belief based upon past experience. These are they who pass over in sure and certain hope of a glorious Resurrection—sure and certain because founded upon the very Being of God Himself, that inherent Life of the All-creating Divine Spirit which is the perpetual interaction of the Eternal Love and Beauty. They have grasped the Life-giving Truth, only they have postponed its operation, because they have the fixed idea that its present fruition is an absolute impossibility.

But if we ask the reason for this idea it always comes back to the old materialistic argument from the experience of past conditions, while the whole nature of advance is in the opening up of new conditions. And in this advance the Bible is the pioneer book. Its whole purport is to tell us most emphatically that death is *not* the will of God. In the story of Eden God is represented as warning man of the poisonous nature of the forbidden fruit, which is incompatible with the idea of death as an essential feature of man's nature. Then from the point where man has taken the poison all the rest of the Bible is devoted to telling us how to get rid of it. Christ, it tells us, was manifested to bring Life and Immortality to light—to abolish death—to destroy the works of the devil, that is the death-dealing power, for "he that hath the power of death is the devil." It is impossible to reconcile this life-giving conception of the Bible with the idea that death at any stage or in any degree is the desire of God. Let us, therefore, start with the recognition that this negative force, whether in its minor degrees as disease or in its culmination as death, is that which it is the will of God to abolish. This also is logical; for if God be the Universal Spirit of Life finding manifestation in individual lives, how can the desire of this Spirit be to act in opposition to its own manifestation? Therefore Scripture and common-sense alike assure us that the will of God toward us is Life and not death.[8]

We may therefore start on our quest for Life with the happy certainty that God is on our side. But people will meet us with the objection that though God wills Life to us, He does not will it just yet, but only in some dim far-off future. How do we know this? Certainly not from the Bible. In the Bible Jesus speaks of two classes of persons who believe on Him as the Manifestation or Individualisation of the Spirit of Life. He speaks of those who, having passed through death, still believe on Him, and says that these *shall* live—a future event. And at the same time He speaks of those who are living and believe on Him, and says that they shall never die—thus contemplating the entire elimination of the contingency of death (John xi. 25).

Again St. Paul expresses his wish not to be unclothed but to be clothed upon, which he certainly would not have done had he considered the latter alternative a nonsensical fancy. And in another place he expressly states that we shall not all die, but that some shall be transmuted into the Resurrection body without passing through physical death. And if we turn to the Old Testament we find two instances in which this is said to have actually occurred, those of Enoch and Elijah. And we may note in passing that the Bible draws our attention to certain facts about these two personages which are important as striking at the root of the notion that austerities of some sort are necessary for the great attainment. Of Enoch we are expressly told that he was the father of a large family, and of Elijah that he was a man of like nature with ourselves—thus showing us what is wanted is not a shutting of ourselves off from ordinary human life but such a clear realization of the Universal Principle, of which our personal life is the more or less conscious manifestation, that our commonest actions will be hallowed by the Divine Presence; and so the grand dénouement will be only the natural result of our daily habit of walking with God. From the stand-point of the Bible, therefore, the attainment of physical regeneration without passing through death is not an impossibility, nor is it necessarily relegated to some far off future. Whatever any one else may say to the contrary, the Bible contemplates such a dénouement of human evolution as a present possibility.

Then if we argue from the philosophical stand-point we arrive at precisely the same result. Past experience proves nothing, and we must therefore make a fresh start by going back to the Original Creative action of the Spirit of Life itself. Then, if we take this as our starting point, remembering that at the stage of this *original* movement there can be no intervention by a second power, because there is none, why should we mentally impose any restriction upon the action of the Creative Power? Certainly not by its own Law of Tendency, for that must always be toward fuller self-expression; and since this can only take place through the individual, the desire of the Spirit must always be toward the increasing of the individual life. Nor yet from anything in the created substance, for that would either be to suppose the Spirit creating something in limitation of its own Self-expression, or else to suppose that the limiting substance was created by some other power working against the Spirit; and as this would mean a Duality of powers we should not have reached the Originating Power at all, and so we might put Spirit and Substance equally out of court as both being merely modes of secondary causation. But if we see that the Universal Substance must be created by emanation from the Universal Spirit, then we see that no limitation of Spirit by substance is possible. We may therefore feel assured that no limitation proceeds either from the will of the Spirit or from the nature of Substance.

Where, then, does limitation come from? Limiting conditions are created by the same power which creates everything else, namely, the Self-contemplation of Spirit. This is why it is so important to realize that the individual mind forms a center from which the self-contemplating action of Spirit is specialized in terms of the individual's own mode of thinking, and therefore so long as the individual contemplates negative conditions as being *of the essence* of his own personality, he is in effect employing the Creative Power of the Self-contemplation of Spirit invertedly, destructively instead of constructively. The Law of the Self-contemplation of Spirit as the Creative Power is as true in the microcosm as in the macrocosm, and so the individual's contemplation of himself as subject to the law of sin and death keeps him subject to that law, while the opposite self-contemplation, the contemplation of himself as rejoicing in the Life of the Spirit, the Perfect Law of Liberty, must necessarily produce the opposite results.

Why, then, should not regeneration be accomplished here and now? I can see no reason against it, either Scriptural or philosophical, except our own difficulty in getting rid of the race-traditions which are so deeply embedded in our subjective minds. To get rid of these we require a firm basis on which to receive the opposite suggestion. We need to be convinced that our ideal of a regenerated self is in accord with the Normal Standard of Humanity and is within the scope of the laws of the universe. Now to make clear to us the *infinitude* of the truly Normal Standard of Humanity is the whole purpose of the Bible; and the Manifestation of this Standard is set before us in the Central Personality of the Scriptures who is at once the Son of God and the Son of Man—the Great Exception, if you will, to man as we know him now, but the Exception which proves the Rule. In proportion as we begin to realize this we begin to introduce into our own life the action of that Personal Factor on which all further development depends; and when our recognition is complete we shall find that we also are children of God.

CONCLUSION

We are now in a position to see the place occupied by the individual in the Creative Order. We have found that the originating and maintaining force of the whole Creative Process is the Self-contemplation of the Spirit, and that this necessarily produces a Reciprocal corresponding to the idea embodied in the contemplation, and thus manifesting that idea in a correlative Form. We have found that in this way the externalization of the idea progresses from the condensation of the primary nebula to the production of human beings as a race, and that at this point the simple *generic* reproduction of the idea terminates. This means that up to, and including, *genus homo* , the individual, whether plant, animal, or man, is what it is simply by reason of race conditions and not by exercise of deliberate choice. Then we have seen that the next step in advance must necessarily be by the individual becoming aware that he has power to mold the conditions of his own consciousness and environment by the creative power of his thought; thus not only enabling him to take a conscious part in his own further evolution but precluding him from evolving any further except by the right exercise of this power; and we have found that the crux of the passage from the Fourth to the Fifth Kingdom is to get people so to understand the nature of their creative power as not to use it destructively. Now what we require to see is that the Creative Process has always only one way of working, and that is by Reciprocity or Reflection, or, as we might say, by the law of Action and Re-action, the re-action being always equivalent and correspondent to the action which generated it. If this Law of Reciprocity be grasped then we see how the progress of the Creative Process must at length result in producing a being who himself possesses the power of independent spiritual initiative and is thus able to carry on the creative work from the stand-point of his own individuality.

Now the great crux is first to get people to see that they possess this power at all, and then to get them to use it in the right direction. When our eyes begin to open to the truth that we do possess this power the temptation is to ignore the fact that our power of initiative is itself a product of the similar power subsisting in the All-originating Spirit. If this origin of our own creative faculty is left out of sight we shall fail to recognize the Livingness of the Greater Life within which we live. We shall never get nearer to it than what we may call its *generic* level, the stage at which the Creative Power is careful of the type or race but is careless of the individual; and so at this level we shall never pass into the Fifth Kingdom which is the Kingdom of Individuality—we have missed the whole point of the transition to the more advanced mode of being, in which the individual consciously functions as a creative center, because we have no conception of a Universal Power that works at any higher level than the generic, and consequently to reach a specific personal exercise of creative power we should have to conceive of ourselves as transcending the Universal Law. But if we realize that our own power of creative initiative has its origin in the similar faculty of the All-Originating Mind then we see that the way to maintain the Life-giving energy in ourselves is to use our power of spiritual initiative so as to impress upon the Spirit the conception of ourselves as standing related to It in a specific, individual, and personal way that takes us out of the mere category of *genus homo* and gives us a specific spiritual individuality of our own. Thus our mental action produces a corresponding re-action in the mind of the Spirit, which in its turn reproduces itself as a special manifestation of the Life of the Spirit in us; and so long as this circulation between the individual spirit and the Great Spirit is kept up, the individual life will be maintained, and will also strengthen as the circulation continues, for the reason that the Spirit, as the Original Creative Power, is a Multiplying Force, and the current sent into it is returned multiplied, just as in telegraphy the feeble current received from a distance at the end of a long line operates to start a powerful battery in the receiving office, which so multiplies the force as to give out a clear message, which but for the multiplication of the original movement could not have been done. Something like this we may picture the multiplying tendency of the Originating Mind, and consequently the longer the circulation between it and the individual mind goes on the stronger the latter becomes; and this process growing habitual becomes at last automatic, thus producing an endless flow of Life continually expanding in intelligence, love, power and joy.

But we must note carefully that all this can only proceed from the individual's recognition that his own powers are a derivative from the All-originating Spirit, and that they can continue to be used constructively only so long as they are employed in harmony with the inherent Forward Movement of the Spirit. Therefore to insure this eternally flowing stream of Life from the Universal Spirit into the individual there must be *no inversion* in the individual's presentation of himself to the Originating Power: for through the very same Law by which we seek Life—the Life namely, of reciprocal action and re-action—every inversion we bring with us in presenting ourselves to the Spirit is bound to be faithfully reproduced in a corresponding re-action, thus adulterating the stream of Pure Life, and rendering it less life-giving in proportion to the extent to which we invert the action of the Life-principle; so that in extreme cases the stream flowing through and from the individual may be rendered absolutely poisonous and deadly, and the more so the greater his recognition of his own personal power to employ spiritual forces.

The existence of these negative possibilities in the spiritual world should never be overlooked, and therefore the essential condition for receiving the Perfect Fulness of Life is that we should present ourselves before the Eternal Spirit free from every trace of inversion. To do this means to present ourselves in the likeness of the Divine Ideal; and in this self-presentation the initiative, so far as the individual is consciously concerned, must necessarily be taken by himself. He is to project into the Eternal Mind the conception of himself as identical with its Eternal Ideal; and if he can do this, then by the Law of the Creative Process a return current will flow from the Eternal Mind reproducing this image in the individual with a continually growing power. Then the question is, How are we to do this?

The answer is that to take the initiative for inducing this flow of Life individually it is a *sine qua non* that the conditions enabling us to do so should first be presented to us universally. This is in accordance with the general principle that we can never create a force but can only specialize it. Only here the power we are wanting to specialize is the very Power of Specialization itself; and therefore, paradoxical as it may seem, what we require to have shown us is the Universality of Specialization.

Now this is what the Bible puts before us in its central figure. Taking the Bible statements simply and literally they show us this unique Personality as the Principle of Humanity, alike in its spiritual origin and its material manifestation, carried to the logical extreme of specialization; while at the same time, as the embodiment of the original polarity of Spirit and Substance, this Personality, however unique, is absolutely universal; so that the Bible sets Jesus Christ before us as the answer to the philosophic problem of how to specialize the universal, while at the same time preserving its universality.

If, then, we fix our thought upon this unique Personality as the embodiment of *universal* principles, it follows that those principles must exist in ourselves also, and that His actual specialization of them is the earnest of our potential specialization of them. Then if we fix our thought on this potential in ourselves as being identical with its manifestation in Him, we can logically claim our identity with Him, so that what He has done we have done, what He is, we are, and thus recognizing ourselves in Him we present *this* image of ourselves to the Eternal Mind, with the result that we bring with us no inversion, and so import no negative current into our stream of Life.

Thus it is that we reach "the Father" through "the Son," and that He is able to keep us from falling and to present us faultless before the presence of the Divine glory with exceeding joy (Jude 24). The Gospel of "the Word made flesh" is not the meaningless cant of some petty sect nor yet the cunning device of priestcraft, though it has been distorted in both these directions; but it can give a reason for itself, and is founded upon the deepest laws of the threefold constitution of man, embracing the *whole* man, body, soul and spirit. It is not opposed to Science but is the culmination of all science whether physical or mental. It is philosophical and logical throughout if you start the Creative Process where alone it can start, in the Self-contemplation of the Spirit. The more carefully we examine into the claims of the Gospel of Christ the more we shall find all the current objections to it melt away and disclose their own superficialness. We shall find that Christ is indeed the Mediator between God and Man, not by the arbitrary fiat of a capricious Deity, but by a logical law of sequence which solves the problem of making extremes meet, so that the Son of Man is also the Son of God; and when we see the reason why this is so we thereby receive power to become ourselves sons of God, which is the dénouement of the Creative Process in the Individual.

These closing lines are not the place to enter upon so great a subject, but I hope to follow it up in another volume and to show in detail the logic of the Bible teaching, what it saves us from and what it leads us to; to show while giving due weight to the value of other systems how it differs from them and transcends them; to glance, perhaps, for a moment at the indications of the future and to touch upon some of the dangers of the present and the way to escape from them. Nor would I pass over in silence another and important aspect of the Gospel contained in Christ's commission to His followers to heal the sick. This also follows logically from the Law of the Creative Process if we trace carefully the sequence of connections from the indwelling Ego to the outermost of its vehicles; while the effect of the recognition of these great truths upon the individuality that has for a time put off its robe of flesh, opens out a subject of paramount interest. Thus it is that on every plane Christ is the Fulfilling of the Law, and that "Salvation" is not a silly shiboleth but the logical and vital process of our advance into the unfoldment of the next stage of the limitless capacities of our being. Of these things I hope to write in another volume, should it be permitted to me, and in the meanwhile I would commend the present abstract statement of principles to the reader's attention in the hope that it may throw some light on the fundamental nature of these momentous questions. The great thing to bear in mind is that if a thing is true at all there must be a reason why it is true, and when we come to see this reason we know the truth at first hand for ourselves and not from some one else's report—then it becomes really our own and we begin to learn how to use it. This is the secret of the individual's progress in any art, science, or business, and the same method will serve equally well in our search after Life itself, and as we thus follow up the great quest we shall find that on every plane the Way, the Truth, and the Life are *One*.

"A little philosophy inclineth a man's mind to atheism, but depth in philosophy bringeth men's minds about to religion."—*Bacon. Essay xvi* .

THE DIVINE OFFERING

I take the present opportunity of a new edition to add a few pages on certain points which appear to me of vital importance, and the connection of which with the preceding chapters will, I hope, become evident as the reader proceeds. Assuming the existence in each individual of a creative power of thought which, in relation to himself, reflects the same power existing in the Universal Mind, our right employment of this power becomes a matter of extreme moment to ourselves. Its inverted use necessarily holds us fast in the bondage from which we are seeking to escape, and equally necessarily its right use brings us into Liberty; and therefore if any Divine revelation exists at all its purpose must be to lead us away from the inverted use of our creative faculty and into such a higher specializing of it as will produce the desired result. Now the purpose of the Bible is to do this, and it seeks to effect this work by a dual operation. It places before us that Divine Ideal of which I have already spoken, and at the same time bases this ideal upon the recognition of a Divine Sacrifice. These two conceptions are so intimately interwoven in Scripture that they cannot be separated, but at the present day there *is* a growing tendency to attempt to make this separation and to discard the conception of a Divine Sacrifice as unphilosophical, that is as having no nexus of cause and effect. What I want, therefore, to point out in these additional pages is that there is such a nexus, and that so far from being without a sequence of cause and effect it has its root in the innermost principles of our own being. It is not contrary to Law but proceeds from the very nature of the Law itself.

The current objection to the Bible teaching on this subject is that no such sacrifice could have been required by God, either because the Originating Energy can have no consciousness of Personality and is only a blind force, or because, if "God is Love," He could not demand such a sacrifice. On the former hypothesis we are of course away from the Bible teaching altogether and have nothing to do with it; but, as I have said elsewhere, the fact of our own consciousness of personality can only be accounted for by the existence, however hidden, of a corresponding quality in the Originating Spirit. Therefore I will confine my remarks to the question how Love, as the originating impulse of all creation, can demand such a sacrifice. And to my mind the answer is that God does not demand it. It is Man who demands it. It is the instinctive craving of the human soul for *certainty* that requires a demonstration so convincing as to leave no room for doubt of our perfectly happy relation to the Supreme Spirit, and consequently to all that flows from it, whether on the side of the visible or of the invisible. When we grasp the fact that such a standpoint of certainty is the necessary foundation for the building up in ourselves of the Divine Ideal then it becomes clear that to afford us this firm basis is the greatest work that the Spirit, in its relation to human personality, could do.

We are often told that the offering of sacrifices had its origin in primitive man's conception of his gods as beings which required to be propitiated so as to induce them to do good or abstain from doing harm; and very likely this was the case. The truth at the back of this conception is the feeling that there is a higher power upon which man is dependent; and the error is in supposing that this power is limited by an individuality which can be enriched by selling its good offices, or which blackmails you by threats. In either case it wants to get something out of you, and from this it follows that its own power of supplying its own wants must be limited, otherwise it would not require to be kept in good temper by gifts. In very undeveloped minds such a conception results in the idea of numerous gods, each having, so to say, his own particular line of business; and the furthest advance this mode of thought is capable of is the reduction of these various deities to two antagonistic powers of Good and of Evil. But the result in either case is the same, so long as we start with the hypothesis that the Good will do us more good and the Evil do us less harm by reason of our sacrifices, for then it logically follows that the more valuable your sacrifices and the oftener they are presented the better chance you have of good luck. Doubtless some such conception as this was held by the mass of the Hebrew people under the sacrificial system of the Levitical Law, and perhaps this was one reason why they were so prone to fall into idolatry—for in this view their fundamental notion was practically identical in its nature with that of the heathen around them. Of course this was not the fundamental idea embodied in the Levitical system itself. The root of that system was the symbolizing of a supreme ideal of reconciliation hereafter to be manifested in action. Now a symbol is not the thing symbolized. The purpose of a symbol is twofold, to put us upon enquiry as to the reality which it indicates, and to bring that reality to our minds by suggestion when we look at the symbol; but if it does not do this, and we rest only in the symbol, nothing will come of it, and we are left just where we were. That the symbolic nature of the Levitical sacrifice was clearly perceived by the deeper thinkers among the Hebrews is attested by many passages in the Bible—"Sacrifice and burnt offering thou wouldest not" (Psalms xl: 6, and li: 16) and other similar utterances; and the distinction between these symbols and that which they symbolized is brought out in the Epistle to the Hebrews by the argument that if those sacrifices had afforded a sufficient standpoint for the effectual realization of cleansing then the worshiper would not need to have repeated them because he would have no more consciousness of sin (Hebrews x: 2).

This brings us to the essential point of the whole matter. What we want is the certainty that there is no longer any separation between us and the Divine Spirit by reason of sin, either as overt acts of wrong doing or as error of principle; and the whole purpose of the Bible is to lead us to this assurance. Now such an assurance cannot be based on any sort of sacrifices that require repetition, for then we could never know whether we had given enough either in quality or quantity. It must be a once-for-all business or it is no use at all; and so the Bible makes the once-for-allness of the offering the essential point of its teaching. "He that has been bathed does not need to be bathed again"

(John xiii: 10). "There is now no condemnation to them which are in Christ Jesus" (Romans viii: i).

Various intellectual difficulties, however, hinder many people from seeing the working of the law of cause and effect in this presentment. One is the question, How can moral guilt be transferred from one person to another? What is called the "forensic" argument (i.e., the court of law argument) that Christ undertook to suffer in our stead as our *surety* is undoubtedly open to this objection. Suretyship must by its very nature be confined to civil obligations and cannot be extended to criminal liability, and so the "forensic" argument may be set aside as very much a legal fiction. But if we realize the Bible teaching that Christ is the Son of God, that is, the Divine Principle of Humanity out of which we originated and subsisting in us all, however unconsciously to ourselves, then we see that sinners as well as saints are included in this Principle; and consequently that the Self-offering of Christ must actually include the self-offering of every human being in the acknowledgment (however unknown to his *objective* mentality) of his sin. If we can grasp this somewhat abstract point of view it follows that in the Person of Christ every human being, past, present, and to come, was self-offered for the condemnation of his sin—a *self* - condemnation and a *self*-offering, and hence a cleansing, for the simple reason that if you can get a man to realize his past error, really see his mistake, he won't do it again; and it is the perpetuation of sin and error that has to be got rid of—to do this universally would be to regain Paradise. Seen therefore in this light there is no question of transference of moral guilt, and I take it this is St. Paul's meaning when he speaks of our being partakers in Christ's death.

Then there is the objection, How can past sins be done away with? If we accept the philosophical conclusion that Time has no substantive existence then all that remains is states of consciousness. As I have said in the earlier part of this book, the Self-Contemplation of Spirit is the cause of all our perception of existence and environment; and consequently if the Self-Contemplation of the Spirit from any center of individualization is that of entire harmony and the absence of anything that would cause any consciousness of separation, then past sins cease to have any part in this self-recognition, and consequently cease to have any place in the world of existence. The foundation of the whole creative process is the calling into Light out of Darkness—"that which makes manifest is light"—and consequently the converse action is that of sending out of Light into Darkness, that is, into Notbeing. Now this is exactly what the Spirit says in the Bible—"I, even I, am He that blotteth out thy transgressions" (Isaiah xliii: 25). Blotting out is the sending out of manifestation into the darkness of non-manifestation, out of Being into Not-being; and in this way the past error ceases to have any existence and so ceases to have any further effect upon us. It is "blotted out," and from this new standpoint has never been at all; so that to continue to contemplate it is to give a false sense of existence to that which in effect has no existence. It is that Affirmation of Negation which is the root of all evil. It is the inversion of our God-given creative power of thought, calling into existence that which in the Perfect Life of the Spirit never had or could have any existence, and therefore it creates the sense of inharmony, opposition, and separation. Of course this is only relatively to ourselves, for we cannot create eternal principles. They are the Being of God; and as I have already shown these great Principles of the Affirmative may be summed up in the two words Love and Beauty—Love in essence and Beauty in manifestation; but since we can only live from the standpoint of our own consciousness we can make a false creation built upon the idea of opposites to the all-creating Love and Beauty, which false creation with all its accompaniments of limitation, sin, sorrow, sickness, and death, must necessarily be real to us until we perceive that these things were not created by God, the Spirit of the Affirmative, but by our own inversion of our true relation to the All-creating Being.

When, then, we view the matter in this light the Offering once for all of the Divine Sacrifice for the sin of the whole world is seen not to be a mere ecclesiastical dogma having no relation of cause and effect, but to be the highest application of the same principle of cause and effect by which the whole creation, ourselves included, has been brought into existence— the Self-Contemplation of Spirit producing corresponding manifestation, only now working on the level of Individual Personality.

As I have shown at the beginning of this book the cosmic manifestation of principles is not sufficient to bring out all that there is in them. To do this their action must be specialized by the introduction of the Personal Factor. They are represented by the Pillar Jachin, but it must be equilibriated by the Pillar Boaz, Law and Personality the two Pillars of the Universe; and in the One Offering we have the supreme combination of these two principles, the highest specialization of Law by the highest power of Personality. These are eternal principles, and therefore we are told that the Lamb was slain from the foundation of the world; and because "thoughts are things" this supreme manifestation of the creative interaction of Law and Personality was bound eventually to be manifested in concrete action in the world conditioned by time and space; and so it was that the supreme manifestation of the Love of God to meet the supreme need of Man took place. The history of the Jewish nation is the history of the working of the law of cause and effect, under the guidance of the Divine Wisdom, so as to provide the necessary conditions for the greatest event in the world's history; for if Christ was to appear it must be in *some* nation, in *some* place, and at *some* time: but to trace the steps by which, through an intelligible sequence of causes, these necessary conditions were provided belongs rather to an investigation of Bible history than to our present purpose, so I will not enter into these details here. But what I hope I have in some measure made clear is that there is a reason why Christ should be manifested, and should suffer, and rise again, and that so far from being a baseless superstition the Reconciling of the world to God through the One Offering once-for-all offered for the sin of the whole world, lays the immovable foundation upon which we may build securely for all the illimitable future.

OURSELVES IN THE DIVINE OFFERING

If we have grasped the principle I have endeavored to state in the last chapter we shall find that with this new standpoint a new life and a new world begin to open out to us. This is because we are now living from a new recognition of ourselves and of God. Eternal Truth, that which is the essential reality of Being, is *always* the same; it has never altered, for whatever is capable of passing away and giving place to something else is not eternal, and therefore the real essence of our being, as proceeding from God and subsisting in Him has always been the same. But this is the very fact which we have hitherto lost sight of; and since our perception of life is the measure of our individual consciousness of it, we have imposed upon ourselves a world of limitation, a world filled with the power of the negative, because we have viewed things from that standpoint. What takes place, therefore, when we realize the truth of our Redemption is not a change in our essential relation to the Parent Spirit, the Eternal Father, but an awakening to the perception of this eternal and absolutely perfect relation. We see that in reality it has never been otherwise for the simple reason that in the very nature of Being it *could* not be otherwise; and when we see this we see also that what has hitherto been wrong has not been the working of "the Father" but our conception of the existence of some other power, a power of negation, limitation, and destructiveness, the very opposite to all that the Creative Spirit, by the very fact of Its Creativeness, must be. That wonderful parable of the Prodigal Son shows us that he never ceased to be a son. It was not his Father who sent him away from home but his notion that he could do better "on his own," and we all know what came of it. But when he returned to the Father he found that from the Father's point of view he had never been otherwise than a son, and that all the trouble he had gone through was not "of the Father" but was the result of his own failure to realize what the Father and the Home really were.[9]

Now this is exactly the case with ourselves. When we wake up to the truth we find that, so far as the Father is concerned, we have always been in Him and in His home, for we are made in His image and likeness and are reflections of His own Being. He says to us "Son, thou art ever with me and all that I have is thine." The Self-Contemplation of Spirit is the Creative Power creating an environment corresponding to the mode of consciousness contemplated, and therefore in proportion as we contemplate ourselves as centers of individualization for the Divine Spirit we find ourselves surrounded by a new environment reflecting the harmonious conditions which preexist in the Thought of the Spirit.

This, then, is the sequence of Cause and Effect involved in the teaching of the Bible. Man is *in essence* a spiritual being, the reflection on the plane of individual personality of that which the All-Originating Spirit is in Itself, and is thus in that reciprocal relation to the Spirit which is Love. This is the first statement of his creation in Genesis—God saw all that He had made and behold it was very good, Man included. Then the Fall is the failure of the lower mentality to realize that God IS Love, in a word that Love is the only ultimate Motive Power it is possible to conceive, and that the creations of Love cannot be otherwise than good and beautiful. The lower mentality conceives an opposite quality of Evil and thus produces a motive power the opposite of Love, which is Fear; and so Fear is born into the world giving rise to the whole brood of evil, anger, hatred, envy, lies, violence, and the like, and on the external plane giving rise to discordant vibrations which are the root of physical ill. If we analyze our motives we shall find that they are always some mode either of Love or Fear; and fear has its root in the recognition of some power other than Perfect Love, which is God the *One* all-embracing Good. Fear has a creative force which invertedly mimics that of Love; but the difference between them is that Love is eternal and Fear is not. Love as the Original Creative Motive is the only logical conclusion we can come to as to why we ourselves or any other creation exists. Fear is illogical because to regard it as having any place in the Original Creative Motive involves a contradiction in terms.

By accepting the notion of a dual power, that of Good *and* Evil, the inverted creative working of Fear is introduced with all its attendant train of evil things. This is the eating of the deadly tree which occasions the Fall, and therefore the Redemption which requires to be accomplished is a redemption from Fear—not merely from this or that particular fear but from the very Root of Fear, which root is unbelief in the Love of God, the refusal to believe that Love alone is the Creating Power in all things, whether small beyond our recognition or great beyond our conception. Therefore to bring about this Redemption there must be such a manifestation of the Divine Love to Man as, when rightly apprehended, will leave no ground for fear; and when we see that the Sacrifice of the Cross was the Self-Offering of Love made in order to provide this manifestation, then we see that all the links in the chain of Cause and Effect are complete, and that Fear never had any place in the Creative Principle, whether as acting in the creation of a world or of a man. The root, therefore, of all the trouble of the world consists in the Affirmation of Negation, in using our creative power of thought invertedly, and thus giving substance to that which *as principle* has no existence. So long as this negative action of thought continues so long will it produce its natural effect; whether in the individual or in the mass. The experience is perfectly real while it lasts. Its unreality consists in the fact that there was never any real need for it; and the more we grasp the truth of the all-embracingness of the *one* Good, both as Cause and as Effect, on all planes, the more the experience of its opposite will cease to have any place in our lives.

This truly New Thought puts us in an entirely new relation to the whole of our environment, opening out possibilities hitherto undreamt of, and this by an orderly sequence of law which is naturally involved in our new mental attitude; but before considering the prospect thus offered it is well to be quite clear as to what this new mental attitude really is; for it is our adoption of this attitude that is the Key to the whole position. Put briefly it is ceasing to include the idea of limitations in our conception of the working of the

All-Creating Spirit. Here are some specimens of the way in which we limit the creative working of the Spirit. We say, I am too old now to start this or that new sort of work. This is to deny the power of the Spirit to vivify our physical or mental faculties, which is illogical if we consider that it is the same Spirit that brought us into any existence at all. It is like saying that when a lamp is beginning to burn low the same person who first filled it with oil cannot replenish it and make it burn brightly again. Or we say, I cannot do so and so because I have not the means. When you were fourteen did you know where all the means were coming from which were going to support you till now when you are perhaps forty or fifty? So you should argue that the same power that has worked in the past can continue to work in the future. If you say the means came in the past quite naturally through ordinary channels, that is no objection; on the contrary the more reason for saying that suitable channels will open in the future. Do you expect God to put cash into your desk by a conjuring trick? Means come through recognizable channels, that is to say we recognize the channels by the fact of the stream flowing through them; and one of our most common mistakes is in thinking that we ourselves have to fix the particular channel beforehand. We say in effect that the Spirit cannot open other channels, and so we stop them up. Or we say, our past experience speaks to the contrary, thus assuming that our past experiences have included all possibilities and have exhausted the laws of the universe, an assumption which is negatived by every fresh discovery even in physical science. And so we go on limiting the power of the Spirit in a hundred different ways.

But careful consideration will show that, though the modes in which we limit it are as numerous as the circumstances with which we have to deal, the thing with which we limit it is always the same—it is by the introduction of our own personality. This may appear at first a direct contradiction of all that I have said about the necessity for the Personal Factor, but it is not. Here is a paradox.

To open out into manifestation the wonderful possibilities hidden in the Creative Power of the Universe we require to do two things—to see that we ourselves are necessary as centers for focussing that power, and at the same time to withdraw the thought of ourselves as contributing anything to its efficiency. It is not I that work but the Power; yet the Power needs me because it cannot specialize itself without me—in a word each is the complementary of the other: and the higher the degree of specialization is to be the more necessary is the intelligent and willing co-operation of the individual.

This is the Scriptural paradox that "the son can do nothing of himself," and yet we are told to be "fellow-workers with God." It ceases to be a paradox, however, when we realize the relation between the two factors concerned, God and Man. Our mistake is in not discriminating between their respective functions, and putting Man in the place of God. In our everyday life we do this by measuring the power of God by our past experiences and the deductions we draw from them; but there is another way of putting Man in the place of God, and that is by the misconception that the All-Originating Spirit is merely a cosmic force without intelligence, and that Man has to originate the intelligence without which no specific purpose can be conceived. This latter is the error of much of the present day philosophy and has to be specially guarded against. This was perceived by some of the medieval students of these things, and they accordingly distinguished between what they called Animus Dei and Anima Mundi, the Divine Spirit and the Soul of the Universe. Now the distinction is this, that the essential quality of Animus Dei is Personality—not A Person, but the very Principle of Personality itself—while the essential quality of Anima Mundi is Impersonality. Then right here comes in that importance of the Personal Factor of which I have already spoken. The powers latent in the Impersonal are brought out to their fullest development by the operation of the Personal. This of course does not consist in changing the nature of those powers, for that is impossible, but in making such combinations of them by Personal Selection as to produce results which could not otherwise be obtained. Thus, for example, Number is in itself impersonal and no one can alter the laws which are inherent in it; but what we can do is to select particular numbers and the sort of relation, such as subtraction, multiplication, etc., which we will establish between them; and then by the inherent Law of Number a certain result is bound to work out. Now our own essential quality is the consciousness of Personality; and as we grow into the recognition of the fact that the Impersonal is, as it were, crying out for the operation upon it of the Personal in order to bring its latent powers into working, we shall see how limitless is the field that thus opens before us.

The prospect is wonderful beyond our present conception, and full of increasing glory if we realize the true foundation on which it rests. But herein lies the danger. It consists in not realizing that the Infinite of the Impersonal *is* and also that the Infinite of the Personal *is* . Both are Infinite and so require differentiation through our own personality, but in their essential quality each is the exact balance of the other—not in contradiction to each other, but as complementary to one another, each supplying what the other needs for its full expression, so that the two together make a perfect whole. If, however, we see this relation and our own position as the connecting link between them, we shall see only ourselves as the Personal Factor; but the more we realize, both by theory and experience, the power of human personality brought into contact with the Impersonal Soul of Nature, and employed with a Knowledge of its power and a corresponding exercise of the will, the less we shall be inclined to regard ourselves as the supreme factor in the chain of cause and effect Consideration of this argument points to the danger of much of the present day teaching regarding the exercise of Thought Power as a creative agency. The principle on which this teaching is based is sound and legitimate for it is inherent in the nature of things; but the error is in supposing that we ourselves are the ultimate source of Personality instead of merely the distributors and specializers of it. The logical result of such a mental attitude is that putting ourselves in the place of all that is worshiped as God which is spoken of in the second chapter of the Second Epistle to the Thessalonians and other parts of Scripture. By the very hypothesis of the case we then know no higher will than our own, and so are without any Unifying Principle to prevent the conflict of wills which must then arise—a conflict which must become more and more destructive the greater the power possessed by the contending parties, and which, if there were no counterbalancing power, must result in the ultimate destruction of the existing race of men.

But there is a counterbalancing power. It is the very same power used affirmatively instead of negatively. It is the power of the Personal with the Impersonal when used under the guidance of that Unifying Principle which the recognition of the *One*-ness of the Personal Quality in the Divine Spirit supplies. Those who are using the creative power of thought only from the standpoint of individual personality, have obviously less power than those who are using it from the standpoint of the Personality inherent in the Living Spirit which is the Source and Fountain of all energy and substance, and therefore in the end the victory must remain with these latter. And because the power by which they conquer is that of the Unifying Personality itself their victory must result in the establishment of Peace and Happiness throughout the world, and is not a power of domination but of helpfulness and enlightenment. The choice is between these two mottoes:— "Each for himself and Devil take the hindmost," or "God for us all." In proportion, therefore, as we realize the immense forces dormant in the Impersonal Soul of Nature, only awaiting the introduction of the Personal Factor to wake them up into activity and direct them to specific purposes, the wider we shall find the scope of the powers within the reach of man; and the more clearly we perceive the Impersonalness of the very Principle of Personality itself, the clearer our own proper position as affording the Differentiating Medium between these two Infinitudes will become to us.

The Impersonalness of the Principle of Personality looks like a contradiction in terms, but it is not. I combine these two seemingly contradictory terms as the best way to convey to the reader the idea of the essential Quality of Personality not yet differentiated into individual centers of consciousness for the doing of particular work. Looked at in this way the Infinite of Personality must have Unity of Purpose for its foundation, for otherwise it would consist of conflicting personalities, in which case we have not yet reached the *One* all-originating cause. Or to put it in another way, an Infinite Personality divided against itself would be an Infinite Insanity, a creator of a cosmic Bedlam which, as a scientific fact, would be impossible of existence. Therefore the conception of an Infinite of Personality necessarily implies a perpetual Unity of Purpose; and for the same reason this Purpose can only be the fuller and fuller expression of an Infinite Unity of Consciousness; and Unity of Consciousness necessarily implies the entire absence of all that would impair it, and therefore its expression can only be as Universal Harmony. If, then, the individual realizes this true nature of the source from which his own consciousness of personality is derived his ideas and work will be based upon this foundation, with the result that as between ourselves peace and good will towards men must accompany this mode of thought, and as between us and the strictly Impersonal Soul of Nature our increasing knowledge in that direction would mean increasing power for carrying out our principle of peace and good will. As this perception of our relation to the Spirit of God and the Soul of Nature spreads from individual to individual so the Kingdom of God will grow, and its universal recognition would be the establishing of the Kingdom of Heaven on earth.

Perhaps the reader will ask why I say the Soul of Nature instead of saying the material universe. The reason is that in using our creative power of Thought we do not operate directly upon material elements—to do that is the work of construction from without and not of creation from within. The whole tendency of modern physical science is to reduce all matter in the final analysis to energy working in a primary ether. Whence this energy and this ether proceed is not the subject of physical analysis. That is a question which cannot be answered by means of the vacuum tube or the spectroscope. Physical science is doing its legitimate work in pushing further and further back the unanalyzable residuum of Nature, but, however far back, an ultimate unanalyzable residuum there must always be; and when physical science brings us to this point it hands us over to the guidance of psychological investigation just as in the Divina Commedia Virgil transfers Dante to the guidance of Beatrice for the study of the higher realms. Various rates of rapidity of motion in this primary ether, producing various numerical combinations of positively and negatively electrified particles, result in the formation of what we know as the different chemical elements, and thus explains the phenomena of their combining quantities, the law by which they join together to form new substances only in certain exact numerical ratios. From the first movement in the primary ether to solid substances, such as wood or iron or our own flesh, is thus a series of vibrations in a succession of mediums, each denser than the preceding one out of which it was concreted and from which it receives the vibratory impulse. This is in effect what physical science has to tell us. But to get further back we must look into the world of the invisible, and it is here that psychological study comes to our aid. We cannot, however, study the invisible side of Nature by working from the outside and so at this point of our studies we find the use of the time-honored teaching regarding the parallelism between the Macrocosm and the Microcosm. If the Microcosm is the reproduction in ourselves of the same principles as exist in the Macrocosm or universe in which we have our being, then by investigating ourselves we shall learn the nature of the corresponding invisible principles in our environment. Here, then, is the application of the dictum of the ancient philosophy, "Know Thyself." It means that the only place where we can study the principles of the invisible side of Nature is in ourselves; and when we know them there we can transfer them to the larger world around us.

In the concluding chapters of my "Edinburgh Lectures on Mental Science" I have outlined the way in which the soul or mind operates upon the physical instrument of its expression, and it resolves itself into this—that the mental action inaugurates a series of vibrations in the etheric body which, in their turn, induce corresponding grosser vibrations in the molecular substance until finally mechanical action is produced on the outside. Now transferring this idea to Nature as a whole we shall see that if our mental action is to affect it in any way it can only be by the response of something at the back of material substance analogous to mind in ourselves; and that there is such a "something" interior to the merely material side of Nature is proved by what we may call the Law of Tendency, not only in animals and plants, but even in inorganic substances, as shown for instance in Professor Bose's work on the

Response of Metals. The universal presence of this Law of Tendency therefore indicates the working of some non-material and, so to say, semi-intelligent power in the material world, a power which works perfectly accurately on its own lines so far as it goes, that is to say in a generic manner, but which does not possess that Personal power of *individual selection* which is necessary to bring out the infinite possibilities hidden in it. This is what is meant by the Soul of Nature, and it is for this reason I employ that term instead of saying the material universe. Which term to employ all depends on the mode of action we are contemplating. If it is construction from without, then we are dealing with the purely material universe. If we are seeking to bring about results by the exercise of our mental power from within, then we are dealing with the Soul of Nature. It is that control of the lower degree of intelligence by the higher of which I have spoken in my Edinburgh Lectures.

If we realize what I have endeavored to make clear in the earlier portion of this book, that the whole creation is produced by the operation of the Divine Will upon the Soul of Nature, it will be evident that we can set no limits to the potencies hidden in the latter and capable of being brought out by the operation of the Personal Factor upon it; therefore, granted a sufficiently powerful concentration of will, whether by an individual or a group of individuals, we can well imagine the production of stupendous effects by this agency, and in this way I would explain the statements made in Scripture regarding the marvelous powers to be exercised by the Anti-Christ, whether personal or collective. They are psychic powers, the power of the Soul of Man over the Soul of Nature. But the Soul of Nature is quite impersonal and therefore the moral quality of this action depends entirely on the human operator. This is the point of the Master's teaching regarding the destruction of the fig tree, and it is on this account He adds the warning as to the necessity for clearing our heart of any injurious feeling against others whenever we attempt to make use of this power (Mark xi: 20-26).

According to His teaching, then, this power of controlling the Soul of Nature by the addition of our own Personal Factor, however little we may be able to recognize it as yet, actually exists; its employment depends on our perception of the inner principles common to both, and it is for this reason the ancient wisdom was summed up in the aphorism "Know thyself." No doubt it is a wonderful Knowledge, but on analysis it will be found to be perfectly natural. It is the Knowledge of the cryptic forces of Nature. Now it is remarkable that this ancient maxim inscribed over the portals of the Temple of Delphi is not to be found in the Bible. The Bible maxim is not "Know thyself" but "Know the Lord." The great subject of Knowledge is not ourself but "the Lord"; and herein is the great difference between the two teachings. The one is limited by human personality, the other is based on the Infinitude of the Divine Personality; and because of this it includes human personality with all its powers over the Soul of Nature. It is a case of the greater including the less; and so the whole teaching of Scripture is directed to bringing us into the recognition of that Divine Personality which is the Great Original in whose image and likeness we are made. In proportion as we grow into the recognition of *this* our own personality will explain, and the creative power of our thought will cease to work invertedly until at last it will work only on the

same principles of Life, Love and Liberty as the Divine Mind, and so all evil
will disappear from our world. We shall not, as some systems teach, be
absorbed into Deity to the extinction of our individual consciousness, but on
the contrary our individual consciousness will continually expand, which is
what St. Paul means when he speaks of our "increasing with the increase of
God"—the continual expanding of the Divine element within us. But this can
only take place by our recognition of ourselves as *receivers* of this Divine
element. It is receiving into ourselves of the Divine Personality, a result not
to be reached through human reasoning. We reason from premises which we
have assumed, and the conclusion is already involved in the premises and can
never extend beyond them. But we can only select our premises from among
things that we know by experience, whether mental or physical, and
accordingly our reasoning is always merely a new placing of the old things.
But the receiving of the Divine Personality into ourselves is an entirely New
Thing, and so cannot be reached by reasoning from old things. Hence if this
Divine ultimate of the Creative Process is to be attained it must be by the
Revelation of a New Thing which will afford a new starting-point for our
thought, and this New Starting-point is given in the Promise of "the Seed of
the Woman" with which the Bible opens. Thenceforward this Promise became
the central germinating thought of those who based themselves upon it, thus
constituting them a special race, until at last when the necessary conditions
had matured the Promised Seed appeared in Him of whom it is written that
He is the express image of God's Person (Heb. I: 3)—that is, the Expression of
that Infinite Divine Personality of which I have spoken. "No man hath seen
God at any time or can see Him," for the simple reason that Infinitude cannot
be the subject of vision. To become visible there must be Individualization,
and therefore when Philip said "Show us the Father," Jesus replied, "He that
hath seen me hath seen the Father." The Word must become flesh before St.
John could say, "That which was from the beginning, which we have heard,
which we have seen with our eyes, which we have looked upon, and our hands
have handled, of the Word of Life." This is the New Starting-point for the true
New Thought—the New Adam of the New Race, each of whom is a new center
for the working of the Divine Spirit. This is what Jesus meant when he said,
"Except ye eat the flesh and drink the blood of the Son of Man ye have no life
in you. My flesh is meat indeed, and my blood is drink indeed—" such a
contemplation of the Divine Personality in Him as will cause a like receiving
of the Divine Personality into individualization in ourselves—this is the great
purpose of the Creative Process in the individual. It terminates the old series
which began with birth after the flesh and inaugurates a New Series by birth
after the Spirit, a New Life of infinite unfoldment with glorious possibilities
beyond our highest conception.

But all this is logically based upon our recognition of the Personalness of
God and of the relation of our individual personality to this Eternal and
Infinite Personality, and the result of this is Worship—not an attempt to
"butter up" the Almighty and get Him into good temper, but the reverent
contemplation of what this Personality must be in Itself; and when we see it
to be that Life, Love, Beauty, etc., of which I spoke at the beginning of this
book we shall learn to love Him for what He IS, and our prayer will be "Give

me more of Thyself." If we realize the great truth that the Kingdom of Heaven is *within* us, that it is the Kingdom of the innermost of our own being and of all creation, and if we realize that this innermost is the place of the Originating Power where Time and Space do not exist and therefore antecedent to all conditions, then we shall see the true meaning of Worship. It is the perception of the Innermost Spirit as eternally subsisting independently of all conditioned manifestation, so that in the true worship our consciousness is removed from the outer sphere of existence to the innermost center of unconditioned being. There we find the Eternal Being of God pure and simple, and we stand reverently in this Supreme Presence knowing that it is the Source of our own being, and wrapt in the contemplation of This, the conditioned is seen to flow out from It. Perceiving this the conditioned passes out of our consideration, for it is seen not to be the Eternal Reality—we have reached that level of consciousness where Time and Space remain no longer. Yet the reverence which the vision of this Supreme Center of all Being cannot fail to inspire is coupled with a sense of feeling quite at home with It. This is because as the Center of *all* Being it is the center of our own being also. It is one-with-ourselves. It is recognizing Itself from our own center of consciousness; so that here we have got back to that Self-contemplation of Spirit which is the first movement of the Creating Power, only now this Self-contemplation is the action of the All-Originating Spirit upon Itself from the center of our own consciousness. So this worship in the Temple of the Innermost is at once reverent adoration and familiar intercourse—not the familiarity that breeds contempt, but a familiarity producing Love, because as it increases we see more clearly the true Life of the Spirit as the continual interaction of Love and Beauty, and the Spirit's recognition of ourselves as an integral portion of Its own Life. This is not an unpractical dreamy speculation but has a very practical bearing. Death will some day cease to be, for the simple reason that Life alone can be the enduring principle; but we have not yet reached this point in our evolution. Whether any in this generation will reach it I cannot say; but for the rank and file of us the death of the body seems to be by far the more probable event. Now what must this passing out of the body mean to us? It must mean that we find ourselves without the physical vehicle which is the instrument through which our consciousness comes in touch with the external world and all the interests of our present daily life. But the mere putting off of the body does not of itself change the mental attitude; and so if our mind is entirely centered upon these passing interests and external conditions the loss of the instrument by which we held touch with them must involve a consciousness of desire for the only sort of life we have known coupled with a consciousness of our inability to participate in it, which can only result in a consciousness of distress and confusion such as in our present state we cannot imagine.

On the other hand if we have in this world realized the true principle of the Worship of the Eternal Source from which all conditioned life flows out—an inner communing with the Great Reality—we have already passed beyond that consciousness of life which is limited by Time and Space; and so when we put off this mortal body we shall find ourselves upon familiar ground, and therefore not wandering in confusion but quite at home, dwelling in the same light of the Eternal in which we have been accustomed to dwell as an atmosphere enveloping the conditioned life of to-day. Then finding ourselves thus at home on a plane where Time and Space do not exist there will be no question with us of duration. The consciousness will be simply that of peaceful, happy being. That a return to more active personal operation will eventually take place is evidenced by the fact that the basis of all further evolution is the differentiating of the Undifferentiated Life of the Spirit into specific channels of work, through the intermediary of individual personality without which the infinite potentialities of the Creative Law cannot be brought to light. Therefore, however various our opinions as to its precise form, Resurrection as a principle is a necessity of the creative process. But such a return to more active life will not mean a return to limitations, but the opening of a new life in which we shall transcend them all, because we have passed beyond the misconception that Time and Space are of the Essence of Life. When the misconception regarding Time and Space is entirely eradicated all other limitations must disappear because they have their root in this primary one—they are only particular forms of the general proposition. Therefore though Form with its accompanying relations of Time and Space is necessary for manifestation, these things will be found not to have any force in themselves thus creating limitation, but to be the reflection of the mode of thought which projects them as the expression of itself.

Nor is there any inherent reason why this process should be delayed till some far-off future. There is no reason why we should not commence at once. No doubt our inherited and personally engendered modes of thought make this difficult, and by the nature of the process it will be only when *all* our thoughts are conformed to this principle that the complete victory will be won. But there must be a commencement to everything, and the more we habituate ourselves to live in that Center of the Innermost where conditions do not exist, the more we shall find ourselves gaining control over outward conditions, because the stream of conditioned life flows out from the Center of Unconditioned Life, and therefore this intrinsic principle of Worship has in it the promise both of the life that now is and of that which is to come. Only we must remember that the really availing worship is that of the Undifferentiated Source *because It is the Source*, and not as a backhanded way of diverting the stream into some petty channel of conditions, for that would only be to get back to the old circle of limitation from which we are seeking to escape.

But if we realize these things we have already laid hold of the Principle of Resurrection, and in point of principle we are already living the resurrection life. What progress we may make in it depends on our practical application of the principle; but simply as principle there is nothing in the principle itself to prevent its complete working at any moment. This is why Jesus did not refer resurrection to some remote point of time but said, "I am the resurrection and the life." No principle can carry in itself an opposite and limiting principle contradictory of its own nature, and this is as true of the Principle of Life as of any other principle. It is we who by our thought introduce an opposite and limiting principle and so hinder the working of the principle we are seeking to bring into operation; but so far as the Principle of Life itself is concerned there is *in it* no reason why it should not come into perfect manifestation here and now.

This, then, is the true purpose of worship. It is to bring us into conscious and loving intercourse with the Supreme Source of our own being, and seeing this we shall not neglect the outward forms of worship. From what we now know they should mean more to us than to others and not less; and in especial if we realize the manifestation of the Divine Personality in Jesus Christ and its reproduction in Man, we shall not neglect His last command to partake of that sacred memorial to His flesh and blood which He bequeathed to His followers with the words "This do in remembrance of Me."

This holy rite is no superstitious human invention. There are many theories about it, and I do not wish to combat any of them, for in the end they all seem to me to bring us to the same point, that being cleansed from sin by the Divine Love we are now no longer separate from God but become "partakers of the Divine-Nature" (II Peter I: 4). This partaking of the Divine Nature could not be more accurately represented than by our partaking of bread and wine as symbols of the Divine Substance and the Divine Life, thus made emblematic of the whole Creative Process from its beginning in the Divine Thought to its completion in the manifestation of that Thought as Perfected Man; and so it brings vividly before us the remembrance of the Personality of God taking form as the Son of Man. We are all familiar with the saying that thoughts become things; and if we affirm the creative power of our own thought as reproducing itself in outward form, how much more must we affirm the same of that Divine Thought which brings the whole universe into existence; so that in accordance with our own principles the Divine Idea of Man was logically bound to show itself in the world of time and space as the Son of God and the Son of man, not two differing natures but one complete whole, thus summing up the foundation principle of all creation in one Undivided Consciousness of Personality. Thus "the Word" or Divine Thought of Man "became flesh," and our partaking of the symbolic elements keeps in our remembrance the supreme truth that this same "Word" or Thought of God in like manner takes form in ourselves as we open our own thought to receive it. And further, if we realize that throughout the universe there is only *One* Originating Life, sending forth only *One* Original Substance as the vehicle for its expression, then it logically follows that *in essence* the bread is a portion of the eternal Substance of God, and the wine a portion of the eternal Life of God. For though the wine is of course also a part of the Universal Substance, we must remember that the Universal Substance is itself a manifestation of the Life of the All-Creating Spirit, and therefore this fluid form of the primary substance has been selected as representing the eternal flowing of the Life of the Spirit into all creation, culminating in its supreme expression in the consciousness of those who, in the recognition of these truths, seek to bring their heart into union with the Divine Spirit. From such considerations as these it will be seen how vast a field of thought is covered by Christ's words "Do this in remembrance of Me."

In conclusion, therefore, do not let yourselves be led astray by any philosophy that denies the Personality of God. In the end it will be found to be a foolish philosophy. No other starting-point of creation is conceivable than the Self-Contemplation of the Divine Spirit, and the logical sequence from this brings us to the ultimate result of the Creative Process in the statement that "if any man be in Christ he is a New creature," or as the margin has it "a new creation" (II Cor. v: 17). Such vain philosophies have only one logical result which is to put *yourself* in the place of God, and then what have you to lean upon in the hour of trial? It is like trying to climb up a ladder that is resting against nothing. Therefore, says the Apostle Paul, "Beware lest any man spoil you through philosophy and vain deceit, after the tradition of man, after the rudiments of the world, and not after Christ." (Col. II: 8.) The teaching of the Bible is sound philosophy, sound reasoning, and sound science because it starts with the sound premises that all Creation proceeds out of God, and that Man is made in the image and likeness of his Creator. It nowhere departs from the Law of Cause and Effect, and by the orderly sequence of this law it brings us at last to the New Creation both in ourselves and in our environment, so that we find the completion of the Creative Process in the declaration "the tabernacle of God is with men" (Rev. xxi: 3), and in the promise "This is the Covenant that I will make with them after those days (i.e., the days of our imperfect apprehension of these things) saith the Lord, I will dwell *in them* , and walk in *them*, and I will be their God, and they shall be my people, and I will put my laws into their hearts, and in their minds will I write them, and their sins and their iniquities will I remember no more" (Heb. x: 16. II Cor. vi: 16. Jeremiah xxxi: 33).

Truly does Bacon say, "A little philosophy inclineth a man's mind to atheism, but depth in philosophy bringeth men's minds about to religion." —Bacon, Essay, xvi.

FOOTNOTES

Footnote 1: See my Doré Lectures, 1909.

Footnote 2: See my Edinburgh Lectures on Mental Science.

Footnote 3: See my Doré Lectures, 1909.

Footnote 4: For the relation between conscious and sub-conscious mind see my "Edinburgh Lectures on Mental Science."

Footnote 5: See "Self-Synthesis" by Dr. Cornwall Round.

Footnote 6: For the relation between subjective and objective mind see my "Edinburgh Lectures on Mental Science."

Footnote 7: This view, it may be remarked, is not necessarily incompatible with the conception of reincarnation, on which theory the final resurrection or transmutation of the body would terminate the series of successive lives and deaths, thus bringing the individual out of the circle of generation, which is the circle of Karma. I may, perhaps, have the opportunity of considering this subject on some future occasion.

Footnote 8: See my "Bible Mystery and Bible Meaning."

Footnote 9: See "Bible Mystery and Bible Meaning" by the present author.

www.ingramcontent.com/pod-product-compliance
Lightning Source LLC
Chambersburg PA
CBHW030919090426
42737CB00007B/248